MW00940701

"From Judas to me", by Anthony Sparzo is a narration of his life, and a chronicle of his battle with alcoholism, drug abuse, and gambling addiction. I found this book to be an excellent account of one man's journey from adolescence to adulthood while struggling with addiction, and its affect on his family, and personal life. From the beginning the book takes you on a wild ride of drugs, alcohol, problems with the law, and destroyed personal and family relationships. It describes the author's personal issues from teenage pregnancy, to a terrible car accident, to his decision to make himself a better person, and the struggle he fought to do so. The motivation behind this book is for the author to share his story of how addiction destroys it victim's lives, and to show younger readers how addictions take hold, and where ignoring their problems could lead them and how it will affect their lives. I feel that this book is an excellent lesson to anyone who is dealing with their own addiction, and should be seen as motivation to change their lives before it is too late. "From Judas to Me" is a wild, and emotional ride that should be read by anyone who wants, or needs inspiration to battle their own addiction problems.

—Timothy DeGiuli, former high school teacher

FROM JUDAS TO ME

Anthony Sparzo and
Michael Cossette

iUniverse, Inc.
New York   Bloomington

From Judas to Me

Copyright © 2010 Anthony Sparzo and Michael Cossette

All rights reserved. No part of this book may be used or reproduced by
any means, graphic, electronic, or mechanical, including photocopying,
recording, taping or by any information storage retrieval system
without the written permission of the publisher except in the case
of brief quotations embodied in critical articles and reviews.

iUniverse books may be ordered through booksellers or by contacting:

iUniverse
1663 Liberty Drive
Bloomington, IN 47403
www.iuniverse.com
1-800-Authors (1-800-288-4677)

Because of the dynamic nature of the Internet, any Web addresses or
links contained in this book may have changed since publication and
may no longer be valid. The views expressed in this work are solely those
of the author and do not necessarily reflect the views of the publisher,
and the publisher hereby disclaims any responsibility for them.

ISBN: 978-1-4502-4056-7 (pbk)
ISBN: 978-1-4502-4057-4 (cloth)
ISBN: 978-1-4502-4058-1 (ebk)

Library of Congress Control Number: 2010909477

Printed in the United States of America

iUniverse rev. date: 7/15/2010

For Heather, Joseph, Cheyenne, Juliano, Brandon and Amanda

In Memory of Dino Radogna

A Taste of Things to Come

Lance failed miserably as a co-pilot and within fifteen minutes, we were officially lost. In a drunken state of mind, I let my irritation towards the situation get the best of me and so I started speeding recklessly to make up for lost time. After all, I wanted to party. As I rounded a turn in a dimly lit residential neighborhood, I took the corner too tightly, causing my front right tire to hit the curb. The tire grabbed instantly, pulling my car up somebody's driveway, and vaulting us airborne. Sheer terror shot through my veins. At fifty plus miles per hour, this was not looking positive. A sudden bone-shattering crunch rang through my skull as my car landed upside down and proceeded to slide with fierce momentum. I had been too drunk and stubborn to be wearing a seatbelt, so I witnessed my final moment as I dropped face first into the sunroof. The sunroof had shattered upon impact, spearing shards of glass into my face. For the next sixty feet my head was at the mercy of the asphalt, which spared no time in shredding the skin clean off of my face. Shock kicked in midway through the slide, causing me to completely blackout. What happened from there after is completely based upon Lance's recollection.

Supposedly, as the car finally settled, Lance, who amazingly only suffered minor injuries, pulled me from the wreckage. I had two extremely large chunks of my head missing, replaced solely by blood, bits of asphalt and empty space. The left side of my face had disappeared completely, with bits and pieces of it scattered throughout the street and sidewalk. Lance claims that he kept screaming for me to keep thinking of Angel and Daniel and that I was going to make it through this. Maybe I heard him, but more than likely not. According to Lance, it was inevitable that I would give up the ghost before any help could arrive. Although through God's grace alone, I did not perish in the arms of my friend on those blood-soaked streets. Unconscious but alive, I was care flown by angels to John C. Lincoln Memorial Hospital.

The next thing that I remember was opening my eyes to Gerard standing over me. Several days had passed since the accident and I was still in agonizing pain, feeling as though thousands of fire ants were consuming my face. My appearance was so grotesque that both my mom and sister could not even bear to look at me, muffling their cries behind hand-shielded eyes. I demanded that someone brought me a mirror. Gerard, a man who was not one to wince at trauma, looked overwhelmed with disgust. Once the doctors were able to locate a mirror, Gerard stepped up to me, took a deep breath and held it up over my head. "Unfuckinbelievable," was all that I could say. My entire face was gone, vanished, lost into oblivion. The blank canvas of a bulky white cast was now my new head. The whole hospital floor echoed with my screams as the pain and frustration rushed through my veins, and that sudden burst of anxiety left me struggling to breathe. *What the fuck had I done to myself?*

Contents

My Early Vision

On August 5, 1967, I was born onto this world as a single vision representing everything that the Summer of Love stood for.

My parents, Gerard and Melinda, were young and full of optimism towards starting a family together. The two of them had met and fallen in love two years earlier while in high school. My father had grown up in New York with his parents, two brothers and sister. With the projects of Brooklyn proving to be too limiting, they moved to Highland Park, California in hopes of finding a better life. Highland Park is located just a brief ten minutes drive from downtown Los Angeles and as my dad would say, it was paradise compared to the projects of Brooklyn. My mother's family had relocated from Chicago, Illinois to Highland Park roughly around the same time and brought with them a family of three daughters and a son.

My parents' romance blossomed in high school, as all true love usually does, and within the year they were fully dedicated to each other as a married couple. Their love was a phenomenal thing, yet the only thing that lacked in their lives was some collegiate ambition. There were no doctors, no lawyers, not even a college graduate in our family, just an average set of individuals trying to carve a niche out in a new locality.

My dad's father, Nick, was of Italian heritage and his mother, Vera, was Irish. When it came to religion, Nick was a devoted attendee to the Catholic Church and raised all of his children in the shadow of the Lord. Their faith was a key factor in keeping the family close-knit. When the focus was not centered on the Holy Scriptures, it was spent at the house being loud and boisterous. In order to be heard in any of our households, someone had to be able to out-talk everyone else in the room and that was no easy task. Though it took me much time to perfect, the loudness that surrounded my family was one that would last throughout the years.

My dad's siblings consisted of his two brothers, Rico and Joseph, and his sister, Barbara, yet of the three, his favorite was by far Joseph. From my earliest memories, I can always remember my dad and Uncle Joe doing everything as a pair. I truly can not believe they ever found enough time to have a relationship with anyone other than themselves. If either one of them walked through the door, it was a sure bet that the other was close behind. I admired the bond that they shared and strived to emulate it by being closer than ever with Joseph's son, Benny. Benny was born only six weeks after me and the brotherhood that we shared made both of our dads proud.

Every Sunday, we held the ritual of gathering for dinner at my dad's parents' house. The adults would all sit around the dining room table and drink the night away, laughing with a deafening roar on what seemed like every minute on the dot. The kids, on the other hand, were ushered to the couch by my grandpa who would comically tell us, "Hush up and watch TV." As humble of a giant as he was, Nick had little patience for anything, including children and alcohol. His only Zen was in the aridly aromatic kitchen making his prized Pasta Vazool. I loved his Pasta Vazool and even saying it made my smile larger than that of the Cheshire Cat's. Even though my dad detested the stuff, citing that he was forced to eat "Pasta-for-Fools" far too often as a kid, I was still nil fazed since I knew that every time Grandpa Nick made it, he made it especially for me.

My grandma, on the opposite side of the spectrum, was usually found amongst the men knocking down beers faster than bowling pins in a strike. A case of Budweiser would vanish, reappear and then the process would repeat itself throughout the evening. By the time dinner was finished, most of the men were well inebriated, all of the kids were antsy to go home and the women were getting prepared to handle the task of driving their kids home, some of which included their intoxicated husbands. The Sunday routine was simple yet it never failed to provide pure, unscripted entertainment.

As fun as I made Sundays out to be, Saturdays in my family were by far the highlight of my week. Everyone congregated at Eagle Rock Park where a grand feast was barbecued while the men entertained the masses with a hard-fought baseball game that always ended up in some variant of a riot. I would get to spend the whole day with Benny, admiring our dads as they took a ground ball to the chest and still made the play, never complaining once.

Saturday mornings were usually started with my mom waking my little sister, Cassandra, and I up early to watch our cartoons while she snuck out to the store only to return and surprise us with donuts. I loved how predictable she was, yet she still acted like it was a new surprise each and every time. With immense anticipation for each Saturday's fun, I genuinely believed that I had the greatest life of any kid in the world. My mom was amazing at how far out of the way she would go to make sure everything was special in my life. The bond between my mother and I was wonderful, making me feel like I was the number one person in her life and jointly, my dad always seemed to favor Cassandra over me. Even if he was in a fit of rage over some shenanigan I was involved in, he could completely collect his composure and speak calmly to Cassandra. This is why I put all of my attention and admiration into my mother who never once failed me when I needed her.

My life showed nothing but promising times of happiness in my future, until the cruel mistress of fate decided to deal me my first Lesson card. Just like every Saturday, my mother woke us up with her usual cheerful self and just like every Saturday, I arose with a powerful smile. *How could I not with a mother like that?* Well on this Saturday, I was beyond anxious because it was the first day of the junior bowling league my parents had signed me up for. My mom's sister, Dina, came over to give me a ride to the bowling alley and my mom stopped her at the door, wanting to go with us and make sure that I got a lucky chocolate bar. I thought it was a great idea and so off we went to the corner shop.

Halfway down the block, Dina realized that our dog, Mr. Bojangles, was chasing her car. I will briefly call to note that my dad idolized The Rat Pack and the only real part he took in the dog's life was naming it. Other than that, he was never really too thrilled about pets in our household. So anyways, Dina brought the car to a screeching halt and for reasons unknown shifted it back into reverse. Just as she muttered the words "Open the door so he can jump in...," the shrill sound of Mr. Bojangles' death whimper cut her coldly short as the weight of the car pressed him firmly into the asphalt. The three of us burst from the car where much to our astonishment, the rugged little pup was alive. Then the screams set in, first from my mom and Dina, then from Cassandra who had witnessed the whole event from the front yard.

With piercing screams echoing throughout the neighborhood, my dad took control of the situation by escorting my mom and me over to the curb and then moved the car back into the driveway. After seeing my mother cry the way she did, I could not shake the thought that somehow this was entirely my fault. This strange feeling of guilt was very unpleasant, so I sulked into the house where I watched silently from the window. My dad simply picked Mr. Bojangles up and placed him snuggly in the backseat of the car. Once the coast was clear, I moved back outside and looked in on Mr. Bojangles. There he lay with an open smile and bright eyes, showing no symptoms of pain. I started laughing because after all of the drama that had just taken place, he was alright and merely resting. Well I soon found out that he was not and I felt horrible for laughing. The guilt that I had experienced from laughing at another creature's pain stayed with me for years to follow. This was my first lesson in suffering, and finding the means that I needed to cope with it.

Around the same time that Mr. Bojangles was leaving us, I saw my dad's temper flare to frightening levels for the first time. Like any child in this blessed country, the hypnotic jingle of the ice cream truck brought sheer excitement and I was no exception. I rushed inside, grabbed all of the change that my dad stored loosely on his dresser and bolted back outside just as the ice cream truck arrived curbside. I hastily told Cassandra to "sit tight" while I went across the street to grab us both some treats. I was barely ten seconds into my mission when I heard the gut-wrenching squeal of braking tires, followed by the horrific thud of flesh hitting tarmac. I turned around to see my sister sprawled in an awkward position under the bumper of a brown station wagon driven by a greasy man with long hair. In a petrified state of panic, I ran into my house, yelling at the top of my lungs for my dad's assistance. I finally found him in the bathroom and with little need for explanation, he rushed right past me. I trailed close behind him as he pushed his way through the sea of people encircling my fallen sister.

Supposedly, the guy who hit Cassandra had tried to take off but was immediately stopped by the ice cream man. Several neighbors were needed to restrain my dad who was intent on causing the guy some serious health damage. My mom had arrived within minutes and came sprinting from her van with screams about her baby. Once again, I could not shake the feeling that this was my fault and the guilt was overwhelming. Although Cassandra was okay and made a full recovery, I had neglected to keep proper supervision over my little sister and my dad was sure to let me know of it. The rage that resided within his eyes was more terrifying than any monster or ghost and from that day on, that fear stayed with me.

Now while Sunday nights were spent in exile on my grandparents' couch and watching the adults grow exceedingly annoying, Sunday mornings were the exact opposite and spent at my mom's parents' house. Meme and Papa, as I called them, were an absolute delight to visit. All of the kids were free to run wild outside and play while the adults watched and laughed joyfully from the patio. Just as I had my brother Benny on my father's side, my mother's side brought my cousin, Bobby, and I together. Bobby was a year younger, which gave me the responsibility of playing the role as his older brother and the nice thing about this mindset was that he looked at me the same way. Bobby and I had endless fun together. Bobby had a sister, Collette, who was roughly the same age as Cassandra and the similarities between us made us more or less an extended immediate family.

My uncle, Ted, who was my mom's brother, was undeniably the one person that I desired to be the most like in every way. He drove a motorcycle and was the epitome of the word "cool". Ted was the real deal when it came to being as cool as the Fonz, who happened to be my idol. Ted was a burly man, towering above the rest of the family at six feet six inches and weighing in at two hundred and fifty pounds. To boot, he took no slack from anyone and his reputation was solid and well known. Bobby and I looked up to him immensely and he gave us all the attention we wanted. Aside from Ted and Dina, my aunt, Karen, who was Bobby and Collette's mother, was the last of the siblings to round out my mom's family. Bobby's dad, Bob Sr., was a pure Italian who had moved to the United States as a young kid. This link in heritage only made my bond with my brother Bobby that much stronger. Not even diamonds could cut these ties.

The only person who could compete with him was Meme, who was without a doubt the ideal grandmother that any kid would wish for. Having experienced her splendor first hand, I can now see clearly where my mom got her pure soul from. Everything that my grandma did was for the joy of her children and grandchildren. Meme had been sponsored and brought over to an American family from Germany during the Second World War. She stood firmly at five feet zero inches and spoke with the sweetest German accent. Her voice was so lyrical that it sent shivers down my spine after every word she delivered. I loved Meme so much.

My grandpa, however, was difficult to connect with since he was a truck driver, a gambler and a drinker who did all of which with great passion. By the time I was old enough to remember things in my life, I had never seen him drink, but some of the stories that I heard were outrageous. He used to work as a bookie and at one point in time, had all four of his children working for him. I always thought that was so cool. Along with that, Papa had been enlisted into the Marines at the age of sixteen and subsequently had a variety of military and personal tattoos covering his body. I would tell my dad that I wanted tattoos because of grandpa and my dad would tell me that if I did, it would be the last thing I ever did. He was not kidding, but hey, neither was I.

I had started to bowl every Saturday and soon saw myself as a bowling prodigy, which gave me yet another highlight to look forward to during the week. As excited as I would be to tell my dad about my stellar games, I usually ended up being bummed out because I never saw him much. With juggling two jobs and attempting to complete some community college courses, he did not have much free time. If, by chance, he did, it was spent alongside his brother Joe, choreographing new comedy routines. Their forte was in celebrity impersonations and whenever the two of them were "on stage", they kept the audience rolling on the floor laughing. I thought it was incredible that one minute my dad could be Johnny Carson and within seconds, switch to Howard Cosell. His prized impression though was of Muhammad Ali, who was my dad's all-time hero. When it came to sports, he loved Ali, but a majority of his heart resided in music and the talents of Frank Sinatra and Elvis Presley.

I began to appreciate my dad's taste in music, especially for Elvis. Elvis was so cool that he could have been directly related to the Fonz and Ted. Another musical inspiration in my earlier years was The Beatles. My dad loved The Beatles and therefore, so did I. Anything that I could find to have something in common with the man who should have been my role model turned out to be a step in the right direction. Then again, it was still my mom who I went to when things were wrong and more than not, she managed to make things right.

When my parents were not home, our time was joyfully spent with Dina, who was only sixteen years old and a blast to be with. Not only was Dina cool, but her friends were equally as awesome and whenever she was over, they were close to follow. As soon as my parents were gone, the party began and whenever I wanted to be entertained, I would just watch her friends push their drunken selves to the limits. The only problem with Dina was that once she had a solid buzz, the mean streak in her came out.

At the innocent age of six, my most prized possession in the entire world was a Ronald McDonald doll. Looking back now, I know it was lame, but back then it was the greatest toy ever. When Ronald got a rip in his side one evening, I was beyond upset, so I took him to Dina so that she could repair him. With a smile and look of sincerity, she promised to get him back to his original state. A few hours later, she returned Ronald back to me, but a few key limbs were misplaced. I received a Ronald McDonald doll with his hands and feet sewn to his head. I completely freaked out. Dina definitely had a solid chuckle towards the whole prank, yet after watching me cry for several minutes, she put him back to normal. As traumatic of a situation as it panned out to be, I never forgot the way that she made everything right again. Dina always took great care of us and with both my parents away at jobs, she was my favorite family member to have watching us.

To be perfectly honest, I was raised in a wonderful atmosphere with a family who was not blessed with the splendors of wealth, but kept a tight bond amongst each other and that was more than enough to be content with. Grandpa Nick started taking a more prevalent role in my life by being my escort to Saturday morning's bowling league and I loved to accompany him on the one mile walk to the alley. His tradition was always to stop at the coffee shop along the way where I could order my favorite, pancakes, and he ordered his, French toast. Being with my grandpa was a comfortable and happy time that I could never get enough of.

For some blessed reason, he took better care of me than he did his other grandchildren. I was always told that it was because I was the first grandson in the family and that was something very special to my grandpa. My uncle Rico had a son about my age, Little Ray, but he had passed away at only two years old. I figure my uncle never recovered from it. I only bring this up to say that I have never forgotten that Ray lived and I personally felt it was the right thing to mention his name. He was my family and he will always be missed.

As for my bowling, I was getting better and better, even to the point where I got my name printed in the newspaper. I would love to believe that my mom still has that sports segment. The highlight of my bowling career came on the night of our league banquet and an astonishing nine trophies were awarded to me. My favorite one out of the bunch was by far the plaque built for a desk with two gold pens that I received for perfect attendance. This award of recognition stood out so prominently because it was the only attendance honor I would ever receive.

When bowling was not occupying my free time, my dad took the opportunity to introduce me to the sport of baseball. I instantly knew that this was the one thing that I wanted to do more than everything else combined. My dad was amazing on the baseball field and nobody could outplay him. He took great pride in teaching me his mindset of the game and signature style of play. The one thing that he was truly animate about instilling into my brain was my inability to complain, even when a grounder took a wicked hop and busted my nose. I was to see every play through to the end, practices included. Baseball soon occupied my every thought and as I would sit there at the bowling alley, waiting for my next frame, I would think about grounders galore.

On one regular Saturday at the bowling alley, while daydreaming of baseball, I remember hearing the faint sound of someone crying. As the crying grew louder, I stood up on my chair like all of the other kids to see what was wrong and realized that it was Dina. As curious as I was, I quickly could feel everyone staring wide-eyed at me. The first thought in my mind was that this was just another one of her clever pranks, yet when she finally reached me, I knew that something was seriously wrong. She grabbed me by the arm with no concern over the death grip she was applying and rushed me to her car. All that I could think about was the two strikes and two spares in five frames I was leaving behind.

We soon arrived at Meme and Papa's house where I was the last of my extended family to arrive. I made my way into the house and was immediately swarmed by wave after wave of crying relatives. I did not know what was wrong but the intensity of the scenario made me cry as well. Meme confronted me and explained that Uncle Bob had gone to Heaven to be an angel. As simple as she was making it out to be, the concept of death made absolutely no sense to me. The only thing that crossed my mind was the sympathy I had for Bobby and the hug that he so desperately needed. The moment was very sincere, but after an extended mourning period, we quietly started to play. We did not play too seriously but just enough to feel normal. Normal was suddenly such a distant emotion and I had no idea of what being normal really meant.

I had very few memories of my uncle Bob and I guess the most vivid one was of him in Chicago driving his Volkswagen. This image tied into his final demise as I envisioned him reaching up on the dashboard to grab his aviator sunglasses and losing control.

That was the story my mom described for me and that was the same story I told Bobby.

Two things were true after that day, I was never going to see my uncle Bob again and I would never bowl again. The times were changing for me and my family and six years old was far too young to feel the grip of pain death has on a soul. My parents and family had done everything within their power to make things appear still optimistic for me, but unfortunately as so many will know, when the shadow of pain falls upon us, it falls with a heavy vengeance.

PAIN AND PINSTRIPES

When the Brooklyn Dodgers decided to relocate to the West Coast, it left an immense hole in my dad's heart. The only time of salvation came on the day when he walked into Yankee Stadium and witnessed Mickey Mantle hitting two homeruns and he claims that after that very moment, he never thought about the Dodgers again. Well at eight years old, none of this reminiscing made any sense to me since Dodger Stadium was only five minutes away from my house and the Dodgers were the only team that I knew about. However, my dad would have nothing to do with my opinion and enforced Yankee Pride in our household. His sole argument was through the stories involving Joe, the Yankees and him. After hearing him speak about the Yankees with such conviction, I had no choice but to follow them whole-heartedly.

Baseball became all that I could think about. Benny and I were lucky enough to be put on the same team, thanks to our dads and the name of our team was the Syd Streakers. Our team was a dynamite group of champions who won the Burbank league in our first season and earned the privilege of riding on a float in the Burbank parade. I was so ecstatic and all I could think was that this was how it felt to be a major leaguer, a dream I now saw possible.

With my life on an upswing, I took full enthusiasm towards all of my obligations, which included studying for my first church communion. The classes were somewhat confusing but I managed to do what I was told and excelled in praising the Lord. When my parents were too busy with work to attend, I used to sneak over to a separate church that was located on the adjacent corner to our block and I mostly went because a majority of my friends were dragged there by their parents. For some reason, I seemed to understand religion a whole lot better while I was there than I did through the classes I took every Tuesday. Somehow, religion just proved to be too difficult, so I continued with my thoughts on baseball.

The miraculous time arrived in my life when my dad and Joe finally agreed to take Benny and me to a Dodgers game. We were ecstatic because this would be our first baseball game and it was all that I could think about for the remainder of the week. On the day of the game though, the weather took a foul turn for the worse, but the pinstripes were still intent on playing. The chance of showers was only around forty percent and my dad was guaranteeing me that there were never any rainouts in Los Angeles. Well by the time we arrived at the stadium, the rain was coming down like a Biblical flood. Nevertheless, all four of us were committed to seeing the game and our dads left us in the van while they went to the ticket vendor.

Benny and I just sat there, in the dark, listening to the rain beat against the roof of the van like a machine gun's fury. We locked all the doors and huddled in the back, waiting for their return. The both of us were occupying our minds with idle baseball chat when a rapid pounding on the van doors made us jump so high we both hit our heads. Once we realized that it was only our dads, we opened the doors to two very drenched and upset fathers. They spared no time in venting their frustrations towards the game that was indeed rained out. Go figure, there has been maybe four or five games in the history of the Dodgers in Los Angeles that has been cancelled and we had to pick one of those days. The hype and excitement that I was building to majestic heights was crushed down to mere rubble. When I looked at Benny, who was sitting speechless next to me, I could tell that he was equally as heart-broken. After a chance to cool down and dry off, our dads promised to take us to see the Yankees and hopefully before the end of the season. Suddenly, any previous anticipation that I had seen crushed was now back and skyrocketing.

Baseball became the dominate subject in all of my thoughts and it was not long before I started to organize pickup games with some of the neighborhood kids. Surprisingly, it caught on very well. Rickie Dominguez lived next door to me and he had the biggest backyard on the block. We shared a colorful future which within only three years would include incinerating his garage. Next door to him lived Timmy Middlebrook, who was one of my best friends. Timmy's parents had built him the coolest tree house and I was so jealous of him, even while I was in it. Our close group of neighborhood kids made the perfect baseball team and everyone contributed to its success. Timmy would take pillow cases and stuff them to make our bases, while I would collect all of my used T-shirts and make team uniforms for everyone. Our backyard league was top notch and my anticipation for the weekend games was so immense that I would regularly be up and ready to play by seven thirty in the morning. The games were very intense and often went all day long and into the lavender twilight of dusk. I always wore the number fifteen, for Thurman Munson, who was my favorite player. Even though I was deep in Dodgers territory, I still made all the numbers after Yankees players. Besides, none of them had the same passion for their teams as I did for the Yankees and the fact that I still had not seen a game lurked in the back of my mind.

I loved the stories that my dad would tell me about the Yankees and the more I heard, the more that I myself wanted to be a Yankee. One memorable story occurred in the 1961 World Series when all of the fans stormed the field and my dad and Joe were part of the mob scene. They may not have been the most exciting stories, but at nine years old, they gave me hope and a positive outlook on life.

The year was 1976 and my dad was absolutely certain that the Yankees were going to win the Pennant. He also mentioned that the Yankees were going to be in town and that there was no way in the world we were going to miss that game. His sincerity was so genuine and I had no doubts that I would be disappointed again. My excitement rose higher than I ever thought possible and that same anticipation held up as strong as an ox for the next five months. Every time Benny and I got together that game was all that we talked about, how we were going to both catch homeruns and the Yankees would win by a landslide.

Waiting for the game tested every last bit of my patience and any free moment that I had I spent playing baseball. Baseball had my complete commitment. I went to tryouts and ended up being selected by the Chicago Cubs. I was extremely upset that I was not a Yankee but since it was Chicago, I felt in a way that I was still representing my mom's team. So I went into the season with full enthusiasm and my passion for the sport paid off tremendously. Within a few games, I emerged as one of the top players on the team and it made me feel great. Everything about the sport excited me, especially wearing the uniform, because in some innocent childish mentality, I felt like a pro. Baseball became everything to me and it brought me a level of happiness that I had struggled to find anywhere else.

School, conversely, was not as mentally stimulating. I showed many of the symptoms associated with Attention Deficit Disorder and found my only niche through playing the role as the class clown. I absolutely loved to make people laugh, which was usually at the teachers' expense. Sure my antics got me into more than my fair share of trouble, but it was all worth it. Going to school in my opinion was strictly a social event and the attention that some of the girls gave me only fueled my ego. There were girls, and then there was the one girl that stood out like a diamond amongst the granite, Jennifer Green. She was the most beautiful girl in the entire school and I had an instant crush on her. Little did it matter that I was only nine, my stomach ran rampant with butterflies and I always anticipated going to school the next day just to see her. I mention her briefly just to call note to my first crush and an astonishing girl that I can never forget.

Aside from her, I made the best out of my school and first communion studies, finding them as temporary solutions to keep me occupied until May and the Yankees. Only two weeks stood in the way of me and that game. All of my classmates gave me grief about being a Yankees fan and I loved every second of it. I loved my loyalty for a team that everyone else seemed to hate. My dad's stories became my own and I used to tell the other kids about how amazing Yankee Stadium was, even though I had never actually experienced it.

Benny and I sat at the park watching our dads play ball and talking nonstop about our big day. A checkmark on the list of my life was about to be achieved and the five day separation was growing far too nerve-racking. On this average Saturday, our dads decided that we could have a "big man's drink" and they slapped us each in the hands with a tall can of Coors Light and kicked us along our way. We had attempted to sneak heavy swings from their beers over the past year, but this time we got to be the big shots. They just told us to make sure that our moms did not see, so we smuggled our beers over to some nearby trees. There we sat and enjoyed every sip of our tall cans, laughing at how great this Saturday was. There was no one that I would rather be with than Benny.

The week ahead seemed as though it would never end and all that I could think about was Thursday and the game, followed by Saturday's first communion. Much to my dismay, my dad and Joe had decided to go to a Wednesday game and we were not invited. I tried to be mad but I was still so excited for Thursday that I did not want to risk saying anything that would spoil it. I could not sleep that night, waiting for my dad to come home and give me a play-by-play of the game. The hours seemed to drag on forever and then I finally heard my uncle's car mosey up the driveway. I ran to the front door and hung out over the balcony, screaming at the top of my lungs to get my dad's attention.

As they emerged from the car, my uncle and dad were laughing hysterically and it was apparent that they had a great time. My uncle told me to keep up the good behavior and that he was looking forward to tomorrow night. I told him not to worry and to tell Benny that I loved him. Smiling, he complied and drove away. So there I sat, waiting for my dad to come up the stairs. He was well beyond drunk but was still in great spirits. He gave me the rundown on the game, screaming with delight as he informed me that it was a Yankees victory. I continued with at least a hundred questions, but he mentioned that tomorrow was a very big day so I needed to get some sleep and that it made him happy to see me so excited.

The next morning, I awoke earlier than usual and it was clearly due to the immeasurable level of adrenaline flowing through me. All that I had to do was keep myself occupied until I could get through the day. I found some brief distraction by walking with my sister to school, but that was short lived and my thoughts went right back to the game. I bragged incessantly to all of my friends about how lucky I was. They were obvious in their disinterest, claiming that I was a traitor to God's team. Laughingly, I corrected them, stating that the Yankees are God's true team. Their words were simple nonsense and I brushed them to the side, putting the rest of my focus into watching the clock tick slowly by. When the final bell rang, I jumped from my seat and ran to find my sister. We scurried our way home and upon arriving, my mom insisted that I took a nap since I was going to be up late. I tried to argue with her but she was deaf to my words, so I plopped myself heavily on the couch right next to the front door. I knew that the moment my dad came through the door, I would instantly be woken up and it would be time for the game.

Hours later, I was awoken by a thump to my head and as I lazily opened my eyes, I took a second to comprehend why I was on the couch. Then I remembered and started to smile, but the mood was swiftly changed as I saw my mom crying. From the other room I heard my dad yelling "What're you fuckin' talking about?" My mom cried back, "Joseph's dead. You're brother's dead." My heart fell into my stomach. None of this made any sense. I had just seen my uncle Joe less than eighteen hours ago.

My sister and I were quietly but urgently walked downstairs to our babysitter's apartment. There I sat, in the front window, wondering what was happening all around me. Every minute seemed like an eternity as I waited for my dad to pull up with Joe and Benny so we could finally go to the game. The longer I waited, the more confused I became, wondering why they would play around like this. The game was about to start and we needed to get to the stadium. Mrs. Ortiz, my babysitter, told me to come to the table and eat my dinner, but I had no appetite to eat. I just wanted to go to the game already. She then stated that even though I may know what was going on, Cassandra did not and by me not being there, it would only confuse my little sister more. Understanding her mentality, I obliged and went to the table. I asked Mrs. Ortiz if my mom was going to be back anytime soon and she promptly responded that everything would work out as it should.

Nightfall came and my parents were still not back, so Cassandra and I were sent to the spare bedroom to get some sleep. Twice now I had been told to get some rest when I did not want to, so all that I did all night was stood up on the bed and stared out the window. Every car that passed made my hopes jump thinking that it might be them and each time I was let down. I gazed up into the stars and prayed to Jesus for Uncle Joe to be safe and back with his loving family. If Joe was alright then we could still catch the closing innings of the game. As pure and naive as my innocence was, regrettably Jesus was not listening that night and my uncle was not coming home. The last thing I remember thinking that night was who was going to watch over Benny now and whether or not the Yankees were winning.

The next morning, my mom showed up to get us and once we were back in our home, she sat me down to explain that Joe was gone forever. I asked her where Dad was and she said that he was still over at Joe's house. She went on to reveal that my uncle Joe had slipped in the shower and struck his temple on the faucet, dying instantly. Speechless, I took a moment to reflect on my thoughts. *How does someone die in the shower of all places? What if I was next?* So much of this dreary event was difficult to understand and all that I knew was that I would never take a shower again. Although that mentality was short lived, I did still take a chair in with me every time that I showered for the next three years.

The next morning my mom woke me, however this time there was no "Rise and shine, Sweetie", just a cold and dismal "Please get up". After looking at her gloomy face, any positive feelings that I had were immediately lost. She asked me to get dressed and ready for my communion, but unfortunately I could not see my dad yet. My mood dropped just as low as hers and after getting myself cleaned up, I sat down on the couch and waited for further instruction. My mom then came into the living room and told me that my dad wanted to see me in his room.

As I walked in, he was sitting on the floor with his back propped up against the wall. The look on his face was what I can only describe as sheer loss. Unblinking, he stared at a picture of his brother and him that he held lethargically in his lap. All that I could say was, "Dad, I love you." Without even looking up to acknowledge my presence or my sentiment, he continued to sit there, until he finally moved his left hand to his tape recorder which he then tossed over to me. I was puzzled at his intentions since after all, this was his prized possession that he recorded all of his impressions on. Then, he spoke only the small words, "That's all I have." I listened to the recorder and listened to the two of them as they laughed and laughed, joyfully locked into the moment. Then it made sense to me what he meant by that. After a soft and sincere "Thank you", I left the room with my mom and we made our way for the church.

Honestly, I did not want anything to do with church, communion, or the celebration that was sure to follow. There was nothing to celebrate. Life was happening all around me but my mind was shrouded with the reality of death. All that I could think about was my dad and what he must be going through. Although my spirit was absent, my body took its first communion and once it was all over, the sadness filled right back in. Afterwards there was no celebration, just a crowd of solemn faces. This should have been a happy and positive day for me, but instead my family was consumed with the task of arranging my uncle's funeral. I still was yet to see Benny and I thought that if I could just be with him then everything would be better. However, at this point in time, that was not an option and things continued to spiral downward.

One night, I came into the house and my dad was posted up behind his bar. He had a couple of friends with him and they were all drinking heavily. Directly above my dad's bar was the shirt that Uncle Joe was intended to be buried in. I had seen this shirt on him so many times and it looked so empty and naked up there on the wall. I did not know what to make of it. Any comment that started to rise was swiftly silenced and I was sent on my way, which was usually outside to play in the alley or at a neighbor's house.

The only time there was ever any laughter was when I went to Meme's house. Only in the presence of Meme was everyone collected enough not to cry, everyone that is, except for my father. Looking back, I can not remember a single time during this whole tragedy that my dad was not crying. I could not blame him. Everyday, day after day, he was locked in his chamber of a room or bar. Life at home was as dark as a casket. We were constantly on guard from my dad's radical outbursts since he was still in complete shock and denial. He had no proper means for channeling such intense emotions. Surprisingly, he managed to work everyday despite his mounting despair. Through all his personal turmoil, he never stopped taking care of his family and I recognized this as how a real man should act. His steadfast dedication to us was truly amazing.

The only time I ever saw a glimmer of light come back into his eyes was in October when the Yankees made it to the playoffs. I was still very new to all of this, but my dad kept reminding me of how long he had waited for this very thing. Thirteen painstaking years had passed since the Yankees were last present in the post-season. Seeing me now as the only male figure he had to enjoy the Yankees with, my dad told my mom to let me stay up late and talk with him via the phone about game five.

With every inning that went by, I grew more and more excited. Even though he was watching from a local bar, he still managed to make me feel like I was part of the experience. We talked more over the phone in that short three hours than we did in the previous five months. Then, in the bottom of the ninth inning with the score tied at four to four, Chris Chambliss cracked the smoothest looking homerun just to the right of the center-field fence and I erupted from the couch. This was undeniably the most excitement I had ever felt in my life. Before I could even get my feet planted, the phone rang and I was still screaming as I answered it. My dad kept chanting back, "The pinstripes are back! The pinstripes are back!" My body was overrun with so much joy, I actually started to cry. The Yankees were the greatest team on the planet and to all of the skeptics out there, this was the proof.

However, my joy turned to deep pain a week later when we were swept by the Cincinnati Reds. Even in this time of great happiness trampled by immense sorrow, my dad was honored to say that I was now a true Yankees fan since I experienced first hand the agony of a playoff loss. His encouraging words were all that I needed to fill the giant void I had in my life. The Yankees became my world. My room was decorated in everything that had a Yankees symbol, yet my poster of Thurman Munson and my Yankees banner really stole the scene. Just having these items made me feel like I was an honorary member of the clubhouse.

The presence of joy and pain in my life was similar to that of an active yo-yo, although this time the pain that I felt was felt around the world. The news traveled fast that the king himself,

Elvis Presley, had died of heart failure. I was only a kid, but the effect it had on me was equally traumatic. His music was all that I would sing every time I walked with my sister to school. Like I mentioned earlier, Elvis was the symbol of everything that was cool. The night he died, I prayed for Jesus to protect his soul and before the prayer was over, I had created what I called my "Heaven Club". As juvenile and absurd as it sounded, it was my special way of putting everyone that I had lost into the same prayer. Once in the club, they could look out for each other and by me calling to their existence kept their spirits alive. Somehow, I found it easier to have this mindset than to think that I would never get to see any of them again.

After school one day, my mom directed me to the master bedroom where my dad was waiting. My brain summarized up my day, trying to decipher what I could have done wrong. Much to my relief he was not upset, but instead sat me down and handed me an envelope. I opened it up and my eyes grew large as I pulled out two tickets. My grin then grew even larger than my eyes as I read the words "World Series", followed by "Yankees versus Dodgers". I exploded into laugher as I flicked the two tickets together over and over. These tickets represented my first Yankees game and it was going to be during the World Series. I could not wait to tell all of my friends at school but once I did, none of them believed me. Oh well, I did not care a single bit about what they thought, I was too happy.

After four long days of school and every brutal comment my friends could say about the Yankees, the time had finally come. My dad and I jumped delightfully into his car and sped off to Dodger Stadium. Despite all of the drama and hardship we had experienced in the last year, this was a joyous occasion and we were going to make the most of it. My dad led me into Dodger Stadium, where he bought me my first Yankees helmet and World Series banner. A smile was permanently tattooed to my face.

Surrounded by a sea of Dodgers fans, we definitely heard our fair share of taunting, but my dad kept shooting back the fact that the Dodgers would always stand second to the Yankees. This was a solid fact that even they could not argue with. Being there amongst thousands of rivals was quite intimidating, but having my dad by my side gave me all of the confidence that I needed to root on my Yankees loud and proud. Almost every inning, I took a deep breath and absorbed all of the magnificence associated with the Yankees and Major League Baseball in general.

At one point in the game, I turned to look at my dad and he seemed very happy. I could not help but wonder if he was thinking about his brother. How could he not? Yet at least whatever thought he had stuck in his mind kept him smiling. Then I pondered if the seat I was sitting in actually belonged to Joe. At that moment, I really hoped that I was dedicated enough to the Yankees to be worthy of that World Series seat. I decided I was and I will never forget that moment. By the seventh inning, we were down by seven and with the fans not giving us any leniency, we made our exit early. My dad's final words to those cursed fans were that assuredly, the Yankees would be the champions and with the help of Reggie Jackson, we were indeed champions. The real world was a tough and troublesome place, but for that week, everything in the world was right.

A year later, we returned to Dodger Stadium in one of the most phenomenal games I have ever witnessed. This was game four of the series with the Dodgers holding on to a four to three lead. With Munson on first, Reggie came to the plate to face Bob Welch. Reggie's at bat lasted an astonishing eight minutes with foul ball after foul ball igniting every seat in the stadium. My dad was right there with them, screaming to me, "Do you believe?" Nodding, I screamed back, "Hell yeah I believe!" I then looked around at all of the Dodgers fans whom I knew could sense the same homerun looming in the air that we could. So the battle between Welch and Reggie continued and with every swing, the anticipation in the stadium grew louder.

Half of my senses were shot, but my eyes still worked and I kept them glued to Reggie. The next pitch brought a thunderous swing, and before I could even react, it was all over. Reggie had struck out. I was dumbfounded, feeling beyond all certainty that Reggie was going to crush the ball out of the park. Then it sank in, we lost and the magnitude of Dodgers fans let us know it. Still, we walked out of the stadium with our heads held high. My dad, in a very drunk confidence, was yelling at the top of his lungs, "Yankees in six. Yankees in six." Even after suffering such a heartbreaking loss, we both continued to have a great time and the fun spilled out into the parking lot.

My dad was so drunk that he could not remember where he had parked so we spent the next two hours roaming the parking lot aimlessly. As we circled the stadium, my dad incessantly kept chanting, "Yankees in six. Yankees in six." How my dad did not get jumped that night I will never know, but what I do know is that the Yankees indeed won it all in game six. That crazy drunkard was right. I know without a doubt that at least half of those Dodgers fans remembered my dad's rant after game six ended. The time I spent with my dad was some of my favorite childhood memories and I truly thank the pinstripes for offering such a positive male-bonding atmosphere.

The Yankees were the only light in the cavern of pain that was my life. However, ten months later the pain and light were brought together when the Yankees World mourned the loss of our Captain, number fifteen, Thurman Munson. My dad was the first to reveal the tragic news to me and he did so with a somber but straight-to-the-point approach. My heart felt weak and empty.

I had experienced more hurt in the past three years than any twelve year old should experience over their entire lifetime. The pain was so real and showed no signs of subsiding. I found myself jaded with what life had to offer and if times did not start to change, and quickly, I was going to lose all faith in optimism. That night, I welcomed a new member into my "Heaven Club", and with a meek smile, I went to sleep knowing that all of the people that I cared about would be safe. After all, they now had the Captain to guide them.

KEY TO THE GATEWAY

*A*s I entered into middle school with endless heaps of advice and promise for the future, I still found myself haunted daily by the past. I was trailed by the constant reminder of what my family and I had gone through in such a short period of time. As a result, my behavior at school grew exceedingly worse and I paid for it dearly at home. My dad had zero tolerance for failure and was absolutely livid any time the referrals came home. Due to his anger, I started to develop a growing resentment towards my dad and began feeling alienated from the activities that once formed our bond. I took a break from my love for baseball and put some time into establishing a new group of kids to run amuck with. I developed an immediate level of friendship amongst some of my classmates and the attention they showed me kept the pain that plagued me at bay.

Although when those kids were gone, I had to find a different means for suppressing the hurt and it came in the convenient form of alcohol. At first, it started as a couple of beers here and there that I smuggled from my dad's supply, but within several months, I had moved on to multiple shots from my dad's bar. Alcohol is rarely seen as the gateway drug, marijuana usually gets that blame, but for me, it was indeed alcohol. *Is this really how easily such a drastic disease starts? Was I in the process of finding yet another skeleton to lurk in my shadows?* The answer quickly proved to be yes and by the end of the school year, my personality had become darker than the depths of the abyss that I was trapped in.

With a solid level of liquor in my system, I soon discovered that most music had some deeper, alternative meanings. There was a certain freedom in the lyrics of Led Zeppelin that allowed me to dream of magical places far beyond Earth's limitations. Black Sabbath let me know that my dark side was perfectly acceptable, but it was a book my mom gave me that changed me in ways that I never thought were possible. The book was centered on the life and death of Jim Morrison, the lead singer for The Doors. After reading it just once, I was hooked and after reading it for the fifth time, I was convinced that Jim's darkness was my own.

I reflected every side of Jim Morrison, from his enmity towards his father to his insolence towards authority. He was constantly shocking people with his fatuous behavior and seeing exactly how far he could push the tolerance of society. Just a year earlier, as a kid, my hero was Thurman Munson, but now that I was a teenager, I had chosen Jim as my idol. Jim had lived the life of a true rock star and had been stripped from this world at the youthful age of twenty-seven. My mindset then became that I would be lucky to survive past my twenty-seventh birthday, so I was going to live as freely as Jim did.

Drinking became a daily need for me, even though I hid it well, but the more I drank, the more reckless I became. Many of the aspects in my life that had mattered up until now became a distant, blurred out memory. Baseball, my all-time love, was far too complicated to play with liquor running through my system, so it took an immediate back seat. I threw away a wonderful, natural talent for a detestable, lifelong disease. My dream of baseball and all its sober glory was forever lost the day I chose to stay at home and drink instead of going to practice and excelling.

I started to make a habit of creating excuses to cover up for my mistakes and many adults would respond that we were just kids being kids. Sadly though, we were far more than that, we were future junkies and alcoholics destroying the last of any skills or dreams God had set in store for us. So with an addicted system, I was convinced that I had all the answers and therefore did not need the guidance of my parents or teachers. I was headed down the wrong road in a hurry and it was all because I read a book glamorizing a deceased rock star. I neglected to put any thought into the reason why he died at twenty-seven, I just saw the means he used to silence his pain and I wanted to mimic them.

I had brushed baseball completely to the side and it was all because the pain I carried was too unbearable for the sober Tony. Looking back, it cuts me to my core to think about how far I could have gone in baseball. The same could be said about my academics. My behavior was so ludicrous that there was no preventing my role as the class clown. *Who needs an education when there is plenty of instant entertainment?* My drinking pushed my attitude beyond any level of control and I found a new hobby through habitual lying. I could drink a beer, lie about it and all was forgotten. My delivery was so precise that there was no way I could be argued against. To boot, once alcohol became too easy to mask, I moved on to cannabis and trailing not too far behind that was cocaine.

I was only thirteen years old and I already had a mixture of ingredients driving me directly into failure. I should have been running down fly balls, but instead I was running down the clock on my opportunity to change for the better. I looked at the other kids who studied hard, taking their education seriously and I thought they were such losers for being puppets to the system. However, it was actually me who was losing everything and they were the real winners. I blamed my dad for my failures and anyone else who tried to steer me right, but that was short lived and grew stale quickly.

I recognized that I had the key this whole time to unlock my future, and what scared me the most was that I used it to unlock the wrong door. I then passed through that door and each one of my steps down that path of vices took me further away from reality. Faintly, I could see what appeared to be my mom trying to bring me back into the light, accompanied by my teachers, yet all that I could do was continue my stride. I should have turned around and ran back to the people who had my best interests in their hearts, but instead I befriended a group of individuals who were walking down the same path.

Their times with me were on separate stop watches, nevertheless, each one of their demises would prove to be dismal and tragic. For some it would be prison, for others, a sturdy casket, but for me, I was just along for the ride with my misled companions. I was walking down a road with individuals as scared as I was, scared to be hurt and scared to be alone. Somewhere behind me, off in the silent distance, I heard a heavy door slam.

THE TRUTH SHALL SET HIM FREE

The evening was quiet, unusually quiet, and that was mainly because my dad had to be up by two o'clock in the morning. At this stage in my life I was no longer able to live in the same room as my sister, so I was relocated to the couch. So there I sat, watching Monday Night Football when Howard Cosell interrupted with the shocking news that John Lennon had been shot. With the volume just loud enough to be heard from his room, my dad burst out with disbelief and planted himself directly in front of the television. "Unfuckinbelievable," he cried. Now this was by far the most prevalent word used in my house, especially by my father. To his credit, this was the one night that he had a right to; I guess the whole nation had a right to. Still to this day, there is no sane explanation for the tragic shortness of Lennon's life. The world was truly less of a better place with him gone.

Three days later a memorial was held in Griffith Park. My dad, Uncle Ted, his friend John and I went, along with at least ten thousand other grieving fans. There was so much sadness that day. I was only thirteen and I felt it too, but hardly on the same magnitude as these people. Most of them had actually grown up with Lennon in their lives. This opened my eyes to the understanding of a true sadness, a hurt the whole world could feel. These were life's lessons instantly forced upon us, upon me.

When our family was not grieving in one aspect or another, a systematic routine was the everyday life at my house. Both my folks struggled with two jobs, and I do admire them since they were both highly devoted workers. Amazingly, my mom still managed to maintain a clean house, which actually rubbed off on me. My great latter profession in life was along the lines of a cleaning service. That aside, I did most of my part to keep up on the chores. My sister, on the other hand, made it certain that she contributed very little. I love my sister Cassandra to death, yet she succeeded in making my world as rough as possible. She took no shit from me and we would battle constantly throughout the years. Nowadays, Cassandra is a success with a great family and she continues to persevere against her fears. I truly am proud to be her brother, but back as kids, life was different.

The nice thing about my parents' schedules was that it made our house the place where friends could hang out. I constantly heard my share of lectures from my mom, but she rarely became upset at me to the point of using profanity. If she did swear though, chances are one of us messed up big time. On one particular incident, she caught me making what she perceived as being a "drug deal" over the phone. To me, it was just a small sack of weed between two friends, but to her, it was a third degree felony. My mom came around the corner and instantly snatched the phone from my hands. She proceeded to dangle the phone over my head, combined with yelling her choice words of profanity. To be honest, her use of these taboo words was so funny that I could not stop laughing, thus further infuriating her. Although her rage would not last long, these were the everyday occurrences that happened in our house.

Furthermore, there were also the confrontations where luckily I was not directly involved. Mostly it was the fights twixt my father and my uncle Sal, who lived down the street with my aunt Barbara. One time he and my dad wrestled each other into the glass coffee table, while my friend David and I stood there laughing hysterically. Another time Sal showed up on our front lawn, drunken beyond tolerability, wielding two machetes and daring my dad to come out and "play." Wisely enough, my dad opted to stay inside that day.

My dad was a complex man. He was a delivery driver for a cookie company and never missed a day of work. On the weekends he delivered newspapers for the Los Angles Times. On special occasions, he would allow me to tag along and throw the newspapers for him. Being a part-time paperboy may sound like a fun job for a kid, but it was not fun for me. The job consisted of freezing half to death in the back of his pick-up truck at three in the morning, throwing the Sunday edition of the LA Times for two dollars an hour. All work aside, my dad, who never tried to go back onstage after his brother's death, was a guy who had many sides. Some were really good, like his humor, which was outstanding and some were really bad, like his anger, when fueled by alcohol, which was scary. Never more so than the day that changed me in just about every way.

As I arrived home from school, my mom caught me at the doorway and informed me that Dad was "D", which was her code for drunk. "Whatever," was my response, but once inside, I noticed it was a Chivas Regal night. *Hard alcohol makes the old man very mean.* Immediately, I put myself on the defensive. He wasted very little time getting started, first about school, which I could not stand to hear, then about chores. From there he moved on to my mom, complaining about dinner and what ever else he seemed irritated by. These were the nights that I hated, and the nights that I hated him the most.

The trigger this night was about his brother Joe and it only grew worse as the bottle emptied. By now it was around eight or nine at night when my dad sternly screamed "Tony, get your ass out on the porch." I was just getting out of the shower and usually did not tell my dad to "Hold on," but hey, this time I did. He just screamed louder. Under my breath I mumbled, "Mother Fucker can wait while I air dry." I got dressed, still drying my hair, and walked out to see what the big deal was. He started jabbing me in my chest, telling me the standard parental phrase, "When I tell you to do something, you do it." "Okay…Dad!" Half sarcastic, but I hid it well. He proceeded on and on about his brother dying. "You don't understand," he tells me. I tried to say what a thirteen year old son is supposed to say. "Yes I do, Dad. I am sorry your brother is gone." Blah, blah, blah, I had already put up with five years of this drama. Well he wanted my attention a little more so he quickly grabbed the collar of my shirt with his clenched fists and lifted me about a foot off the ground. "This is how my brother died," he screamed. "He hung himself you dumb son of a bitch." The rage…the pain in his eyes was both frightening and heartbreaking. I started to wriggle around, gasping for air, so he let me down. I did not understand what I was hearing. "How did he hang himself? Why?" My dad shot back, "He didn't deliberately kill himself. He died during a moment of self-gratification." He chose to explain the nightmare that he had kept concealed for the past five years. Uncle Joe's body was found hanging in his bathroom, death from self-asphyxiation.

None of this twisted shit made any sense. All that I could think was how I needed to talk to Benny, and get the fuck away from my dad. So I ran down the street to the cemetery, tucked behind a mausoleum, and struggled to untangle the web of thoughts that were going on in my head. I sat alone, picturing Joe hanging there in his bathroom. This new vision of my uncle was so strange, so ugly. I guess the thing that bothered me more personally was the lying. This mistrust gave me a reason to have the upper hand, but this was not necessarily an advantage.

A few hours later, I finally went home, knowing how long it took for my old man to pass out from drinking. I immediately called Benny to tell him that I had something important for him to hear. By the sound of my voice, he already knew exactly what I was going to say. He mentioned to me that he had found out the truth just a couple months ago. We talked all night about it and together we cried. I loved my cousin so much and we now shared a great pain, a great secret.

About two months passed relatively quietly, until yet another fit of rage spawned from my father. My resentment towards him grew so badly that I hated my dad almost every moment of every day. Well on this dreadful afternoon he began his usual tirade of complaints and ended up throwing my uncle Bob in my face. My dad did not like my uncle Bob. I told him, "At least Bob didn't go out like a freak." My dad blew up at my absurd allegations. He then grabbed me and threw me to the ground. My dad put his index finger to my head, using his hand to simulate a gun, and then stared me down the deepest that I have ever seen. "Your fuckin' hero of an uncle blew his brains out. The coward took his own life. There was no car accident. This was your precious Bob." He sealed his words by spitting directly into my face.

My whole world became pitch black. I did not know what to believe anymore. Two days later I confronted my mom, asking her if Bobby or his sister Collette knew. She became frantic, realizing that I had discovered the truth. She did not know what to say, so she only told me that nobody else could know. I began to sense that I could not trust my mom either. I managed to uphold my word for about another two years but somebody had to tell Bobby about his father, and that somebody was me. I believed that the truth would set him free, if there was any freedom in the truth.

Looking back at my dad, he was trapped in a deep prison, one that no words or confessions could save him from. He surely tried on that day when he shared his nightmare, and all that I benefited from it was simply another way to have the upper hand. All of this new knowledge became my rage, a fire in my soul at the tender age of thirteen. No matter how much I tried, I could not shake the images of my uncle Bob or my uncle Joe and the way that they departed this world. All that I could comprehend was that Bobby and Benny did not have dads and I still did, yet I wanted nothing to do with mine. Life was on the verge of becoming grossly interesting. I knew that things would never be the same and that I would never be the same. I could see my dad had deep regrets for what he had revealed and there was no way that I was going to let him off the hook that easy. I muttered the only words that I knew would cut him the deepest. "Fuck...the... Yankees." Each word felt just as powerful as the next. I did it to hurt him, it worked, and it felt great.

Being a Teen Rager

Shortly after the death of his father, Benny moved with his family to West Covina. The haunting memory of his dad and that house became too much for them to bear and the move was an appropriate decision. We constantly were devising ways to be together by sneaking into each other's car at the end of the day, hoping that our mothers would not notice. Needless to say, it never worked, but the effort was always there. I begged my mom constantly to let me have more time with Benny and although she agreed that I was usually on my best behavior around him that unfortunately the distance made regular visits too difficult to commit to. I argued with her everyday, yet since she was always so wise about every situation, I accepted the fact that my cousin was now less of an immediate figure in my life.

With my cousin now distanced from me and finding out the truth about my uncles, Joe and Bob, mistrust was created in my heart and head for all adults, including my parents, my teachers and above all, the law. I remember coming home from school and my uncle Sal's house was surrounded by the police. The vision looked like a pitiful yard sale as most of his furniture was out on the street. The cops had raided my uncle's house in hopes of finding a large cache of drugs. There were no drugs, but what they did find was some Vicodin and a few unregistered weapons, which was clearly not enough to satisfy these cops.

All of my friends were showing up, curious to know what had went down with my uncle and I loved every bit of the attention. The fact that my family was so dysfunctional did not matter because the notoriety that it brought me outweighed everything else. My family and I were known to be the troublemakers amongst the neighborhood. My friends' parents did not want their kids associating with me or my family. As for Sal, he got some weekends in jail and some large fines, and my aunt Barbara got some new furniture. That was the point when I accepted that there was nothing normal about my family.

The combination of such events taught me the valuable lesson that I could get away with anything and that I was smarter than anyone with any level of authority. In my mind, both my parents and the cops were at my complete disposal. My teachers as well had nothing to offer me. School was strictly for entertainment, a chance to be the class clown. Going to school gave me an opportunity to be with my friends who at this point were far more important than my family. My close clique consisted of David, Oscar, Carmen and Debi. These were the people that created my family away from home. I was free from my parents and I took advantage of everything. I could do anything that I wanted and then lie to get away with it. My poor mother would believe anything that I said simply because she wanted to believe in me, and from my standpoint, an occasional beat down from my dad was no serious punishment.

Alcohol and drugs became the main focus of my life. Oscar and I would begin our day by smoking a joint or two before school, followed by a couple of bottles of cheap wine. These vices gave me the courage that I needed to do the crazy shit that Sparzo was known for. Fighting with teachers, disrupting class, getting suspended, I would do anything for the attention. Along with that, being a flawless liar was a key feature in how I made my early income. I started as an everyday panhandler guilt-tripping people for money. I could sit on the bench outside of a grocery store with an empty look of misery and abandon on my face and the spare change would just come rolling in. I would also sell the gifts that my parents had given me and then use the instant cash to buy more drugs and alcohol.

For about two months in ninth grade I had convinced the girl at the snack line to give me free food and I, in turn, would sell the snacks to my friends at a discounted rate and make a small profit. I was easily able to turn a single dollar into five, thus making about one hundred and fifty dollars per day just by selling juice and donuts. The more money that I made the more drugs and alcohol I consumed, and it worked out to be a simple and seamless process for a young entrepreneur.

Being under the influence gave me the notion that I was invincible and I often tested my limits by pushing the buttons of every cop that I encountered. I absolutely loved to taunt the law. After all, I was only fourteen, what were they going to do to me? I definitely was an antagonist towards them and they treated me accordingly. They were constantly searching me, harassing me, pulling me over, and no, not in the car, but on foot. By the time that I was fifteen, all of the cops knew me and I loved it. Again, my world revolved around attention.

I managed to put in a halfway decent attempt at school and my teachers took pity on me, giving me straight D's in an effort to get me to the next level. I did not realize how much I really needed that education, I did not care. I just wanted to get stoned, get drunk, cause trouble and lie to get away with all of it. My favorite was when I would tell my mom that she needed to give me some money for a charity at school. She genuinely believed that I was doing something good and gave me the money, even though realistically she could not afford it. My mom tried so hard to make things right in our house, but in all honesty, her efforts were far too late.

Everything that I had seen and the absurd truth about my family did nothing but turn me into an angry teenager. My friends had all of the answers, which came in the form of drugs, and if they did not, their older brothers or sisters did. I knew that it was wrong but I could care less. Marijuana relaxed me and that was precisely what I needed to settle the rage that was inside. I was so hyper and out of control that my nickname quickly became Spazo instead of Sparzo. Teenagers can be so cruel, but none of them were crueler than me. I recall the first time that I told my mother to "fuck off". The words broke her heart, mostly out of fear of what my dad would do to me and reluctantly she said nothing to him. Again I was given the upper hand and I ran with it, separating myself from anyone who cared. Plus, if things ever got too bad, I could just bullshit my way back into her heart. As a juvenile, this mentality made perfect sense to me and I did not care who I hurt. My immunity, however, was short lived.

The first time that I ever got arrested was an experience I can never forget. Steve, Mike and Sean and I went out for a delicious dinner turned dine-n-dash at the Los Arcos Mexican Restaurant. Sean had obtained a fake drivers license stating that he was twenty-two so he started ordering round after round of margaritas even though we were already belligerent, having just left from a nearby house party. Soon enough, our dinner bill was almost at the hundred dollar mark, so the only option now was to ditch the place, and fast. In complete unison, we all made a break for the door. Two bus boys ended up tackling Steve and took his boom box which he had chosen to bring in with him. Mike and Sean got away, as did I. However, this situation was not over with just yet. This was an opportunity to do what I did best, cause havoc. So I went back into the restaurant, demanding for them to give us the radio back. They refused and informed me that the police were on their way, but once again I did not care. Pompous with attitude, I proceeded to destroy the place, kicking in doors, throwing a chair through the window, smashing tables. To this day, I still can not believe that somebody there did not beat me down severely. The cops arrived and of course arrested me. I talked shit about their mothers, their wives, anything to get a reaction. The cops only laughed. Maybe it was the same cops that busted my uncle so they already knew my family, or maybe they just did not care.

When my mom came to pick me up, she was so irate and still I had no remorse. I just regurgitated the tainted truth to her, about how I was the victim, how Sean never told us that we were going to run, how I was just trying to receive my best friend's radio and that I never caused any damage. She said that she believed me and I felt a sense of relief. Just as usual, my dad found out nothing about this, and he never would. I had my mom right where I wanted her. All that I could think was just how much I could not wait until Monday so I could tell my story to the masses that waited to hear it. I was fourteen and I had all of the solutions to any problem. I could play the victim and get away with it, every time. Life was finally figured out, right? Boy was I wrong, so very wrong.

To Love and Respect

The concept of "Love at First Sight" never really made an impact on me until the day that I first met Desiree. Instantly, I knew that this was the girl that I wanted to spend the rest of my life with. Her beauty was so pure and unmatched that it made my heart leap from my chest and beat with a furious insanity. The only downfall to this potential romance was the fact that she was thirteen and I was fifteen, yet the age issue only fazed me for about a fraction of a second. Desiree was very soft spoken and wisely humble with her words. She had a spine-tingling smile and an unbelievable body. There was no denying that at fifteen, the female physique was easily priority number one. My main focus became to turn her attitude, since I was certain that she did not feel the same way as I did, and chances were she never would. I was determined to do anything to show her the light.

As I established myself within the community, I began to develop a tight group of friends to hang out with and everyone was equally as misdirected as I was. My entourage consisted of Desiree, her sister Jennifer, Rick, Rick's brother, who was also Desiree's ex, and myself. Every so often Benny would come to visit from West Covina and that would make my days that much brighter. Meeting up with Benny was a major event and it always involved a heavy weekend of drinking. My alcohol and drug use had become an everyday occurrence and aside from the occasional encounters with the cops, I felt like I was doing just fine. I used my vices as the courage medium that I needed to try and win Desiree over. Desiree was everything to me, my every waking thought, but she evidently wanted nothing to do with me. Desiree had her own issues. Both Desiree and her sister were habitual runaway children who were constantly in trouble with the law to the point where they were both on probation. At the time that we met, she had an amazing father by the name of James. James was by far one of the purest, most honest men that I have ever encountered. Raising two teenage daughters was not an easy task, yet he always maintained the good nature that still made guests feel welcome. Desiree's mom, Gloria, was completely on the opposite end of the spectrum. She was undeniably the most miserable person to be around. Gloria had a look of disgust on her face every time that I saw her, and it was directed towards everyone. I am convinced though that her distaste for me was still just a little bit greater than that of my peers. I chalked her right there in my books next to my parents who I already could not stand, so pushing her aside took little, if not, no effort at all. So in order to be around Desiree, I put up with her intolerance and the same could be said about Gloria. In order to be with her daughter, she had to put up with us, and mostly me.

Truth be told, we were all delinquents on a one way path to juvenile hall. Desiree seemed to be the only one who was growing bored with our lifestyle. However, what could be boring about a lifestyle of having random strangers buy us liquor, meandering down the lawless alleys, arriving at Pelaconi Park and raging until sunrise? When the vibe was right, some of us would get beyond wasted, wait for the train to come rolling through and then either play a risky game of chicken or just hop on and take a ride downtown. The only issue with the latter was the walking back part, which was a real hassle since we had to pass through a culturally dark part of Los Angeles known as "Frogtown". An insane idea for any white kid, but then again, what did I care? This was just another opportunity for me to prove my valor.

Desiree was different and not very impressed with my antics. She was a few years younger than me but ten years ahead of me mentally. Desiree was an old soul no doubt, and to this day, one of the strongest women that I have ever known. To make Desiree my girlfriend meant that I had to become somebody that I was not, I had to develop a false persona. She was a lot more open-minded to the world than I was and did not let the everyday pressures of life get her down. I also failed to see the positive attributes in others the same way that she did. Any change on my behalf was going to be tough, but for her it was worth it.

Around the same time that I was putting all of my energy towards Desiree, I met a guy my age by the name of Martin. Martin's family had moved from Hollywood to Glendale in an attempt to keep Martin off of the crime-infested streets. Martin started shooting dope at the age of twelve and in many ways it had already demonstrated its damage. Damaged or not, he instantly became my new best man and a fresh face to my close group of friends. He was the prefect ally for my drunken outbursts and the first night that we hung out resulted in both of us getting beaten black and blue.

Martin decided that it was a grand idea to try and steal a car while we were roaming around late night in Lake Hollywood. The main holdback to our escapade was that the owner of the car was passed out in the backseat. He awoke in an enraged daze just as Martin, who was a master at hotwiring cars, was connecting the ignition. The silence was broken as a glass bottle was planted across Martin's face. As I witnessed the blood flooding into Martin's eyes and down the bridge of his nose, a trigger in the back of my mind signaled that it was time to retaliate. I went absolutely ballistic, boiling inside with rage mixed with alcohol. The situation soon panned out to Martin and me up against four college brutes. Man, we got fucked up. The relentless beating finally subsided when our friend who did not get involved until that point decided to assist by smashing a tire iron over one of the meathead's skull. A crimson river of blood spilled out across the asphalt, staining our shoes. A group of girls who were watching the fiasco screamed bloody murder. The shrill sound of their screams pierced my ears, creating a sudden and relentless ringing. Everyone dispersed quickly, leaving nothing behind but blood-drenched tarmac. I recall hearing sometime later that the guy who was tire ironed suffered permanent brain damage. Upon reflecting back on the incident, I was not bothered a single bit, but Desiree was completely appalled. Like I said, she was better than all of us.

Consequently, my behavior had me permanently barred from Desiree and her house. I was devastated and soon found myself increasing my consumption of alcohol and cannabis in a desperate attempt to numb my soul. I also started reminiscing harder on my uncle Joseph, constantly drawing back to the vision of him hanging himself and wondering why he did it. I still had not experienced intercourse and struggled to grasp why someone would deliberately hang their self just to get off. On one particularly drunken night, I convinced a friend to give me a ride across town to the house where my uncle had died. I knocked on the door and an elderly gentleman answered. I apologized for burdening him and explained that my uncle had passed away there and that I needed to find some final peace with him. Surprisingly, he agreed and welcomed me in. The house had a dark and deeply gloomy atmosphere despite the many paintings and photographs of smiling faces in every direction that I looked. As I entered the master bedroom, my eyes immediately bolted towards the bathroom. There I stood, picturing him in his death pose, like a lifeless ornament that only the Devil would use. This vision suddenly frightened me and I had to leave at once. In no way was this therapy, but more like teenage drama. However, it did give me a chance to say goodbye to him and let him know how chaotic things had become for our family. Nothing was ever the same after he died.

A month or so passed before I finally felt a gleam of light come back into my life. The time had come for me to lose my virginity, and at the age of fifteen, not twelve like I had told all of my friends. Her name was Jenny, and Jenny was a girl my age that actually had an interest in me. The feeling was nil reciprocated since I was already in love with Desiree, but it tore me to know that I could not have anything to do with her, so it was nice to at least be wanted by somebody. Jenny was of Guatemalan descent, with dark, wavy hair that flowed all of the way down to the small of her back. She was a short girl, with a greatly developed physique far ahead of her age.

I convinced Jenny to cut out after fourth period class and join me over at my parents' place. Once the bell rang, we swiftly made our way. We went upstairs to my dad's bar, took several shots of Cuervo Gold tequila and then hit the couch. Inside, I felt terrified, but I tried to act all smooth by putting up the illusion that this was not my first time. Jenny, on the other hand, had already engaged in the act so she instantly took control. She warmed me up by jumping on top, thrusting her hips rhythmically into mine. Although the feeling of exaltation quickly turned to shame as halfway through the experience Jenny leaned over and grabbed a cigarette. My supreme pride was torn to shreds, followed by a sudden sense of guilt and remorse. My deflowering should have been with Desiree, but instead I had joined spirits with a girl that I felt nothing towards. Since the truth was unentertaining, I lied to everyone, spurting out nonsense like, "I lit her up with multiple orgasms." Ha! The only thing lit up that afternoon was her fucking cigarette. I am sure that she told the truth since her version was accurate, yet I never stuck around long enough to hear the ridicule.

Hypothetical eons had passed before I was finally allowed back into Desiree's life and home, promising to develop a better relationship with her family. Her mom still denied acceptance of me, but I could Eddie Haskell any parent and did so with great success. To Desiree, I was viewed solely as a friend, so I used this as a foot-in-the-door for developing a strong bond between us. We became joined at the hip and partied together everyday. The time that I spent with my friends decreased and Desiree noticed an obvious improvement in my demeanor. Every time that I was with her I fell harder in love. All of the cliché symptoms of love blindsided me and I could not eat, I could not sleep, I could not do anything. Still, no matter how persistent my actions were, there was no reaction on her part.

Frustrated and hurt, I found myself making out with her sister at a party one weekend. A couple of her friends stepped up to me, questioning about how I could do that to Desiree. I argued back that Desiree wanted nothing to do with me, so I needed to move on. Her close friend Justin slapped me across the face and proceeded to tell me the exact opposite, which in truth Desiree did have an interest in me. Still numb from the slap, my jaw dropped in amazement. Two seconds later, I was out the door and sprinting down the street. Exhausted and panting for air, I finally made it to her house. With clasped hands, we laid on the grass in her backyard and with the celestial sky glistening above us, the mood was finally right. I whispered a sweet nothing to her and then we started to kiss. Hallelujah. Desiree was so beautiful, an angel amongst devils, there to prove God's omnipotence. I was in Heaven, forever lost in that solitary moment.

Monday morning rolled through and that was the day that I had to be at the police station before continuation school. The only nice thing about this was that they were right across the street from each other so it made it easy to fulfill both obligations. I arrived at the station to pick up the boom box that was taken from Steve at the dine-n-dash a year earlier. I thought it was great that they had to give it back even after all of the destruction that I had caused. Detective Richard Price escorted me down the elevator to the basement where the evidence locker was. My attitude towards cops had only grown worse and this was an opportunity to show Detective Dick Price what Sparzo was made of.

The disrespecting started the moment we got out of the

elevator. The detective just laughed, calling me a tough guy. "That's right Dick," I sneered, "Do your job and give me back my radio." Again he just laughed and after signing the necessary paperwork, the detective escorted me back onto the elevator. As we started back up, he oddly slammed the elevator "Stop" button. Blankly, I looked at him. Abruptly, he grabbed me by the throat and held me up against the elevator wall. Dick explained to me that I was lucky that no charges were filed, and he really believed that he should be allowed to beat some discipline into me. Dick then cleverly added that I was not going to be a minor forever. Well he established my attention for certain. Gasping, I demanded for him to let me go, and he released his grip, giggling like a retarded schoolgirl. We continued to the main floor where I rushed out the door and across the street to the continuation school. I was outraged at the fact that Dick Price got the best of me.

Too distracted to focus, I ditched my class and met up with my friend Jimmy. We were initially planning to trade the boom box for some cocaine, but instead we wound up with some heroin. Somehow, I knew that Jimmy had what he really wanted. I could not stand anything having to do with heroin due to the fact that it had its ugly hand on my uncle Ted and it was the same substance that caused my uncle Bob to put the trigger to his skull. But then again, here I was, sitting in an alley a block away from both the school and the cop shop, with a belt around my left arm and a needle going into my vein. I was scared to death but managed to keep my emotions contained. This was the first time that I ever felt the influence of peer pressure since usually it was me on the other side of the situation. All that I wanted was simply to hang out with Jimmy, so I closed my eyes and let him take me on the ride. Before I knew it, I was throwing up all over myself. This was not the kind of experience that I was hoping for, but I played it cool and soon enough my mindset mellowed out. Ultimately, I tried it two more times, but word traveled way too fast and soon Desiree found out. She told me to get lost, again. *Why the fuck does this keep happening to me?* I had finally started to establish a positive bond with her and now this. My life was avalanching downhill.

At the fragile age of fifteen, I started to feel that if I could not have her, then what was the point of living? Hour after hour, day after day, I spent calling her house but she refused to speak to me. After about a week of relentless effort, she actually accepted one my calls. Surprisingly enough, it was her father who convinced her that a friend never turns their back on another friend in a time of need. I went straight over to her house where we talked well into the dusk. I told her everything and she forgave me. God bless Desiree. I promised her that I would never do drugs again. Desiree smiled at that thought and with the momentum on my side, I asked her to be my girlfriend. That first kiss sober was unreal. With a tear in my eye, I swore to her that I would love and respect her forever. This was a bold statement for something that I knew nothing about.

Playing Daddy

A new life with Desiree was exactly what I needed to find a better direction in my own life. This was the first time ever that I felt more concerned for someone else's well being than my own. I loved her so much, and really wanted to spend the rest of my living days with her. Every waking moment was spent with Desiree. Curbing my behavior seemed to be the only thing that was not falling in line. I had recently been kicked out of Lincoln High School and sent to Walter B. Harris Continuation School, which truthfully was tolerable since all of my close friends were already there. My drug use had escalated to acid and I was in constant search of doses. Finding the "Meaning of Life" seemed a lot more possible with acid as the medium. Since most of my days were spent focused on me, I spared no time for my family, except for when I needed something. I could then focus in my charm and portray the innocent youth that they could give something to.

As for Desiree and me, we spent most of our days sneaking around, finding the most creative and unique places to share our love. Life was euphoric. This was precisely what I thought it would be like to be with the woman that I loved. However, calling her a woman was an oxymoron in the sense that she was still only thirteen. I heard my fair share of demeaning from my family and friends about her age, yet my deafly selective hearing tuned right past their opinions and advice. On seldom occasions, I would attempt to share some of my personal thoughts with my dad but his sole response was that we as a couple would never last. *Pessimistic fool, what the hell did he know?*

The one person who did actually believe in me was Tony Boyte. Tony was the complete opposite of me, the model son. He played on the first string for the football team, established a quality job for only being sixteen and was a huge success when it came to his academics. He basically did every move right. When living with my parents had escalated to high levels of hostility, I would break free from the concentration camp that was their home and found a solid residence living out on the streets. Tony stepped up by taking me in and I admired his benevolence. Since he was a year older than me, Tony became the big brother that I had always wished for. He struggled like everyone else to get through to me, but I was already the knowledge guru and his advice fell upon deaf ears.

The biggest problem with my life was that my outlook towards my life only grew worse. Not only was I deeply seeded in alcohol and drugs, but I was now a verbal abuser, constantly venting my aggression out on Desiree. I had always despised any man that I ever heard vociferously belittling a female and now here I was doing the exact same. I was a hypocrite. Every time that I screamed at her I would swear to never let it happen again. Her love for me became her biggest weakness and she always forgave me, so this disgusting behavior remained for the greater portion of our relationship.

The storm of rage subsided intermittingly for brief periods of time over the following year and it was during one of these calms that Desiree revealed to me the few words that could freeze me in my tracks, she was pregnant. The twenty pound lump in my throat fell heavily to the depths of my stomach. A stabbing poison of fear and bliss flowed through my veins. The fear then jumped to sheer terror when I considered our parents and what their reactions would be. After all, Desiree was only thirteen.

We decided that the best strategy would be to inform her parents first. When we sat them down to discuss our predicament, they were amazingly calm about it. I was shocked. James should have unloaded on me, but instead he kept his composure and spelled out our options. We unanimously agreed to keep the baby and make my delinquent self step up as a man by securing a quality job. Desiree's parents were incredible. Although, informing my parents of this new blessing was going to be a different story. I determined that it was less stressful to approach my mom first. She too remained calm, joyfully replying to me that this would bring our family closer together. Her acceptance gave me a rush of excitement. Maybe all the resentment that was in my heart would finally give way. This could be the opportunity that I needed to sober up and be an awesome father to my child. Though as great as this feeling was, it, like all good things, was short lived.

Now came the hardest part, telling my dad that he was going to be a grandparent. This was the confrontation that I had dreaded since I first heard the news. I walked up to his bar and without a moments hesitation blurted, "Desiree is pregnant." His face went pale, and then flushed with the deepest red any man's face has ever shown. He held nothing back. "Unfuckinbelievable," he kept screaming. "How could someone as fucked up as you even think you can be a father? You can't even stay in school let alone provide for a child. You're a fuckin' disgrace." I was stung at how right he truly was. I was the last person that should be a father. I had no sense of responsibility, or any motivations to work hard. My life was consumed by the desire to drink and use drugs, which I had no intent of quitting. So I left the bar and tuned him out as his continual screams grew fainter with the distance.

The feeling of a close, tight knit family had not been present in our home for quite some time and all that I wanted was a chance to once again have the ideal family that we lost so long ago. The only way to achieve this was to believe that I was going to be with Desiree forever. My head was so full of misdirection that I lost what a clear path was to me. I should have been in school playing baseball and studying hard with thoughts of college, but instead I was getting ready to play Daddy and in all honesty I was morbidly afraid.

I could instantly see a beautiful change in Desiree and along with that, she prepared herself to be the best mother possible. She quit smoking cold-turkey and started regulating her vitamin intake. Her bedroom became a library of books and guides about being a mom. She was on top of everything. I, on the contrary, had no idea what I was doing. The financial strain that was being put on her parents never crossed my mind and since my parents were never involved, it was completely on them. I gave her parents my word that I would take care of their daughter and my child. They truly wanted to believe in me, but actions speak louder than words and I never grasped that the fun was really over.

Desiree asked for very little change from me, just that I remained sober and established a job. I suddenly found myself looking at Desiree the same way that I looked at my parents and teachers. She was constantly telling me what to do, but I was blind to the fact that she had every right to. Desiree was carrying my baby and I was not doing my part, so I would do what came naturally and lie. Countless times I made the promise to wake up early and scout out a job, yet when the moment actually came, I would just head over to a nearby friend's house to lounge around and get high all day. I complained to whoever would listen, claiming that I was the victim. I wallowed in my own self pity and most of my friends agreed with me. The only person who saw cleanly through my charade was Tony. He said nothing near what I wanted to hear, so we spent less time together because of it. I was too proud to absorb the truth. I wanted to believe that I could do what I wanted, go out when I wanted, then go and play Daddy when I wanted and everything would be fine. Unfortunately, that sort of behavior does not work in the real world. In the real world,

Desiree was getting closer and closer to her delivery date and the reality was beginning to take hold. I had to get my act together.

The two of us went to Harris Continuation School to enroll Desiree in classes after she was recently excused from her junior high. As we came closer to the entrance, I realized that it was a break between classes and that all of my friends were out in the front. So I held back, telling Desiree that I forgot something in the car. I did not have the guts to be seen with a pregnant thirteen year old. To this day, I fully regret my skittish behavior by making her walk alone. I eventually moseyed my way up and Desiree was the first person I saw. Uh oh! She just shook her head and asked, "What the hell are you doing?" For the first time, I had no answer. "Get your shit together and start taking care of business." I agreed with her, showing an overly forced smirk.

I was a mess and a complete failure, a drop out dad to be with no job, no car and nothing to rely on but my lies. After enough searching, I was finally able to land a job bagging groceries and my only real obligation was to occasionally bring home a bag of diapers. A tough task for an up and coming father, yet all that a job was to me was just an ample source in money for alcohol and pot, period. I watched the real world just slide by, when suddenly things made a turn for the worse. Desiree had to commit the last two months of her pregnancy to an unwed-mother's home, which turned out to be more of a hassle than a benefit for her. The home was down on Beverly and Rampart which was a dangerous neighborhood, especially for a girl as quiet yet resiliently strong as Desiree. I missed her so much that I often found myself talking out loud in the third person just to feel like Desiree was around.

Whenever I had the chance to take the bus down there, excitement was the only emotion that I experienced while visiting her, but departing her was brutal. I could feel her eyes watching me as I walked down the hall. I did have a conscience and I did have guilt, yet I always had a method to bypass that guilt. Desiree never complained, giving it one hundred percent of her efforts at all times. At the age of fourteen she had a good idea what the next eighteen years of her life meant and that she was going to be an active mother everyday until she was thirty-two. I, on the other hand, did not think that I would even make it to twenty-eight. I had no idea what I was doing, I just followed her lead. So when she signed up for Lamaze classes, I managed to attend. Moments would flash in my head where I genuinely believed that I could do this, but I was so good at lying by now that I was only deceiving myself.

During our third Lamaze class the inevitable happened, Desiree's water broke. She was having the baby and I was having an anxiety attack. Then again, I was thrilled because at that moment, I realized that this was actually happening. The Lamaze staff assisted Desiree to a vehicle and rushed her to Saint Theresa's Hospital. I was not able to ride in the vehicle with her, so I called my aunt Dina and told her where to meet me. Dina had been quite involved and was more or less the only member in my family who seemed excited. I grabbed Desiree's necessary belongings from her room, threw them in a suitcase and headed down Beverly Boulevard to wait. There I was, sitting in the parking lot of a liquor store at around eight o'clock in the evening and every freak that Los Angeles had to offer was out and about. I fit right in.

Not a moment passed before a guy approached me, looking as though he had just escaped from a hospital. He wore a lime green patient's gown and had wires taped to his body. He tried to sell me an international phone card, but I reluctantly refused and told him that I was waiting for a ride. He was harmless. We started talking when up walked this woman, a fairly attractive black prostitute, covered head to toe in pink and white feathers. She instantly started to flirt with me, but upon closer inspection I realized that She was actually a He. My gut erupted with laughter because only this kind of shit happened to me. I just wanted to get to the hospital, yet instead of my aunt's car, up rolled the LAPD.

The patient and the prostitute bolted away and the boys in blue made a direct motion towards me. I did not belong there, but instead of cooperating like I should have been, I was confrontational as usual. So they shoved me up against the hood of the car and went through Desiree's stuff. One of the cops remarked to his partner, "We have ourselves a cross dresser!" I jokingly replied, "No, you just let that one get away," referring to the transvestite. The cop grabbed me by my hair and drove my face into the hood of his squad car, then pulled me up and slammed me down on the curb. I cursed at him like a sailor on his death bed. He informed me that if I spoke one more word he would gladly pull out his Billy Club and demonstrate some police brutality. So I shut my mouth and waited as they called in to verify my story. The cops then gave me back Desiree's stuff and told me to wait on the corner for my ride, claiming, "If we catch you anywhere else but here you're going straight to jail." Again, I did not say anything, and there I waited.

Within a couple of minutes the patient and the prostitute were back. The prostitute was working for me to wait more comfortably up in his/her place. I said, "Thank you but no thank you." He/She just kept talking, "I have a phone you can use, Sugar." Again, "No thank you." At this point, I was starting to become very anxious and therefore easily agitated. *Where was my aunt?* I knew that Desiree had to be upset since an hour had already passed and I was still not with her. I waited a few more minutes before deciding "Fuck it" and walked over to the Hotel Roosevelt. Once inside, I was able to use a complimentary phone in the lobby to call my aunt. No answer. So once I was back outside, I continued to wait when a guy who was in our Lamaze class walked up and asked me why I was not at the hospital. I explained the last ninety minutes to him, being sure to put a lot of emphasis into my delivery. I was halfway through the part about the transvestite when he/she made an appearance by exploding from the lobby and punching me in the face, knocking me to the ground. The guy that I was talking to immediately ran away. Thanks buddy!

As I gathered my senses and shook the ringing from my ears, I realized that he/she was waving a gun. All that I could do was crawl

what little I could under Desiree's suitcase to shield myself. He/
she kept screaming, "I'm a mother. I'm all woman." He/she then
abruptly finished his/her words, did an unfashionable pirouette
and walked away. Definitely a dude! I jumped up and there,
stopped in the middle of the street, was the two cops laughing
at me. All that I could do was run. About two miles later James
randomly spotted me and picked me up. He was disappointed but
stayed calm. There was no way that I could tell him the truth. We
arrived at the hospital and I finally saw Desiree. She was livid, so I
spent the next eighteen hours of her labor apologizing and helping
her breathe. Desiree was so strong, so beautiful.

At that moment, age had nothing to do with anything.
Desiree was every bit of a woman, giving birth to a healthy
baby girl. My interest was in naming her Lisa Marie, after Elvis
Presley's daughter. Desiree felt that name was a little too simple,
so we compromised and on February 12, 1985, Angel Marie was
born. I had no idea how much of my life changed at that very
moment. There was a new, beautiful Sparzo in the world and she
was as radiant as an angel. I was finally given the opportunity to
play Daddy correctly and I liked it. Maybe it was because of the
attention, or maybe it was a new someone to love and a chance to
be part of something. Although at the same time I was petrified,
confused and riddled with guilt, and the scariest thing of all was
that the harshest times were just beginning. I was seventeen and
already screwed for life. Desiree, she just loved her little girl and
she would prove to be a great mother to Angel everyday of her
life, never quitting. The only thing that she needed to quit was
me, but I would not let her.

Sparzo Lives

*E*arlier than usual one morning, my mom came into my room and demanded that I got up immediately. By the tone of her voice I knew that something was wrong. She asked if I knew of any kids by the name of Leon Trite or Chris Mathis. I nodded, saying that I used to go to school with them. She then asked me about the nine-millimeter handgun that I owned. I thought, almost laughing, *what was she talking about?* From the cold stare in her eyes, I could clearly see that this was a very serious situation. She then explained the phone call that she had just received from Mr. Small, the Dean of Students from my old high school, who believed that I was threatening students with plans to shoot them. I could not believe what I was hearing. Now I was involved with a lot of things at this time in my life, but never guns, they were not my style. Ever since my dad told me about my uncle Bob I hated guns. For once, I was innocent and it was my reputation that had placed me right in the center of an extremely serious situation. Not only that, but some sadistic freak really hated me. Most of the students being harassed used to be my friends in junior high. In high school they became the jocks and the popular kids of the "in-crowd", and I was known to hang out amongst the kids on "School Street". Every school has one, the place where the smokers and the pill-poppers mingled. To hurt any one of them though, that was never a thought that crossed my mind. Despite my outlook towards the well-being of my peers, nobody believed me, not even my own mother. Go figure that my life's actions up until now had actually made an affect on her. I was deeply saddened by her cold-shouldered approach towards this whole scenario, but I refused to show it.

The severity of this situation was growing rapidly and showed no signs of relenting anytime soon. The police were immediately involved, constantly patrolling me like an enraged alpha lion. I felt like a terrorist in my own hometown. However, that was the least of my problems, there was a group of ticked off people who wanted to beat me senseless. The entire football team wanted to kill me, even their water boy. Here I am, a dad for two days and now this. What made it even harder was that I was alone in the corner with nobody to watch my back other than myself. For the first time, I truly was the victim, instead of just pretending to be and I sensed a strong connection with the kids that were actually being threatened.

I spent that evening at the hospital with Desiree and everyone came to visit: my mom, my sister, Desiree's parents and siblings. I acted as though nothing was wrong and tried very hard to suppress the accusations that lurked in my shadow. My main focus was simply to spend as much time as I could on just enjoying the moment, and that was a moment which I hoped would last as long as possible.

Early the next morning, an astoundingly beautiful morning at that, I went to the police department to cooperate with hopes of finding a way to clear my name. This was completely outside of my nature, but this time I needed them. I met with Detective Emily Benson and she played me a recording of the calls that were being made. The calls were so disturbing that they made my stomach queasy. Within the first few words the detective was able to recognize that the caller was not me, but she was still convinced that I knew more than I was saying. Detective Benson proceeded to explain the series of violations that had been occurring, which included not only the calls, but some graphic vandalism as well. Whoever was doing this had put an axe through one of the kid's car window, poured fake blood all over and carved "SpArZo LiVeS" across the hood. Everything that this person did was to terrify these people and frame me as the prime suspect.

Traveling from Desiree's house to my house, or anywhere for that matter, became a real obstacle. My drinking escalated to everyday, and consequently caused me to lose my job. My drinking pattern usually started at around eight o'clock in the morning and continued long into the night. I found that it made my life easier to deal with in lieu of everything that was going on. None of my friends believed me except for Martin. Martin had my back, he always had my back. He also had a safe place for me to stay. So that was how my life went for quite some time, moving from house to house, never staying in any one place for too long and if a friend was incapable of sneaking me in, I found myself a comfortable place to sleep at Pelaconi Park. Pelaconi used to be my party spot, now it was my home. On the positive side though, it was safe, quiet and desolate. Sometimes being there just seemed easier, with nobody to disappoint or burden other than myself. I was a weak person with a weak mentality.

My weakness had taken alcohol and shifted it from a coping habit to a serious disease. I was a seventeen year old alcoholic. My parents tried numerous times to enroll me in Alcoholics Anonymous but I made it impossible for them to help. I was unreceptive to their efforts and it seemed like the more they tried the more I alienated them. I simply thought that this was my issue and therefore nobody could help me but me. My parents had their own issues and their own fears, most of which were due to me. I had put them through a lot but I just neglected to see it that way. That truly was what made being alone acceptable.

Over the years I would follow this pattern of disappearing and reappearing, hurting those that only wanted to help and help was what he called it when I answered the phone at my parents' house one day. Mr. Small was on the other end and he felt determined that he knew who was responsible for all of these accusations. He revealed that my mom had confirmed my whereabouts when the aggressive calls were made and I was therefore no longer a suspect. With a spark in my voice, I told him that I would be there within the hour. I jumped right back on the phone and called Desiree. Desiree and I had an appointment later that day and I told her that I could still make it as long as she could convince her dad to pick me up at Lincoln High School. I was finally able to be cleared of all of this drama and the light at the end of the tunnel was blinding me with such an intense brightness.

So off I was to the institute of education that had banished me two years prior. I never thought that I would come back, especially as an invited guest. Here I was, walking the same steps up to the Dean's office, like I had done countless times, yet this time I had nothing to fear. Mr. Small met me in the hallway with a smile and a firm, extended handshake. He led me into his office and offered me a seat in a very plush chair. He politely asked me how things were going and how the baby was. He sounded by all accounts genuinely concerned. *Maybe all this time I was wrong about Mr. Small?* After a few more minutes of subtle conversation he handed me two yearbooks in which he felt certain that the individuals responsible for this were in.

I was just starting to look through the second yearbook when I heard both of the doors to Mr. Small's office open up behind me and in walked all of my accusers. Coldly, my eyes rose up from the yearbook and directly to Mr. Small, who shuffled rather uncomfortably in his seat. For a moment, I was speechless. He then ordered me to put the yearbook down and confess to what I had done. I peered around at my audience, all of whom were struggling to act intimidating by pounding their fists into their hands. I could barely take a breath to explain that I had done nothing, when Mr. Small suddenly interrupted. "You're a fuckin' liar Sparzo. We know it's you. We want your confession." With a full lung I responded soundly, "FUCK YOU! You a son of a bitch,

I came here because you told me…" He immediately cut me off. "These boys are ready to kick your ass unless you confess." Again, "Fuck you Mr. Small. You asshole." His vision shot right past me and into the eyes of all of the testosterone filled knuckle-heads. "Did this punk Sparzo just threaten my life?" They all agreed. He then picked up the phone with the intent to call the police and accuse me of threatening his life, trespassing and a whole slew of other embellishments. I shot back at him, "Go ahead Smalls, and call the cops. I have nothing to hide." He slammed the phone on his desk and left it dangling over the edge as he demanded for my final confession.

At that moment Desiree's dad, James, walked into the office, obviously startled by the thick tension in the air. He asked Mr. Small if he was finished with me. James had no clue what he just walked in on, but he did so like a blessed champion. I jumped up with a smile on my face. Inside, I was on fire and my blood boiled like red-hot magma, but I did not let a single bit of it show. I had won. A trembling Mr. Small looked me in the eyes and claimed, "I'm gonna nail you one day, Anthony Sparzo." Funny thing is, I never saw that little hairy leprechaun again.

Looking back, I guess I failed more than a few of my teachers, at least the ones who cared. I should have taken the opportunity to accelerate my education. I was actually a smart kid, a kid smart enough to know that even teachers and faculty can be crooked. Mr. Small is the principal now at that same school. Had I been more scandalous I could have taken both him and his career down, I just was not that corrupted, yet.

A month passed with little incident when I was unexpectedly arrested on a weapons charge. Rick and I were drunk in the parking lot of a liquor store, playing a friendly game of "Stick 'Em Up". The cops rolled through and charged me with manufacturing of weapons. Luckily, I had that whole minor thing going on for me and there would be no jail, just basic probation. Two months later, I met with Detective Benson again and she informed me that they had caught the two suspects who were making all of the threats. I never revealed to anyone their identities for fear there would be revenge, and likewise, no one ever cleared my name to the people they terrorized. One would think that an individual would clean up his act, but that was not me. Maybe Mr. Small was right, maybe I was a liar? Not that day though Mr. Small, you were the liar and you were wrong. Oh, and by the way, congratulations on the promotion.

You Are Not a Minor Forever

As I spend my days running a cleaning service for a living, I get plenty of time to reflect on the pivotal moments in my life. This is also an opportunity to realize all of the wasted advice that I did not heed. I was turning eighteen and my idea of being an adult was the same as I had envisioned when I was fifteen. Along with that there was no physical growth, a pattern that would follow me for years to come. I had been out of school for a year, bounced around several temporary jobs, but now the time had come, the time to turn eighteen. I was now legally old enough to vote, old enough to be a Marine, old enough to be a dad and old enough to stay in jail. Since I was eighteen now, I felt that it was appropriate to refer to my parents by their first names instead of as dad and mom. So Gerard and Melinda were really excited for my eighteenth birthday. I spent most of the early part of the day fighting with Desiree, and Gerard was trying to suddenly get involved with my life. However, let us face it, parents are a distant second to a girlfriend or friends, and I could care less about his feelings. I just wanted to go out, get some beer and celebrate, so I left the lame confetti and streamers party that my parents had thrown for me, and met up with Brad.

Brad and I had been close friends for the past year. He was

From Judas to Me

older than me by a year, had a car, unlike me, and shared the same attitude towards life that I did, get high and contribute nothing. The only difference between us was that I had a child, but I was a dad by name only. Child aside, the one thing that Brad and I had the most in common was baseball. Since Brad was a die hard Angels fan, we always had something to argue about. Baseball was such a part of our lives that we even turned it into a drinking game. However many runs either of our team scored, that was how many beers the other person had to consume. We loved our sports and we loved our alcohol.

As an adolescent, I was living on the streets as a bona fide vagabond. Brad would sneak me into his house from time to time and let me crash on his couch. This was all done much to the anger of his parents, who felt quite uncomfortable with their son harboring a homeless dad. With little concern we just continued to do our thing, which in the next few years meant one of us, or both, would end up in jail. We constantly had some form of a scam going on and Brad ran a steady business of dealing the choicest marijuana in the neighborhood. The lone stress factor to our day was merely how we were going to get our alcohol. If actually purchasing the liquor was out of the picture, we would steal. Bootleg beer runs became a weekly thing for us. *What was the point in finding a job and paying for what we could already get for free?* That was our mindset, a very selfish and distorted view. I enjoyed my time with Brad and started spending ninety percent of my time in Highland Park.

Highland Park was an easy place to be since most of my family lived there and none of them were more important than my cousin Bobby. Bobby and I held an incredible bond, how could we not. The only problem was that Bobby and Brad never really got along. Bobby was a different person than most, having been raised without his dad by his mom. Bobby was hands down the funniest person to ever walk this planet, a comedic prodigy. We would tell everyone that we were brothers, sometimes even twins, fighting over who got to be two minutes and forty-nine seconds older that day. I felt good to have that kind of bond. To Bobby, I as well was everything. Our connection was unbelievably close ever since I revealed to him the truth about his father, and he respected me for my strength and honesty. Besides, we were family and Bobby was all about family. My aunt Karen did her best to raise both him and his sister Collette properly. Collette was a knockout, a full on ten out of ten, and I mean that in the most respectful way. My uncle Bob was a pure Italian and they both took after him remarkably. Collette was as beautiful as she was crazy, just like all of us. I had no problem calling her my sister, the less crazy one at that.

That night was going to be perfect by celebrating my eighteenth birthday with my brother, sister and best friend. We obtained some great acid, plenty of alcohol, cannabis, and for dessert, crack cocaine. Our party destination was a place up in Highland Park known as "Flat Top". Flat Top was the perfect place to party since it overlooked the illustrious, never sleeping downtown. On a clear, star filled night, we could even see the lights from Dodger Stadium off in the distance. Everything set up for a perfect evening. The acid was kicking, and there we sat, not a care in the world. The place was packed and everyone was having a great time. While staring off at some distant satellite, a vision came into my head and I started to have a bad trip on the acid. I began analyzing my life as a father and turning eighteen. I had no self-confidence, no home, no goals, and no future. I honestly believed that the acid would enlighten me on this night, but all that it was doing was corrupting my thoughts. The night ended miserably. I was caught sneaking into Brad's house and his parents demanded that I left. I ended up at Pelaconi once again, sleeping in the bushes, crying and tripping myself to sleep.

I awoke earlier than the sun, shivering beyond belief. I ran to Desiree's to tell her and Angel that I wanted to change, that I was ready to be a better dad and I really meant it this time. As a validation for my words, I managed to secure a job at another supermarket, and for a while, I was doing well. However, I was never one to follow through with anything and soon found myself falling back to my old habits. I loved my habits, drinking and using, anything to escape my reality which I had created but could not control. In the blink of an eye, there I was on acid in the same car with the same people doing the same things. The monotony was truly getting old. Minus Bobby; Collette, Brad and I were having a great time trippin' at Flat Top one evening. Fireworks were going off at Dodger Stadium, illuminating the sky and the colors gave me a strong sense of warmth and security.

Then there was a sudden flash and a helicopter showed up with the spotlight on us. Fuck! Everyone started to scatter except for Brad and me. Not giving any care about the cops, we started in with a slow dance under the spotlight, followed by a three… two…one…DROP! The cops in the ghetto bird soon got a bright close-up of our full moons. They instantly responded on the loud speaker, telling us to get in our car and leave. We started screaming obscenities at the helicopter, stretching our middle fingers out as far as possible and throwing beer bottles. We actually nailed the damn helicopter, twice. Loud cheers roared from our lungs, overjoyed in our asinine behavior. With overflowing adrenaline, we jumped in Brad's car and bolted. At the bottom of the hill we ran into some problems with a car load of Chicanos, and it spilled out into a gas station parking lot.

To be honest, I had no clue where everything started from, but after order was restored, we were once again on our way. We dropped Collette off and decided to meet up with Bobby, who was smoking crack all by himself. Crack was Bobby's choice drug by far. I never found it appealing to me, but then again, I already had acid and alcohol in my system, what was a little crack going to do? We smoked heavily for at least an hour, maybe longer. Lightweight Brad quickly passed out, and I could not wake him up for the life of me. I felt stranded due to my incapability to drive. Impairment was not my excuse, but the fact that I did not know how to drive a manual transmission. So after a few more hits of the crack pipe, I felt the courage and clairvoyance that I needed to do this. I turned to Bobby, stating, "Dude, watch this. I'm gonna do it." He burst into laughter as I pulled away, grinding the gears up El Paso Boulevard. I was surprised at how easy a manual transmission actually was.

Three blocks later and I was rolling smooth, and so were the police. My adrenaline shot straight through the roof. They ordered me out and put me through their asphalt acrobatics routine. In my mind, I aced their field sobriety test. Problem is, when a cop says to take eight steps and turn around, and I take twenty-five, I am going to jail. So off I went. A cold shiver ran through my spine as I realized that this time it was for real. No more Glendale City Jail, they were taking me to the "Glass House". I had heard about the place and I can assure one thing, I was terrified. Fried and terrified.

I awoke the next morning in terrible shape. Go figure. Primarily, my hangover felt like that damn Energizer Bunny was trapped inside my skull. Plus, I did not have the slightest clue where I was. Then it all hit me and panic shot through my bones, I had to find a phone and get out of here. I cried to Gerard, or was it Dad now since I was in serious trouble and needed something? Thankfully he obliged to help and at that moment, my dad was my best friend. So on that early Saturday morning he agreed to drive across town to bail me out. Roughly twelve hours passed before the release officer called my name and the anxiety from waiting so long had me on edge.

Alas, I was free, Desiree would never find out I was in jail and everything would be back to normal. A few minutes were spent releasing my property and I was headed out the door, almost laughing at the whole experience. I could see Melinda through the glass door when the booking sergeant halted me, claiming that they had a warrant for my arrest out of Burbank. *What the fuck?* I did my turn on the slick, concrete catwalk and they put me right back into the cell. With a burly mustache grin, the officer told me not to get comfortable because I was headed to county. Now the time to really freak out. I was headed to Los Angeles County

Jail and everyone in the holding cell knew that it was my first time, so they spared no time in messing with my head.

On the steel trap of a bus ride, I struggled to fathom how to tell Desiree what was going on, since the truth was not in any way acceptable. Upon arrival I realized two things: one, that I was not a minor anymore, and two, I could not finagle my way out of this one. After about eighteen hours of processing, I was led up to 9500, a housing unit large enough to sleep two hundred, yet boarding well over five hundred. *And I thought our schools were overcrowded.* They gave me a mat and I found my way to a square of cold concrete under a bunk. There I lay, counting the minutes. Finally, nine hours later, I was able to secure some phone time. I called Gerard to find out when I was getting out and he was straight to the point, telling me that I was going to be there for at least a few days. My ultimatum had come and it was time to call Desiree.

I had no choice but to collect call her and it destroyed me to know that this was just another way to cost her family more money. After all, raising my daughter was not enough. But hey, I was the victim and Desiree never turned her back on me. She was furious and slammed the phone down. Fifteen calls later and she finally responded to me. Before I even had a chance to report the bad news, Desiree promptly had news of her own. She was pregnant, again. I was speechless, followed by an immediate jolt of sheer terror. There I was, sitting in jail, not even sure if I still had a job, one baby in the crib and another en route. I barely finished crushing her hopes with my confession when the sheriff cut the line. I felt relieved that the call was cut short, hearing Desiree's reaction would have just torn me apart more. Five days later and I was officially a free man, plus I did not lose my job. My only punishment was that I had to face Desiree's parents to discuss my intentions with their daughter.

Everyone had grown jaded of my shenanigans, the game was getting old. Everyday I was constantly reminded that I was an adult now and I should start acting like one. Find a new phrase for Christ's sake. I complied and made every promise in the world to Desiree, her parents, my parents, heck, even my grandparents, but deep down I knew that I could not keep those promises and deeper down so did they. I could not get it through my thick skull that I was not fourteen anymore. Life happened too fast and Detective Dick Price was right, I was not a minor forever.

Knowing that Desiree was pregnant again only pushed us further apart and the resentment she was building towards me was growing as quickly as her stomach. I continued to fill her family's heads with promises that I knew I could not keep and I believe her parents saw right through them because they gave me the ultimatum to shape up immediately or be on my way for good. With heartfelt handshakes, I promised some foolish lies and then shot right back to my old ways. I continued to only show concern for myself and day after day, I sunk deeper into the abyss that was my troubles.

With little guidance from any credible role model, my life continued to center itself on my ever growing fascination with Jim Morrison. My intent became to emulate his life in all aspects, which included trying to gobble down as many hits of acid as Jim himself had swallowed. Along with that, my thirst for alcohol, like his, became as equally unquenchable. All substances aside though, the one positive thing that I did get from this unique fascination was the writing of poetry. The rhythmic flow of poetry allowed me to live freely in the world of creative imagination, one that was so much better than the world of my dismal reality. With just a pen and a piece of paper being joined by the words of my heart, my entire soul was suspended blissfully into the comfort of the clouds.

Whenever I would share my sacred words with others, it would really catch them by surprise at how serious and deep I could be. I could sense an aura of happiness that would overcome them when my words would sink into their conscious minds. My poetry became a source for satisfaction in my life that I struggled to find anywhere else. My beautiful words would flow as smoothly as my heartbeat, but each heartbeat was just a pulse away from turning my words of love into daggers of anguish.

I felt as though I could never stay content for too long and the reality of my hurt would spread bare across the pages. Angst once again became the prevailing attitude and I simply figured that this was the same torment Jim had to live with. This desire to mold myself into Jim's image stuck with me for many years and my mindset reached the point where I was on the same exact death march that he had undergone. The only significant difference between the two of us was that I was not a rock star and I had nothing to offer to the world. I was a father of two and I had no right chasing the lifestyle of a death pawn. Then again, I had no way of stopping myself either. Just like Jim, twenty-seven was not too far away, but at least it was an inevitable quick release from a world that I had found cold and mean, just like me.

The only breath of fresh air came on October 10, 1986 when my son, Daniel, was born into this world. He was such a beautiful and healthy baby with the biggest blue eyes. He was in every way a Golden Child, so remarkable that all of the other mothers in the baby ward sighed with envy. This was the sign that I needed to wake up and take advantage of embracing my living lineage. The future of the Sparzo family was just lying there in front of me, so beautiful and wide-eyed. Instead, I ran like a coward back to my dark corner of alcohol and drugs to numb the nervous anxiety. Daniel was barely a ten pound infant on this world and he was already better suited raising himself than relying on a washout like me.

My Betrayal

As I came to grips with my new reality, my life soon began to seem more and more dismal. I was a nineteen year old father of two with no desire to change and no established place to call home. I managed to convince my aunt Karen into providing me with a place to live and even though I had a job, Karen never asked for rent. As an added bonus, I got to be with Bobby, just like we had always wanted. Bobby was one of the only individuals who fully understood my trials and I was desperately in need of any kind of support that I could get.

I quickly grew to love my new life. I was far enough away from the responsibilities of my children and my failing relationship with Desiree that a sense of peace and liberty flowed through me. On top of that, the drugs were changing and in a hardcore way. I still drank everyday and smoked copious amounts of cannabis, but instead of gobbling acid, Bobby introduced me to PCP. Alas, a new wonder drug. A twenty dollar dip could take me even further away from reality than I already was and that was precisely where I wanted to be. The only way to stop the constant desire to pick up the crack and smoke was this freshly cool, dangerous cocktail of madness. PCP instantly became my ritualistic medium for mindlessness.

Bobby and I shared a very similar mindset and no subject was too taboo for our thoughts. Both of us detested authority, cherished our drugs and were able to seduce practically any girl we desired. Bobby tended to be a tad more successful and I figured I just lacked that certain suave, but all minor pride issues aside, life was grand. I separated myself from the plaguing cognition that Desiree was home with my two kids at the age of sixteen, forsaking her teenage years. I had no desire to be reminded of her sacrifices and PCP made certain that it remained that way.

With the accelerating increase in our drug use, our criminal acts heightened as well. When we were younger, the worst that we would do was break into arcade games at the bowling alley, panhandle the winners at the Santa Anita Racetrack, sneak into the cinemas and whatever other petty stuff seemed cool at the time. However, now hardcore drugs were involved and that meant that the stakes needed to be raised. Bobby was a natural at stealing motorcycles, so boosting street bikes became a great way to make some quick cash. On average, we earned three hundred dollars per bike, which was plenty of money to keep us living the lavish life. After hearing just a few of our stories, I was able to convince Brad to start spending more time in Highland Park with us. The three of us would search all night, find a poorly locked bike, steal it and then sell it. From there we would take that money straight to our dealer, buy some crack, smoke every bit of it and then watch the sun rise while coming down with the PCP cools.

Very little time passed before Karen, who had lost all of her patience with me, perceived me as being a bad influence on Bobby and asked that I left. Her perception towards things was a joke in itself, but nevertheless, I was shown the door. Karen was close to being the only adult I had any love for, so in a rare show of respect I decided to make a positive gesture. I thanked her, gave her a genuine hug and off I went.

With life on the curb proving to be too much of a constraint, I soon fell so far into my troublesome ways that everybody I knew shunned me. That is, everybody except for Oscar. Oscar had been living in a house called the Irving Pad with a group of other like-minded adolescents going nowhere fast. We shared a mutual friend, Samantha, who was a unique girl with a devout love for witchcraft, Tarot cards, Ouija boards and anything else of the supernatural genre. Samantha and I had known each other since second grade, so I felt that the Irving Pad was an acceptable place for me to be. After some intense pleading with Oscar, he was able to secure me some space on the floor of his bedroom. This was a great step up from the bed of the El Camino I used to sleep in the last time Oscar came to my aid and I appreciated this new opportunity.

Living with Oscar had changed a lot since our El Camino days. Oscar had grown into an aggressive pro-weapons military man, minus the actual enlistment. I used to antagonize his beliefs with talk of peace, love and joy. Even though I never pursued any of those ideals through practice, I still spoke them firmly, knowing that it would agitate him greatly. Oscar would then counter with words about peace through superior firepower. Despite the obvious separation in our mindsets, we still shared the same thirst for mind-altering substances and Oscar kept the house stocked with enough weed and cocaine to keep all of the Irving Pad floating high above the clouds.

Randomly throughout the week, I would make a presence at Desiree's and play Daddy. Despite the fact that they were only ten minutes away, it might as well have been three thousand miles because I never was there when I truly needed to be. The kids were growing so quickly in front of my very eyes. I loved them beyond belief and I often referred to them as my little wonders of the world. Those moments with Desiree, Angel and Daniel were the only things that were ever truly real to me. I struggled day in and day out to be a positive influence for my family, yet it became more and more evident that it was simply a matter of time before Desiree would be over me. A sharp pain stabbed ever so slightly into my heart. I had honestly believed that she would always be there for me and this first moment of doubt was very unsettling.

Back at the Irving Pad, life was simple. I was surrounded by people with intense addictions and no desire to do anything remotely productive with their lives. I had found my perfect niche and it was sad at how quickly my pine for life disappeared. Any focus towards improving me was deferred by my using. At this point, alcohol and drugs were my only focus. The Irving Pad became just a place to be mindless, my quest for any form of normalcy would never be found there and the scene soon wore thin on me. The only solace that I could find was through Samantha who kept my stomach and mind full by using all sorts of crazy medicines. She was an inspiration for me to know that my manic attitude was actually acceptable and thus it proved that my life could still have a purpose. To this day she remains one of the most important people in my life.

With daily visits from the cops getting to be too uneasy for the owner of the house to handle, she decided to sell the place and all of the occupants were sent out on the streets. This was her only way to get rid of us for good and it worked.

So with Oscar headed off to Pacoima, I was once again on my own and back to the park. Pelaconi had consistently been my home for so many years, but now even I was growing tired of the outdoor life, so with nowhere else to turn, I spent more time at Desiree's. Her family was still so amazing to me, even though I continually neglected all of my promises and never established myself as a father to my children. Their struggles were endless when it came to me, but to this day, I carry such a heavy level of respect for them and this is something that I should have been exhibiting the entire time.

Being in the presence of Daniel, however, was the only thing that made being in that sober household more desirable. Daniel was a beautiful boy with the same playful heart that I possessed at his age. Being with him was more important than any drug or booze that I could consume. Daniel and I would spend all of our time together and he loved me without hesitation. For once, my behavior was showing signs of improvement and I attributed it all to Daniel. He was perfect in every sense of the word, but Desiree, on the other hand, could not stand to be in the same room as me. There was no way that I could blame her, but somehow I managed to always snake my way back in. As much as I desired to, I could never stay consistent and not even Daniel with all of his innocent love could correct my selfish ways. Before too long, I was back to the cold, dark silence of the streets.

Tony Boyte had grown frustrated with my lack of discipline to the point that he ignored all of my phone calls. I would curse him on the outside, but on the inside I was devastated. I looked up to him immensely and I proved to be no more than a constant disappointment. Yet instead of cleaning up my act and earning his respect, I just continued to fall further into drug abuse. Every three months, I would get arrested for something petty, do five to seven days and then be released right back onto the streets. Sometimes I was lucky enough to spend a few weeks up at Wayside Ranch and that would actually get me clean, temporarily that is. I would make a thousand promises to Desiree, to Melinda, to anyone who would accept my collect calls. I knew enough people inside the jail to make it semi-comfortable, yet I could not stand the constant abuse from the sheriffs, who took their jobs a little too seriously. Even from the inside, I could never understand the magnitude of the jail scenario. All of these correctional facilities were filled with inmates who felt extreme enmity towards the prison guards, and then here we were routinely going back to be told what to do. This was an ironic and unfortunate lifestyle from individuals with so much to offer.

Shortly after being released from jail one evening, I was abruptly notified that my grandfather, Nicholas, was close to walking hand-in-hand with the Lord above. He had been in poor health for many months but never showed any signs of losing the fight. I loved him dearly and knowing that he was near his end gave me yet another excuse to get drunk and lose my mind. When the time finally came, it was a torturing experience to stand there and just watch him go.

That evening was unusually cold and gray, the kind of night that is stereotypical for death and loss. While at the hospital, I stood by Gerard as he watched his father leave this world. I blinked, and in that brief moment of closure for my eyes, another soul was gone. I truly had no feeling for Gerard or his pain. All of my thoughts were on Nicholas and I just did what I felt was right and spoke my condolences. Gerard remained expressionless throughout my entire unscripted monologue. I figured nothing could hurt Gerard after his brother had passed away, so I took his stone cold approach towards death and made it my own. Allowing myself to cry for anyone who died was now no longer an option. There is no life without death and vice versa. To further test my emotions, roughly a year later my grandmother joined her soul mate in Heaven. I suppose her heart was broken, to the point where it overruled her desire for life. Once again I refused to cry, I refused to console Gerard, and I refused emotion all together. Although unable to numb it with alcohol, the anger and pain sunk far into my soul.

No one could ever claim that I was weak, but I was weak and deeply addicted to my alcohol and drugs. Everything and everyone took a backseat to my disease. Even my uncle Ted, who I greatly admired, failed to get through to me and my attitude was so warped that I just saw him as another junkie who had no right to lecture me. *Uncle Ted was incapable of staying off of heroin, so who the fuck was he to preach to me?* Nowadays, I know exactly how afraid he was for me since I was on the same path of destruction that he took. However, unbeknownst to him, heroin was not my thing and alcohol was not a drug. That was clearly a pompous attitude from someone who had none of the answers.

I soon found that living on the streets was growing old and accordingly, the whole lifestyle was growing old. Thoughts flowed through my mind that maybe I was trying to die without actually committing suicide. Being nineteen with no direction was starting to take its toll. I reached out to my parents for help and again I was able to convince them that I was ready to change. They clearly stated that they did not want me back in their house, but they were willing to let Mike Rice and me move into my recently deceased grandparents' house until they could sell it. I thought it was incredible to be back in Highland Park and back with Bobby, who immediately moved in. My grandparents' place instantly became drug central. Bobby, Mike and I took full advantage of Gerard's kindness, and the "G House", as we called it, became the new place to be.

Also, much to my interest, Bobby had recently started dating a girl named Lana. Lana was, to say the least, absolutely phenomenal, one of God's masterpieces. She was tall and slender with wavy brunette hair, blue eyes and the most beautifully intimidating smile ever witnessed. I developed an instant crush on her and amazingly we got along really well, even better than her and Bobby. Her background had brought her up from Highland Park amongst some of my cousins. We had crossed paths at random times throughout the past, but reconnecting with her this time was uniquely special. I had feelings for her and Bobby knew it, but did not care. He kept no loyalty for anyone except for me, which made her untouchable. This gave Lana and me an opportunity for our friendship to grow even though my thoughts were far more on the perverse level. Every time she licked her lips, my mind wandered. Every time her skin brushed mine, my mind wandered. Every time she yawned, most definitely my mind wondered.

As the days passed, my drug habits worsened. Mike and Bobby were regularly hitting the crack pipe, much to Lana's disgust. So as her and Bobby's relationship crumbled, I started to say no, with hopes of impressing her. Even though she had no intimate feelings for me, I continued to play the role as her friend. I mostly did so just to have that connection with someone and ours was a connection that would prove beneficial throughout the upcoming years.

Although, as fast as the good times came, they vanished even faster. After an early morning court date, I was now dedicated to sixteen weekends of community service picking up trash on the freeways. My new Saturdays consisted of Melinda picking me up from Highland Park and driving me down to the Cal Trans office in Echo Park to settle my obligations. The judge chose community service in regards to the high level of overcrowding in the jail system. For once, I was shown a form of leniency.

Less than two weeks passed before I was dismissed from the program for showing up intoxicated. Aside from the fact that I was now looking at four months in jail, I was hardly affected. My weekends were mine again and in my head I was beating the system. So what better way to spend my next Saturday than to have a party? Well I threw one and all of the masses came. The sole person that was not on the invite list was Desiree and then right on cue, like a soccer mom on Black Friday, there she was. She was accompanied by Martin and after arguing with Martin as to why he brought Desiree of all people, I submitted and conjured up my two-faced attitude. However, Desiree was not buying it a single bit. She was a scholar to my lies and spared no time in creating a confrontational atmosphere.

Desiree's father had recently fallen very ill and she was confiding in some friends about her fears for him. Well, I did not care to hear a single word of it, so I let her know what my thoughts were right in front of everyone. Midway through my rant, Martin pulled me aside and asked me to meet him in the master bedroom. As I closed the door and turned to find out what his issue was, Martin abruptly struck me numerous times in the face. I was dumbfounded by his audacity but instantly fought back. Bobby charged into the room and split the two of us up. Completely ignorant to my disgusting behavior, I screamed, "What the fuck was that all about, Martin?" He proceeded to give me his judgment on my life. I was enraged to know that this was my very close friend defending her. After enough time passed, I calmed down long enough to realize my faults and I apologized to both of them for my behavior. Needless to say, the incident had put a heavy damper on the party and Desiree just wanted to leave. I had embarrassed her greatly and I gladly showed her the door.

My first thought after her departure was which method I was going to use to clear my head. Bobby and I made haste towards Drew Street and picked up a twenty dip to relax on. As we arrived back at the house, Martin and Collette's boyfriend, Sean, were in the front yard fighting. I was too high to notice that Sean had a gun, Martin had a knife and the two were both high on PCP. Somehow I managed to get both pieces from them and I fired the gun several times in the air, hooting and hollering like Yosemite Sam. As the two of them backed down, I pointed the gun at both of them and demanded peace. Reluctantly, they agreed.

The next morning, I awoke with an immense sense of guilt from the night before. I called Desiree to apologize, hoping it would make me feel better. Her only words were, "Go fuck yourself." I slammed the phone down several times when it suddenly rang again. *Was it Desiree letting me off the hook?* No. Gerard was on the line, furious about the phone call he had received from the G House's neighbors about the previous night's activities, including the multiple gun shots. He told me to stay put because he was coming over. Yeah right! I wanted nothing to do with him and since it was Bobby's birthday, a trip to Tijuana was the perfect solution. So off we went.

The first order of business upon our arrival was to buy Bobby his first drink at a bar. Proudly, I was already in possession of a valid California Drivers License claiming that I was twenty-two, so drinking in a bar was old news to me. Since this day was about celebrating Bobby's eighteenth birthday, we jumped right to it. Bobby was not much of a drinker, pacing at one beer for my every three, but it was still a lot of fun. After several hours of binge drinking, we were approached by two of Tijuana's finest prostitutes, at least in my drunken state of mind. After a brief discussion over the financial responsibilities on our part, we made our way up Revolution Street to the fanciest hotel twenty-five dollars could provide. We were both in Seventh Heaven. At eighteen and nineteen that is all a young male is thinking about doing, never mind the Acquired Immune Deficiency Syndrome epidemic which was sweeping the globe. Neither of us was a needle-pushing junkie or a homosexual, so in our minds we were safe from AIDS. Even though I constantly tested my limits and those around me, karma was never a governing factor in my life.

After a very recreational hour with the two Latinas, we were back at the bars. In honor of our recent endeavor, we invented a drink called a Mexican Hooker which consisted of Khalua, Amaretto, Tequila and cream. Surprisingly, it turned out to be a delicious concoction. By two o'clock in the morning we were both on the dance floor with some Go-Go dancers being cheered on by about sixty drunken Marines. The situation was priceless. Eventually we made our way back to the car, and after a small altercation with the Border Patrol, we were back in our homeland. We made it roughly four exits before Bobby wisely pulled off the freeway and into a vacant lot to get some rest.

A short rest later and we were back on the road. Roughly twenty minutes passed before we spotted and picked up a hitchhiker. His name was Rick Brady and he was a native to Cleveland, Ohio. Rick had a charismatic attitude that left me with positive vibes, so all was well. By the time we reached Los Angeles, we invited Rick to stay a couple of days with us. He was a huge Indians fan and had an in-depth knowledge of the game. Since the Yankees owned the Indians at the time, I had all of the bragging rights. Baseball was the only thing I had left that could always guarantee me happiness. No matter how down in the dumps I was, I always had the Yankees and God, in interchangeable order.

Upon coming home, Mike informed me that Gerard had given us thirty days to move out, so I looked at Rick and asked if he wanted to stay for the whole month. He was ecstatic. I loved making new people happy, unfortunately I chose the wrong people most of the time. I held no understanding towards the definition of priority or loyalty, all that I wanted was immediate satisfaction. In all aspects, I was a complete jerk to any of the people that actually loved me.

Within the week after getting back from Tijuana, Benny

decided to visit from West Covina. Benny and I had started to grow apart and it genuinely hurt him that Bobby, not him, was living at the G House. For some reason, Bobby and Benny rarely got along. I loved them both equally as much, but at this stage in time it appeared that Benny was maturing a lot faster than me and was already above the influence of drugs. So that started to separate us, since again drugs were more important than family and family is what Benny wanted but never got. He did not receive the love from our family that he should have after his father passed away. I have come to realize after many years that our family failed him greatly. Without a doubt, he would have appreciated my parents' love far more than I, then and today.

With only a few weeks left on yet another spoiled opportunity, Bobby, Mike and I continued to disrespect the house my grandparents had treasured. The same dining room table where the entire family used to sit when I was a child was now where we gathered to smoke our dope. The guest bedrooms became bedrooms by the hour. My beloved friends would take a girl in there, demonstrate their carnal rage and then leave. Bobby and I even shared the opportunity to take a girl in. We demonstrated our skills so well that we shattered the bed. I gradually found myself disgusted at what I had done, but then again, it was only sex. My guilt would only be present until the next girl was on top of me, then it was always right back to business. I could not blame anyone but myself.

There was one distinct night at the G House where I experienced a lucid Godfather moment. There is a scene in Godfather where Michael is having a vivid flashback to the past. There I sat, alone in a room full of strangers, but instead of my friends all that I could see was my family. Everybody was there: my grandparents, my parents, Uncle Joe, Uncle Rico, all of the kids. We were in no way normal, but we were happy when united as a family. For the next five minutes I was a child again, fearless and never alone. But that was it and like a light switch I was right back to, "Pass me the pipe." Those were the only words that I could use to forget how wonderful life was and how evil mine had become.

The final night of our reign in the G House was a typical evening of drugs and violence. On this night, I received a heavy beating from Danny, a Highland Park local. I was up in his face about some nonsensical drama and I got what I had coming. The situation felt as though I was in the ring with Muhammad Ali himself. I could barely put up a fight. As I rose back to my feet, I noticed that Bobby was to the side just watching me get knocked around. Any other time in our lives Bobby would have bashed in anybody that did that to me, but this time was different, he simply stood back and sipped his beer. *What happened to my perfect wingman?* Countless thoughts rushed through my head as I keeled over bleeding.

Bright and early the next morning Gerard showed up and started kicking people out by the dozen. Poor Rick was puzzled, having no idea what to do. Turned out, the same Danny that beat me down offered him a place to stay. What a great guy. I heard that within two weeks after we were kicked out, Rick was shot. Supposedly, Danny and Rick were sneaking into Danny's girlfriend's house to get cleaned up after who-knows-what. As they came through the window, her grandfather fired on them. I believe that he was going for Danny's head, but instead he shot Rick in the hip. That poor guy came all the way from Cleveland and gets shot trying to take a shower. Luckily enough, he lived.

As Bobby, Mike and I gathered the last of our pointless belongings I felt a cold stare crawl up the back of my neck. There Gerard stood, unblinking, incinerating me alive with the inferno in his eyes. Never once did Gerard scream, or even talk for that matter, just watched. I believe that if my face had not already been so torn up from the previous night, he had the intentions of giving me an equal beating. I certainly deserved it, but instead he just stared. I knew my betrayal towards the house and his generosity was unforgivable. My actions had disgraced my grandparents' legacy. My soul was now forever emblazoned with the haunting memory of the hurt my betrayal inflicted.

My Name is Judas

Soon after being kicked out of the G House, Bobby and I were able to hustle up enough money to share a weekly motel which was a grave change from the home we had just lost. Since both of us were unemployed and desperate for money, we decided to see if our aunt Virginia had any work we could do. Aunt Virginia was a frail, elderly woman who had trouble achieving even the simplest of tasks. We were able to provide assistance by painting the fence, running errands, preparing her meals and various other household chores. After a long days work, all that she had to do was write the checks. Now here is the catch, her ailment was also her downfall. Aunt Virginia was in the early stages of dementia and it was such an easy ploy obtaining her money. She would write a four hundred dollar check everyday we worked to paint the same fence and so on. I would feel empathetic, that is, until all of the drugs kicked in. We were exploiting here illness to fund our habit. Sadly though, we were so self-absorbed in our own scam that we actually convinced ourselves we were taking care of her.

Karma was on the warpath and it hit us instantly, Bobby more so than I. Bobby found out that he had developed ghaneria, as an added bonus from our trip to Tijuana. He was too prideful to take the blame so he blamed Lana, who was completely clean the entire time. Somehow he found it simpler to single it out on her, and that was when the close group of friends that I hung out with showed their true selves. Lana became the connotative subject in every conversation or activity. My so-called friends' need to feel important and involved became their downfall as credible individuals. They pressed more focus into badmouthing Lana, despite knowing the real truths, and siding with Bobby and his lies. Nobody spoke the truth by revealing that she was innocent. Everything just fit right into place for the typical stereotype with sex. When a female has too much, she is deemed a slut, but when a male is well-traveled, he is idolized and never seen as contaminated. This is an extremely contradictory opinion. Irregardless, I knew the truth yet did nothing to clear her name. I figured the damage was already done and I was not going to turn on my brother. Plus, I figured his karma was his shadow because every time Bobby urinated I could hear the screams from across the motel. I was brutal on Bobby, never allowing him to forget his cheating ways.

After a few weeks of medication Bobby was back to chasing women, any woman. Bobby was never picky. He was a very attractive guy which made him cocky beyond belief yet still maintained a great sense of humor. He had it all, including an escalating drug problem that far exceeded even my own. I still preferred alcohol over drugs although I would walk down that third path from time to time and experiment with nearly anything. I hold this theory that there are three paths in life that we can all choose from, not just the right and wrong. The third is the experimental path in which a good person, or bad, chooses to experiment with something outside of their niche but still within their established realm. Though I was in control, this erratic mentality was what persuaded me to step out of the everyday drug box. Bobby started to concern me and that was scary because caring for somebody else was normally not something that I was known for.

One incident in particular was a night when Bobby was overly spun on crack-cocaine. He felt that he needed some more so he dragged me to an alley in Compton that he frequented to get us some rocks to smoke. This was the fourth or fifth time that he had asked to get it fronted, so at this point his dealer was fed up with his antics. Bobby quickly said, "Give me five minutes," and off he ran into the darkness. Roughly an hour later Bobby came back, opened the side of the van and this six foot ten Samoan-looking gentleman informed me that I was sitting in his van. I looked at Bobby, thinking *what the fuck?* However there was no changing this situation, so I grabbed my backpack and started walking down the alley. Bobby informed me that he had traded his van for an ounce of crack, two glass pipes, two torches and three hundred dollars cash. I did not hesitate to remind him that we were in the fucking middle of Compton. With zero concern, he turned his back to me and kept walking.

Off we strolled for a couple of miles, stopping every block to hit the pipe. We finally got to the point where we came to our senses and found a taxi to take us back to our motel. Once there, we sat up until twelve o'clock the next afternoon smoking and choking on the rock. Bobby suddenly realized how incredibly retarded his barter was from the previous night so he started to scheme. Amazingly, two days later, he showed up with the van. I never asked him how, I just swore that I would never smoke crack cocaine again and true to my word, I never did.

However, being off that drug did not stop my appetite for a high. Since I knew where to get some great acid, I talked Danny into taking the bus down to Hollywood with me. We had made peace after the whole Rick situation and so being around him was okay. Danny and I ended up getting ten hits of some Red Pyramid acid. We spared no time in dropping two hits each. Forty minutes later we started to trip, so we headed back on the bus to the motel. Within a few stoplights on the bus, we started to fry real hard. I decided that it was a brilliant idea to start antagonizing a Marine since he was drinking a quart of beer and the acid had me very parched. I tapped him on the shoulder and asked him to let me have a drink. He politely declined. I called him a fucking asshole. No response. So I just kept running my mouth. Danny then chimed in with some words for the Marine, but I told Danny to wait until our stop. As we approached our destination, we both got up and moved towards the exit of the bus. Without any warning, I started hitting the Marine in the face. He jumped up, popped me squarely in the mouth and I slipped backwards down the steps. Danny tackled the Marine out the door and now all three of us were out on the street. I was the first one to my feet and immediately started kicking this guy in the face. Crunch, crunch, crunch! At one point our eyes met and I could read his thoughts, *why are you doing this to me?* I had no idea why either, I just kept stomping on his face. Danny finally grabbed me and we started to run, laughing at what has just transpired.

We made it several blocks up the street before the LAPD arrived swiftly in two squad cars. They burst out, guns drawn, telling us to put our fucking hands on top of our heads. My first thought was the six hits of acid that were still in my seat pocket. I reached into my pocket with them screaming at me and thrust all six tabs into my mouth. I was barely able to swallow the acid before an officer slammed me head first into the motel wall. This cop was furious and I was so lit that I could not refrain from laughing. The cops threw both Danny and I to the ground and the laughter only grew louder. They finally cuffed us, put us in the car and drove us back to the bus. After a positive identification by the bus driver, we were driven to the Glass House in Los Angeles. The acid was so intense at this point that I could barely stay seated and I had a permanent grin. My jaw was clenched so tight that I thought my teeth were going to shatter. My heart was filled with such hatred that every pulse pushed my anxiety closer to the edge.

By the time we arrived at the station, I was screaming at Johnny Law to give me my rights. He laughed and kept escorting me. I then chose to twist my way into a verbal bashing with the booking officer, going as far as to calling him a "fucking nigger."

The room grew eerily cold and silent, and there was no denying that they had finally had enough. In the depths of my stomach I knew that I had just fucked up royally. Not since I was about to get the beating of a lifetime by the boys in blue, but because that word alone made me feel disgusting and pathetic. I had crossed the line and no apologies were going to save me now. Now it was their turn to set me straight. Six officers dragged me into a side room and made me strip. Snickering the whole time, they then handcuffed my wrists to my ankles. A rapid thought of sheer terror as to what was about to happen to me made my skin crawl. Much to my relief, never once did they touch me. Their sole purpose was to humiliate me, and it worked.

Panic stricken, I eventually made it to my cell where Danny had already obtained us some smokes and some candy. I quickly lit up a cigarette and continued to blaze on the acid for the next eighteen hours. Tripping in prison was no wonderland. The walls were melting all around me and invisible bugs were constantly taunting me in my peripheral. Even closing my eyes filled my head with the ghostly images of those around me. All visuals aside though, the worst part was that I knew I was going back to County on Monday and there was no way I was posting the twenty thousand dollar bail. So in an effort to mellow my mind, I sprawled my body across the cold, stone floor and tried to analyze why I was back here again. I found no concrete answers, but at least it passed the time.

At last, I started to feel sober and coherent on the inmate transfer down to Los Angeles County. The processing portion was an overcrowded time burner. I must have spent at least eighteen to twenty-four hours in the processing cell before I even saw a bed, sandwich and an apple. Three times a day it was a sandwich and apple, never once tasting a hot plate. To top it off, that apple and sandwich was being eyed by thirty-five people in a cell only large enough for ten. A day later, Danny and I finally made it to the holding facility known as 9500. I had already seen it before and all that I wanted was my turn for the phone so I could talk to Desiree. As long as she had my back, I could handle jail.

Fortunately enough, she accepted my collect call and she said that she would support my desires to change. Once again, I had dodged a bullet.

As long as Desiree was still by my side, I knew that I was going to make it through this. I dialed her number every chance that I had, constantly promising that this would never happen again. Although for some odd reason, roughly halfway through my incarceration she stopped accepting my calls and I completely went berserk. I struggled to grasp exactly why she was doing this. Possibly it was the physical abuse, the constant cheating, or as all of the guys in the joint claimed, she had finally found her Sancho. Something was definitely going on, but there was no way that Desiree was with another guy and so they simply were wrong.

Ten days later, Danny and I were released with the basic three years probation, plus I was facing additional time for a warrant relating to the weekends of trash service that I failed to complete. To complicate things even more, I had obtained Rick's identification card and was using the name Rick Brady to help diminish my punishment. The only downfall was that I had to wait to get to Wayside Ranch to fill out the necessary cop-out sheet. With all paperwork aside, my parents took sympathy upon me once again and allowed me to live with them. I hated the concept, but I was prepared to do anything that it took to get Desiree back. I was determined to stay sober, realizing after my whole acid mistake that maybe using was my downfall. I mellowed out on drinking and that was a huge step, yet it still did not make a difference to those that mattered. Desiree had already had enough of my verbal abuse, my lies, and my broken promises. My wrong doings had finally taken hold.

After several months of unsuccessfully trying to win her back, I rejuvenated my thirst in an attempt to forget my Desiree related issues. Upon drinking, I quickly found myself stranded at my parents' house where I did not belong with nothing better to do than get wasted at all hours of the day and night. Occasionally, I was doing drugs with Bobby, who at this point had moved on to slamming speed. Drugs or no drugs, he was the only person that I had left.

As the holidays approached, things really started to take a turn for the worse. On Christmas Eve, Bobby and I drank far too many shots of Kessler whiskey, a bottle each to be exact. There I sat, until the dawn broke through, crying to Bobby about my woes. Exhausted and drained of thought, we started making our way back to my parents' house. Irritated at the fact that I had missed the morning festivities, I felt it was necessary to argue with Cassandra right away. Well halfway through my tirade, Cassandra screamed at me, "You don't think I hate them for what they've done to you?" I just stared at her, asking, "What the hell are you talking about?" The following words froze every cell in my body. "Desiree and Benny are together." For some reason Cassandra thought that I already knew. With a trembling tongue, I vaguely muttered, "Unfuckinbelievable." I went directly to the phone and called Desiree. With heavy resistance, I pleaded with her to tell me the truth. Desiree told me the truth alright, that Benny and her were indeed seeing each other. I could not believe what I was hearing. *How could they do this to me, my own cousin and my girlfriend?* Despite the truth that my priorities had not involved her for quite some time, all that I saw was my own blood betraying me in the worst way possible.

Sick to my stomach, I ran outside and proceeded to vomit profusely. The Kessler burned even worse now than it had before. Bobby rushed outside after me, claiming that all he wanted to do was knock Benny out. No matter how hard I shook my head, my thoughts kept drifting back to visions of the two of them together. Torn with disgust, I kept calling Benny "Judas" for his betrayal of me. I was his brother, his very blood. All accusations aside, it was me who was Judas. I was the great betrayer of everyone and anyone who loved me. My betrayal was karma finally stepping in. Benny had taken her from me. Over a decade passed before I could clearly realize that he did not simply take her from me, he saved her from me.

Discovering New Lows

The crushing blow to my vulnerable heart left me stranded without a clue as to where I could go with my life. Losing Desiree created bitterness in me that would follow me everywhere that I went. Even in darkness, I still had a shadow. My insides burned at every thought of Benny or Desiree and I had no method for turning the pain off. With utter disregard towards my parents and their simple rules, I willingly moved myself back onto the streets. I developed a weekly routine of bouncing between Brad's, Martin's and the park, just like I had been doing for the past three years. I spent my thoughts contemplating on how blind I was to not see all of this downfall coming, not only Desiree, but the whole picture.

I longed for the days when all that I had to do was attend school regularly, finish my chores, and respect my parents. Following their straightforward guidelines surely would have directed me towards college where I would have had the chance of making something with my life. Instead I was homeless, jobless and careless with no desires other than to get high or drunk. My friends chose to take my side, unable to believe what Desiree had done. I accepted their words on the outside, but inside I was still dying with guilt. My guilt rose higher with every connotative word that they used when speaking of her. Desiree did not do anything wrong but find a little bit of happiness. As hard as I tried to be mature about the situation, I could not escape the fact that her happiness only filled me with emptiness. At twenty years old, I had thrown it all away: my education, my girlfriend, my kids, my family, my self-respect. Since my friends were no better off than me, there was never anyone to look up to. I had created a life with no guidance.

One certain mid-afternoon day, I became increasingly exhausted and all that I wanted to do was get some rest. I checked with Brad first and since he was not home, I crossed the street to see if Paul was available. Maybe he would take pity on me. As it turned out Paul, his brother Joe, his girlfriend Cindy and her cousin Heidi, were heading to Mexico for a little getaway. They asked me if I wanted to join them and I quickly agreed. Paul and I had been friends since grade school and it was him who had first introduced me to weed. Paul, like me, was a young dad as well. After losing his mother, Paul was raised by his grandparents who instilled the art of love and patience into him. His dad was never seen since he was doing time in a Mexican prison for drug trafficking. Along with that, Paul had some rough trials, but his grandparents solidly made up for it. Paul was a stone cold fool, a renegade just like me, who once again became an instant close friend.

As we headed south, the confined seating arrangements had put me in the back seat right next to Heidi. Heidi was a beautiful, petite red head who was really cute and really pregnant. She reminded me a lot of Desiree, not in the physical sense but the fact that she was seventeen and pregnant. Despite her obvious baggage, we connected immediately and this new friendship changed my glum demeanor in a heartbeat. I was not alone and that meant that it was time to party. As my mood lightened, I could easily recognize that Heidi was into me and I felt privileged to have her to flirt with me. She later confided in having a crush on me, but a young, pregnant girl was not on my agenda. I wanted a Latina.

By the time we reached Ensenada I had already consumed a twelve pack, with an ever-growing thirst for more. I knew of the perfect place, so I guided Paul to Speedy Gonzalez's Bar. Speedy's was bar none the best place to party. Once inside, Paul, Joe, Cindy and Heidi quickly found a table. Since I was the fifth man at a four seat table, I started to roam around in search for an extra seat. A gentleman in a dimly lit corner gestured for me to come over and take a seat next to him. After a brief glance back at my group, who were showing no attention towards me, I took the seat. We shook hands as we introduced ourselves. He was a clean-cut Mexican local by the name of Jaime Velasquez. Jaime spared no time in buying a few rounds of tequila shots. Ignoring my friends and partying with a stranger was fine by me. Life seemed great because the more that I drank the less I thought about Desiree. After another three rounds, Jaime asked me if I wanted to do some blow. I instantly became paranoid, explaining that whenever I was visiting in Mexico, I usually aimed to be on my best behavior. My heart abruptly stopped when Jaime pulled out his identification with a badge attached. He stated that as a federale, he had access to the top-notch cocaine and he thought that I seemed cool enough to share it with. I was blown away by this whole situation, but I decided to take a chance.

So we hit the bathroom to "tune-up" and then returned back to our seats, feeling very drunk and really energetic. Paul decided to come over to ask if I had any intentions of joining them. I said, "Sure, but meet my bro Jaime first." After six shots, four beers and a few gangsters, Jaime was now my brother. Paul had an obvious attitude towards my new friendship so I told him, "Fuck off! Leave me here if you want." Sulking, Paul went submissively back to his seat. Jaime hesitated, and then asked if I wanted to do some more coke. With a wide grin, I complied, but this time we went down to his patrol car indeed. Without any second guessing, I jumped right in. I truly loved this, doing cocaine in a police car in Mexico. I commented to Jaime at how funny this situation was to me and he agreed, laughing heavily. We snorted three monster rails a piece and then headed back upstairs. We laughed and laughed over a couple more drinks. Once those drinks were down, I thanked him for his righteousness and then stated my need to get back with my friends. Jaime's face showed utter disappointment, but he said he understood and let me go about my way. *I guess not all cops are bad after all?*

When I arrived back to the table it was clearly obvious that everyone was irritated with me and after some light apologies, all was forgiven. As we all sat down for the first time, I congratulated Joe and Heidi on the upcoming baby. Heidi then informed me that she and Joe were not together and that the baby's daddy was already a runaway figure of the past. I apologized for my faux pas, instantly noticing that Heidi could not take her eyes off of me. With my newly found courage through booze and blow, I was now all about her. By the end of the night, Heidi and I were alone in the corner of the bar making out. Cindy was noticeably disgusted but I did not care, I was oblivious to the severity of my actions. After that night, Heidi became obsessed with me and would not leave me alone. I told her that we could never be together, that I was a bad seed and she could do better. Much to her dismissal of my words, Heidi continued to think that I was the greatest thing ever.

Heidi was such an amazing girl. I loved hanging out with her and I loved being wanted. Her constant attention towards me made my break-up with Desiree a lot easier to absorb and that was my style, always looking for the easier way out. Seldom did it matter to me that I was playing with the girl's head, I was simply happy not being alone. That was one thing that I could not handle, being alone. Solitude terrified me and lately I was always alone. Heidi filled that emptiness at the expense of her own heart and I did nothing to stop it. I still believe to this day that Heidi loved me more than any other woman ever has and ever will, a true and unconditional love. Even though she was only seventeen, she knew what she wanted and she deserved every bit of it, she just wanted it from the wrong person.

Aside from Heidi, I spent most of my days wandering around town, looking to get high or drunk as early as possible. I ended up sleeping atop the parking garage at the Galleria the night before and since it was extremely cold, I probably slept for a total of about an hour. So I started my day overly exhausted and irritable. My closest option was to head over to Martin's where I could take a shower and hopefully blaze some cannabis. As I walked down Glen Oaks Boulevard, I noticed a bright new car across the street in a gas station parking lot. More importantly, I noticed the two kids screaming and playing in the back seat. To my surprise, it was Angel and Daniel. Instantly, my face lit up with emotion until I realized that the car must belong to Benny. We had not seen each other in the six months since our grisly falling out.

Despite the shrill sound of my own kids screaming for me, I dropped my head and kept walking. I was far too ashamed at my current appearance to even face my own children. All that I kept my eyes focused on was watching one foot passing in front of the other, the fastest way out of this scenario. Alas, they drove by me. I lifted my head slightly and watched my family grow faint in the distance. Then again, it was not my family, it was Benny's. At that moment, I had forfeited all of my rights as their father. My lowest moment in life had finally arrived and sadly enough, I realized firsthand how it felt to face-plant rock bottom.

NOWHERE IS HOME

The world was growing up around me and I could not seem to find a way to catch back up to its pace. So I decided to make a bold move and follow a girl by the name of Serena up to Klamath Falls, Oregon. After just a few short weeks of countless drugs and endless sex, I had found myself back on the streets with nowhere to go. I would wander aimlessly, screaming at the stars hidden behind dimly lit streetlights to help me get back home. I had no answers for myself, so I relied solely on the Heavens. After a disgraceful week of unsuccessful panhandling, I called up Gerard who reluctantly wired me some money to take a bus back to Los Angeles. On the bus ride home, I vowed to never leave Los Angeles again.

I was not even back in town and back to my parents' for more than a week before I was called up by my buddy Ray. Ray had recently moved to Tucson, Arizona to help lay carpet with a guy that he had met while in jail. He asked if I wanted to work and live with him and I flatly declined his offer. I had no intentions of leaving Los Angeles. After all, the last time I left was a complete disaster. Ray was my best friend and I knew that I was going to miss him, but Arizona was no place for me.

So I kept my mind secured in Highland Park by staying as

high as possible at all hours of the day. I soon found out that Collette and Lana had been staying with this drug dealer by the name of George and this did not settle easily with me. George's reputation was not of just being a huge drug dealer, but he was also that creepy kind of guy who always had younger girls living with him. He was in constant supply of pounds and pounds of both weed and blow and I hated the entrancement that these vices brought upon girls. Cassandra, as well, had fallen under his spell. He would buy her jewelry and clothes, and then kept her high and incapacitated with coke and heroin.

I instantly devised a plan to rob George of all of his stash and all that I needed was an accomplice, but everyone that I asked thought that it sounded like a terrible idea. As much as I hated to hear that from them, I still took their words seriously and chalked the whole idea up as just crazy talk. I did however still go over there to talk with Collette and check the scenario out for myself.

George's house was only a block over from my grandma's house and I had seen it a lot as a kid, but had never actually passed through its doors. Once inside, I was rather surprised at the level of upkeep his house maintained despite the number of random strangers that were constantly moving in and out. I found Collette and nothing about her had changed over the years, she was still a beautiful girl. She offered me some PCP and I jumped right towards the opportunity. For the next thirty seconds I felt perfectly fine, then the whole room collapsed and everything went black. I awoke after what seemed like an eternity to a little Colombian Charlie Manson-looking guy staring at me from across the room. The infamous George was literally nothing like I had expected. There was no way that this five foot three inch furry introvert could get any chicks, but without hesitation he offered me a beer and I rolled with it. Once he left the room, Collette told me to keep my cool and roll with it. I laughed and told her that rolling with this scenario was already on my mind. Plus, there was still a chance that I could hustle this fool out of something.

George returned and with a handful of beers. We knocked them down in a matter of seconds and before too long he was breaking out line after line of cocaine. There was no way that I could say no, but it still infuriated me because I felt like I was one of his girls. A feeling of disgrace and disgust overwhelmed me, yet after the third or fourth line, I did not care anymore. George then approached me with a proposition. Since he had recently moved, he still had some of his product at his old house in Lincoln Heights. The only catch was that the house was being monitored randomly by the cops. However, I was nil concerned with the cops. All that I was concerned with was the two thousand dollars that George was going to pay me and all of the weed and coke that would be included alongside.

I immediately called Collette's boyfriend, Sean, who was very enthusiastic about the idea and we set out that night. We made our way over to Lincoln Heights and once we arrived there my adrenaline skyrocketed. I was so excited and the blow that we found inside was like some glorious drug addict's Christmas. There were four large black trash bags filled almost to the brim with cocaine. As we sat down to sample some of the goods, Sean brought up that George's ex-girlfriend, Jennifer, had died right there in that very living room from a drug overdose. Apparently, word on the street was that Jennifer had too big of a mouth so George served her up with a rig of pure heroin. All that I could say was how fucked up this George character was, but we needed to keep our focus.

Once our brains were well-influenced, we set aside as much of the cocaine as we could possible get away with for ourselves and I guessed it to be around a quarter of a pound each. We had everything in place but every time I checked out the window to make sure the coast was clear, there was a car. I would swiftly close the blinds and then peek through to see if it was a police officer or not. Luckily, it never was and after roughly twenty-five minutes of nerve-racking patience, we made a break for the covering darkness of the alleys. We successfully made the trip back to Highland

Park and George was all too thrilled to see me. He gave me my two thousand dollars and as an added bonus, he tossed in a solid baggie of coke and several ounces of weed.

So with the stash that he gave me, plus the extra smuggled portion that I had to adjust every so often while in the bathroom, I chose to lay low for the time being. Before the end of the week though, I decided that enough was enough and called up Ray in Tucson, bragging to him about my big score. Ray insisted that I make the trip to Tucson and this time I agreed. I said my goodbyes to Collette, Sean and George, not knowing that I would never see Sean or George again. Sean ended up getting busted for armed robbery and is due to sit in his cell for many years still to come. George was shot and killed roughly a year after the last time that I last saw him. So with my stash and money in tow, I headed off to Tucson for no purpose in general, just to get as far away as possible from anything that mattered.

As soon as I got off the bus in Tucson, I immediately started to second guess my decision to be so far away from home and all that the bus ride did was give me a painful head and backache. Nevertheless, I hopped in a taxi and took it directly to Ray's place, but instead of Ray I was greeted by a cute young blonde named Kim. Kim was, to say the least, the epitome of a Hooter's girl. She welcomed me inside, explaining that Ray had to work late and would not be coming home for several hours. With a slight smile from both of us, I made my way to the shower where I was surprised that Kim did not follow me. That attitude lingered until the moment that I stepped out of the bathroom and was halted by Kim wearing nothing but a thin-laced bathrobe. I lifted her up, as her legs wrapped around my waist, and carried her into the bedroom where we spent the next hour romping energetically between the sheets. Exhausted yet very relieved, we then made our way to the kitchen counter where we started chopping up massive lines of coke. Ray had told Kim about my big score and I think that the amazing sex was just her way of guaranteeing she would be well compensated.

When Ray finally showed up, I was really excited to see an old face in a new place. We hugged and then he introduced me to his boss, Gary, who was an Axl Rose look-alike with tattoos sleeved up and down both his arms. Gary had spent two separate terms in prison and had found God along the way, which had turned him towards the sober life. From a first impressions standpoint, I could sense that Gary saw me as a threat to his resurrecting lifestyle of sobriety. I laughed internally, then turned to Ray and told him that we had some partying to do. Ray invited a few of his friends from the housing complex and by the end of the night we were known as the "Dude guys" from California. I thought that the nickname was an absolute riot. I loved my California roots and the immediate recognition that they brought me. Besides, it was better than the guy who nicknamed us, "Tex" from Tucson. After several weeks of non-stop partying, Gary finally submitted and joined us in our celebration of brotherhood. This was received much to the displeasure of Gary's wife who knew exactly where his influenced behavior would lead him. However, there was nothing she could do to stop the momentum of the vice train we were on.

The party continued without relent and as soon as Bobby got wind that I was in Tucson on a party binge, he was on the next bus ride over. When Bobby arrived I was beyond ecstatic since I was with my brother once again. The only person who did not seem too thrilled was Ray, who immediately saw my friendship with him diminishing. This was an attitude that I knew he needed to disregard so I jumped straight back into "Who needs a beer?" and everything was fine again. Now the one main problem with the party lifestyle is that it burns through money like a wildfire through a thicket and it was not too long before Bobby and I were scheming.

On one particular night, the two of us were halfway through a handle of tequila and were suddenly desperate for the influence of some cocaine. We devised a brilliant plan to break into our own house and steal Ray's prized ferret, Zeke. Zeke was worth more than the world to Ray and he loved that ferret indefinitely, but to us, that ferret was worth an eight-ball of coke. He loved Zeke, and so did we. Bobby and I did what we had to do and everything went as planned. Never once did Ray suspect us, he just sulked silently into his reclining chair and slowly smoked from his sack of weed. I apologized with a slight tear in my eye for his loss and offered him some coke to help him cope with his loss. I felt it was the least that I could do. Truth be told, losing that ferret tore him down far more intensely than I had ever anticipated and the Judas that I felt for sure I had banished was present more than ever. Alcohol and drugs gave me no morals or boundaries, just an excuse to turn my back on and humiliate anyone who had ever given me a chance. I soon realized that a two hundred dollar sack of cocaine, that lasted less than a day, jeopardized a lifelong friendship.

After that, it was only a matter of time before the light that was Tucson finally burned out. On one of my final days there, Bobby, Ray, Gary and I decided to start drinking early in the day and roam around the city. The day was progressing smoothly until in a drunken state of mind, Bobby and Gary started a fight with a random group of guys in front of a K-Mart. I thought it would be entertaining to run an empty shopping cart into the testosterone filled mosh-pit and it worked with astonishing results, knocking one of their guys to the ground. The police were quick to arrive and Bobby, Gary and I were sent to jail. I never had a chance to see how Ray escaped. I guess it just must have been a swift move amongst the entire ruckus. So after a minor eighteen hour stint in jail, the three of us were released with a promise to appear in court. Three days later, we were packed up and on the road back to Los Angeles, never to return to Tucson again.

With time to reflect, I genuinely believe that if I had never shown up in Tucson, then maybe Ray actually had a chance to make something out of his life. I personally took him down and I did it without any remorse or justification. Alcohol and drugs fueled my insanity and that same insanity shredded everyone around me. I had become the catalyst for misery and misfortune.

DOWN AND OUT IN PHOENIX

*O*nce I was back in Los Angeles, I finally decided to provide my life with some new meaning, so I put one hundred percent of my focus into self-improvement. With the help of my parents whom had purchased me a cheap Ford, I was starting to put my life back together. I was able to work my way into a year-round job with great pay. I was also dating a beautiful brunette, Mary, who was able to secure me a room in her apartment. Things were finally starting to look positive.

All that I had to do was maintain myself on a consistent routine, which was something that I knew nothing about. I was still drinking heavily but at least I was able to make it to work everyday on time, which was a small wonder in itself. I was even taking the kids a few times a month. I loved them dearly, yet deep inside still lived a hurt that was self-inflicted from all of my previous actions. My life was in no way perfect, but it sure beat living on the streets with all of my possessions stuffed into a backpack. I also enrolled myself into a literature course at the community college and I spent most of my alone time free associating my thoughts into a journal. I enjoyed writing and even contemplated whether or not I could eventually do something with it. Though a small goal, pushing my education gave me hope of more than a nightshift at a bakery.

An old friend, Robert, called me to announce that that he and his longtime girlfriend Sydney were getting married. They were currently living in Phoenix and were planning on flying out to Los Angeles for the ceremony. "Of course I'd be there," I responded. Mary and I had been arguing the morning of the wedding, so in a stubborn rage, she opted not to go. Unfazed, I called up my buddy Lance to see if he wanted to party and of course he was interested.

First things first though, before the fun could begin, I had to make sure that I attended a class I had at the college. Soon after arriving to the campus, I ran into an old friend of mine by the name of Pam. We started to chat and she told me how great it was to see me back in school. A feeling of warmth overwhelmed me. However, her next words she did not choose so wisely. Pam revealed that Desiree and Benny were having a baby. This was breaking news to me, yet as I pretended not to care, that warmth inside me turned to frost. Without hesitation, I ended the conversation and bolted straight back to my car. I never went to class that night and needless to say, I never went back period. The news of their baby became the final stake in the coffin that was Desiree's and my relationship. I buried my past, left a solitary rose and moved on.

So with a lead foot, I picked up Lance and we headed off to Burbank for the wedding. By the time we reached our destination, Lance and I were well influenced by the chronic. As proud as I was for my friend, the sight of Robert and Sydney getting married only fucked with me more. Without fail, the vision of Desiree and Benny arose like a zombie in my thoughts and my flask of whiskey was the only solution to quickly shoot that zombie back down. So by the time of the reception I was feeling good and drunk. With Desiree out of my mind for the moment, it was now time to join everyone in drinking ourselves silly. After all, it was a celebration.

Robert informed me that he and Sydney could not afford to fly, so they were planning on taking a Greyhound bus back to Phoenix and I would hear nothing of it. I had the next three days off from work and loved to travel, even if it was to Arizona again. Without a second thought, Lance was enthusiastic for a road trip too. Lance volunteered to drive since I was clearly too intoxicated and besides, I had more drinking to do. In doing just that, I literally drank all of the way from California to Phoenix and by the time that we arrived there, I had drunk myself sober. All that there was to do now was just take a quick nap.

Once high noon rolled through, I awoke and made an immediate effort to go out and find the local bars. Along the way I made plans to hook up with Scooter, an old friend, yet the only problem was that Lance and I could not stop drinking. We hit roughly eight bars before we finally stumbled into a place called The Library. By now, it was around eleven o'clock at night. In a drunken stupor of false recollection, Lance thought that someone had swiped his money off of the bar and decided to start a fight. Before I could say "One for the road," six bouncers were on both of us. They wrapped us up and threw us to the curb. We were clearly too wasted to fight and it would not have done us any good anyways since these boys looked like they were Linebackers for Arizona State University, the wonders of all steroids. After a loud "Fuck you" to the bouncers, we jumped in my car and I sped off to the nearest liquor store. Lance picked up the beer while I called Scooter and after getting some hazy directions, we were on our way to his house.

Lance failed miserably as a co-pilot and within fifteen minutes, we were officially lost. In a drunken state of mind, I let my irritation towards the situation get the best of me and so I started speeding recklessly to make up for lost time. After all, I wanted to party. As I rounded a turn in a dimly lit residential neighborhood, I took the corner too tightly, causing my front right tire to hit the curb. The tire grabbed instantly, pulling my car up somebody's driveway, and vaulting us airborne. Sheer terror shot through my veins. At fifty plus miles per hour, this was not looking positive. A sudden bone-shattering crunch rang through my skull as my car landed upside down and proceeded to slide with fierce momentum. I had been too drunk and stubborn to be wearing a seatbelt, so I witnessed my final moment as I dropped face first into the sunroof. The sunroof had shattered upon impact, spearing shards of glass into my face. For the next sixty feet my head was at the mercy of the asphalt, which spared no time in shredding the skin clean off of my face. Shock kicked in midway through the slide, causing me to completely blackout. What happened from there after is completely based upon Lance's recollection.

Supposedly, as the car finally settled, Lance, who amazingly only suffered minor injuries, pulled me from the wreckage. I had two extremely large chunks of my head missing, replaced solely by blood, bits of asphalt and empty space. The left side of my face had disappeared completely, with bits and pieces of it scattered throughout the street and sidewalk. Lance claims that he kept screaming for me to keep thinking of Angel and Daniel and that I was going to make it through this. Maybe I heard him, but more than likely not. According to Lance, it was inevitable that I would give up the ghost before any help could arrive. Although through God's grace alone, I did not perish in the arms of my friend on those blood-soaked streets. Unconscious but alive, I was care flown by angels to John C. Lincoln Memorial Hospital.

The next thing that I remember was opening my eyes to Gerard standing over me. Several days had passed since the accident and I was still in agonizing pain, feeling as though thousands of fire ants were consuming my face. My appearance was so grotesque that both my mom and sister could not even bear to look at me, muffling their cries behind hand-shielded eyes. I demanded that someone brought me a mirror. Gerard, a man who was not one to wince at trauma, looked overwhelmed with disgust. Once the doctors were able to locate a mirror, Gerard stepped up to me, took a deep breath and held it up over my head. "Unfuckinbelievable," was all that I could say. My entire face was gone, vanished, lost into oblivion. The blank canvas of a bulky white cast was now my new head. The whole hospital floor echoed with my screams as the pain and frustration rushed through my veins, and that sudden burst of anxiety left me struggling to breathe. *What the fuck had I done to myself?*

My days became consumed with me sitting on that damn hospital bed, waiting for the next skin graft, contemplating how all of this happened, why it all happened? I felt an immense level of remorse for my family and what I was putting them through. All that I could think about was how lucky I was that Lance was not killed, but here I was, deep in the hole now. My reality quickly confronted me. I was completely destroyed inside and out, I had totaled the car that was just purchased for me, jail was a certainty and now I was in store for multiple months of rehabilitation. Scooter, Robert and Sydney came to visit me and Sydney could not refrain from crying. Scooter showed immediate signs of anger and resentment towards me. Their visit proved to be brief and far too silent. Pain soon filled every part of me, not only body, but my mind and soul as well. My main focus became to fight the pain, which was so severe that I had completely lost my appetite. I can sadly assure that at that point I genuinely did not want to live. I held no appreciation for the fact that my benevolent creator had just spared my life. The only feeling that I felt was utterly worthless.

Within a week, an officer showed up, announcing that I was being held up with five different charges and was given a court date. To further dampen my spirits, I still had several surgeries lined up for me. I obviously had no desire to drink but some prescription pills that I was given were starting to do the trick. Knowing that they could not stay forever, my family eventually left to go back to Los Angeles. Some time would pass before I too would get to leave Phoenix. Life was finally starting to catch up to me and my actions had left a permanent scar on me, forever branding me to remember my mistakes. Hell, I was only twenty-one.

Running With Fear

After a grueling three months of strenuous rehabilitation and court dates, I was finally back in Los Angeles and back to the only house that managed to still take pity on me, my parents'. Being there was acceptable simply because I was in horrendous shape and needed a place where I could sleep undisturbed. The doctors mandated that I needed to sleep sitting up because of the intense trauma to my head. After enduring numerous skin grafts my face was starting to heal, but I still made the Hunchback of Notre Dame look like a cover model. The only positive thought in my mind was that it had been three months since my accident and thus three months since my last drink. I became content without alcohol, since I had a slew of pain killers to keep me high, along with a steady dose of weed. This prescription practice not only numbed the pain, it numbed my mind and spirit as well. My body was truly void of all life, a soulless corpse with a pulse. I had no appreciation for my second chance at life, just a deep resentment towards my current condition.

I did have one friend though who for some reason showed more concern than most and her name was Sadie. Sadie and I had met a year earlier through some mutual friends, but she had moved back to Tennessee after things did not work out for her in

Los Angeles. Now she was calling me four times a day, blatantly concerned with my well-being. As out of place as it seemed, once again I could not stand to be alone. Sadie was a catch indeed since she was both beautiful and funny. She also had the ability whenever I was down on myself to lift my spirits and help me sustain that positive mindset throughout the duration of our conversations. Her only point of concern was the two sons that she had from a previous relationship. However I did not let that bother me and very little time passed before we made plans for her to fly back to Los Angeles. Until then, I spent most of my days guarding the couch since even walking became too painful for me to handle. Smoking weed seemed to distract me from the pain and boredom slightly, but it also had me eating my way into some abrupt weight gain. What little ego I still had left became fragile and meek. Nonetheless, I had Sadie coming to visit and her nightly calls were the perfect motivation to get me through my long days.

On one evening in particular, the phone rang and with pure delight I rushed to it. Instead of Sadie like had I expected, it was Samantha calling. This struck me quite off-key because I had not spoken to Samantha since the fallout at the Irving Pad. She was in a frantic rush to speak to me and the tone of her voice made my heart skip with anxiety. Samantha informed me of Joseph, Heidi's son, and his illness which had been ongoing since birth. Samantha's next words were completely unforeseen, Joseph had AIDS. A lump of shock sank into the pit of my stomach, as I was incapable of believing what I was hearing. With a trembling voice, I asked her how this all came about. Samantha remained silent for what felt like an eternity, and then told me that Heidi had found out earlier in the day yet was too afraid to call me. Like a sledgehammer to my chest, a sudden reality hit me. I too must have it. *Was it me that gave it to him? Did Heidi also have it?* Samantha insisted that I calmed down, and proceeded to tell me that Heidi was being tested and that I should go as soon as possible to be tested as well. I asked Samantha to have Heidi call me and then thanked her for all of her help. Once off the phone, I sat there, pondering why God had spared me in my car accident, just so I could turn around and die of AIDS. I knew without a doubt that I too was infected and could instantly feel the virus flowing inside me, making my skin crawl. Heidi was the good girl and did not sleep around. I was the pig, not her.

The phone rang, making me jump and this time it was Sadie. I explained to her the news that I had just received and she was highly concerned. At that very moment, I was beyond certain that the next words out of her mouth would be "Good luck and goodbye." Much to my surprise, all that Sadie said was, "Take care of Heidi and I will take care of you." With pure confidence, those words stuck with me forever. Sadie completely supported me, standing solid as my backbone.

I waited for Melinda to get home from work and when she arrived, I notified her of the situation. She was utterly devastated to say the least, but maintained a solid attitude since I was beyond distraught. Melinda immediately made an appointment for me to be tested later on that week. So many thoughts were exploding in my mind, all of which were linked around the early stories of AIDS and its symptoms. I wanted to clear my head but even alcohol and drugs were useless, I was too petrified to let my fears subside.

Upon my arrival at my appointment, the doctor was very tranquil and easy to be around despite the stressors of his profession. He stated that the results would take a few weeks and that it was important for me to abstain from sexual intercourse. I assured him that abstinence would not be a problem. I can only assume that based upon my appearance, he felt that I should have no issue whatsoever of staying abstinent. My face was still in horrifically bad shape.

Roughly three days later, Heidi called me to announce that she had tested positive for the virus. I gasped loudly in disbelief. *Why her? Nobody deserved this, especially not Heidi. Why Heidi?* Right on cue, my thoughts turned from my concern towards

Heidi to the fear of my own test. The week that stood between me and my results was undeniably the longest week of my life. All that I could do was just continue to watch as the clock ticked from one minute to the next. To lighten my worries, I felt at peace knowing that Sadie was coming in two weeks and I tried to share my excitement as much as possible. I did everything in my power to not let her know my fears. Everyday was a struggle to ignore the nightmare that was unfolding in my life and aside from Sadie, the pills I took helped me with that. Vicodin quickly established itself as my new alcohol, my new escape from sobriety.

Finally the week passed and I was back at the clinic. When the doctor came in and delivered the news that I had tested negative, I was so relieved that I broke down and cried. He reminded me that I was not out of the woods yet though. I was instructed to continue to avoid intercourse and return to be tested again in three months. I assured him that I would remain sex free, but with Sadie coming those promises would surely be broken.

When the time came for Sadie to arrive I was extremely nervous, however she was very accepting of my physical appearance which relieved me in a much needed way. I felt instantly that this was more than a growing friendship. This was an opportunity for me to get her out of Tennessee and into my life. Sadie was everything in a woman that I needed and I was lucky to have her. The next two weeks were like a college party movie composed of binge drinking and tireless sex. I was actually wise enough to use a condom, much to the disappointment of Sadie, who like many of us was oblivious to the real hazards of AIDS. I should have refrained from being intimate with her altogether, but I convinced myself that as long as I wore a condom I was fine. Using protection was only easy because of the fear and belief that I was eventually going to test positive.

Despite how prevalent these thoughts were in my mind,

I still managed to hide them well through the combination of the pills and alcohol. Nobody seemed surprised that I was drinking again. Even Gerard told me that as long as I did not drive, there was no harm in a few beers or shots. What he failed to understand was that drinking was my disease. The two weeks with Sadie were over faster than a shooting star and reluctantly she went back to Tennessee. I missed her terribly, and promised her that I would soon make my way out there to see her.

When Sadie was not available to talk, I would spend my time on the phone with Heidi. Despite her situation, she was still the same Heidi, showing all of her concerns towards her son Joseph. Never once did I hear her question her own dismal future. At eighteen years old, her life had just begun and in the back of our minds, we all knew that it was only a matter of time before her life would cease to exist. All of this heartbreak was too much for me so I did what I always did, I fled. I called Greyhound bus lines and booked myself a one way ticket to Tennessee. Two days before my departure I was randomly hanging out with my buddy Mark Andrews and I convinced him to come along. Mark used to date Cassandra and after they broke up, he and I were able to become friends. Mark was a charismatic guy with an easy going personality. I would jokingly call him Picasso because he was an artist when it came to his culinary skills and the name Picasso instantly stuck. So after convincing Picasso to skip town, we were off on the road to Tennessee.

My parents did not exactly agree with my decision due to the fact that I had only been back from Phoenix for little over a month and still had some therapy to finish. Melinda would burden me with her incessant lecturing, so I did my best to simply tune her out. I had all of the answers, and Tennessee was one of them. Heidi was noticeably hurt by my departure, still believing that we could be a couple. Like I said, she loved me more than any woman ever had, but now all that I could do was get as far away from the whole AIDS crisis as possible.

Upon arriving in Tennessee, I was greeted by Sadie and

her friend Hope. I was exhausted but relieved to be there, two thousand miles from the pain and the gossip. By this time, everyone had accepted that I was HIV positive and these individuals' constant need for gossip and hurtful rumors made me ill. Then again, due to my track record, who could blame them? Sadie and I quickly picked up where we left off, spending the first three days locked in her room, much to the displeasure of her mom. I had no idea that I was in store for a lesson in life, Tennessee style.

Sadie woke me early one morning, telling me that her mom felt it was inappropriate for the two of us to be sleeping together out of wedlock. I thought it was a joke until Sadie told me that in order for us to continue our lustful ways, we needed to get married. I held no real rebuttal to the idea so with a strong sense of pride, I went for it. With delight, Sadie and her mom made swift arrangements for us to be married. Awkwardly enough, this whole situation seemed relatively normal to me.

Being that we were so close to Elvis' house I only had one request, that we be married on August 16, the anniversary of Elvis' death. They agreed and with Picasso as my best man, Sadie and I were married with no predictions or cares for the future, only that we honored her mother's house while we still lived there. Certainly, this was not the way that I had envisioned marriage being, but my life was anything but normal and at least I had done something right.

With a new sense of responsibility, I finally put the alcohol down and put my focus on my family. All that I had to do was figure out how to take care of Sadie and her two boys. My mind also drifted to the fact that I was due within the month to take another AIDS test. The subtly buried fear was slowly coming back. I had traveled over two thousand miles and could not escape the reality that I might be infected and dying. All that I did was go out and get married to a girl I had dated primarily by the phone for two months. When I called my parents with the news of my marriage they quickly made note of my past failures. I argued,

"Why can't you just be happy for me?" So they took my input into consideration and did their best to be supportive. In doing so, they sent me enough money to hop on a Greyhound back to Los Angeles with my new family in tow.

By the time we made it to Los Angeles, the news of my marriage had spread to my friends and family, which left most of them shaking their heads in disbelief. For the first time in my marriage, the thought crossed my mind that I had made a hasty decision and deeper down inside my heart, I knew that I was right. I simply tricked myself into believing that this time I was going to do things differently.

Very little time passed before the honeymoon was over and I was not only back at my parents' house, but now I had a new family to think about. I stayed sober, found a job and steered things in the right direction. The holiday season was upon us and for the first time in three years I was looking forward to Christmas. I was taking Angel and Daniel on a semi-regular basis and my sobriety was proving to be a beneficial tool. At this stage in my life, I was getting very self-righteous and felt that my newly found responsibility had given me the right to think I was the king of the household.

On Christmas day the whole family went to Mimi and Papa's house as part of our annual tradition. Everyone seemed to be enjoying themselves. Part way through our Christmas ham dinner, I excused myself to use the restroom. As I made my way through the hallway, I caught my uncle Ted dropping my grandfather's new leather jacket out of the bedroom window. The jacket had been a Christmas gift from my grandmother. I went absolutely ballistic on Ted. The jacket was going to get him two spoons of heroin, that is, until I walked in. Just like that, the Christmas spirit was gone. I made it a point to expose my uncle's wrongdoings out in front of the entire family. After four months of sobriety I thought that I had all of the answers and maybe so, but I was indeed a hypocrite too. My uncle had never judged me for my actions and now I was pointing the finger of shame at him. As a youth, I idolized him and now here I was, going flip-mode and belittling him in front of everyone. I knew what I did was wrong, but I was establishing myself as the alpha male. In all honesty, that was no way to prove that I was a leader. All that I exhibited was that I was still a scared little man.

Soon after that episode, my marriage to Sadie was starting to show obvious signs of deterioration. We both became sober at the same time and it was starting to create enmity. That and the fact that we were still living at my parents' developed an additional strain in our relationship. My parents had had enough and once again, they went out of their way and co-signed for a loan to help us establish our own place. They also included several pieces of dilapidated furniture for us to use. They did everything they could for my family, but they still could not fix me.

My old ways slowly started to creep up again, which meant less time with the family and more time with my cronies. Sadie had started to use cocaine sporadically and I moseyed my way back to smoking weed. I managed to stay away from the alcohol and actually grew stronger for it, but I still had no right being married. I did not have it in me to not be selfish and in a marriage, neither partner can be selfish. Without the help of counseling, our marriage was over within six months. Sadie and her kids packed up and moved out. Despite the fact that my experiment with marriage was a complete failure, I just went on with my life as though nothing had happened. I failed to notice that my actions had hurt yet another individual.

So with some new space available, Ray and Dino almost instantly moved in and the party lifestyle fell back into full swing. I even put so much emphasis on reconnecting with my friends that I quit my job and started selling weed again. Heidi also lived nearby and she had an attractive roommate named Cassidy, so it made visiting her that much easier. Much to my astonishment, I had taken my third AIDS test and it once again came back negative. I had no idea how, but sadly enough it did little to improve my attitude. My second and third chances at life were wasted on me. Somebody else could have used those chances. Me, I just abused them by running away from any and everybody, with my fears locked securely around my neck.

Tony Boyte tried one final time to help me gain control of my life and again I disregarded his advice. All that he could do from there was simply wish me luck. I figured I would allow him some time to cool off and then things would be back to normal, but times were changing and that was not always a certainty.

LEAVING MY LIFE BEHIND

My new found freedom did not exactly pan out to what I had originally imagined. I was still depressed over my break-up with Sadie, but Ray and Dino helped me get on with my life. I continued to stay away from the alcohol, Ray did as well and Dino was fighting off heroin. Our struggles seemed easier since we were all focused on the path to sobriety. I also started dating Dino's sister, Liza, much to the dismay of Dino who thought it was a bad idea. In all respects, he was right. I had no right being with another woman, I was still legally married to Sadie. Then again, I harbored no interest for the rules of society and I was afraid to be alone. I dabbled with a pointless job but soon found myself unemployed and depending on my pot sales to pay the bills. As great of an idea as it sounded, it never worked out since I always tended to smoke more than I could sell.

Heidi and I began spending more time together and the guilt of knowing what was happening to her made these times even more difficult. Not only Heidi, but her son too was slowly losing the battle to this dreaded disease. The question also still lingered that I as well was HIV positive. I continued to ignore the whispers even though I myself thought the same thing. Besides, I had bigger worries arising.

Oscar had been doing three years for possession of cocaine and evading the police. For once, I noticed that everyone was either coming or going through the system except for me. Sobriety quickly proved to be the key to keeping me out of jail. A soothing burst of accomplishment overwhelmed my body and soul. Sadly though, by the end of the week I received the call that Joseph had passed away from complications due to AIDS. Cassidy mentioned that Heidi was holding up surprisingly well, but was not sure for how much longer. Heidi was so strong that it blew me away. My weak mind would have buckled and went insane. Joseph Murphy was two years old and already released from this Earth. She chose not to have a service for reasons unknown.

With Heidi in no condition to associate with others for the time being, Cassidy ended up staying with my roommates and me. She was from Silver Lake and she fit right in. Dino had grown up with her, and Liza and Cassidy were best friends. I was still seeing Liza on a limited basis, but that was going nowhere in a hurry. So my focus of interest shifted and I set my eyes on Cassidy. I started things on a very mellow pace. Cassidy was absolutely stunning, standing just over five feet tall, with emerald green eyes, blonde hair and an attitude that took no strife from anyone. The moment I showed interest in her, she reciprocated it right back. A few of my friends that knew her told me she was not worth the effort but I did not listen. To me she was searching for the same thing that I was, a better way of life.

Aside from my growing relationship with Cassidy, I had some intense problems in store for me. Oscar's prison term was coming closer to an end and I was in debt to him three-thousand dollars. I should not have been holding the basket by myself, but two other so-called-friends threw me under the bus and pinned all of the money on me. So I started taking my money from my weed sales and putting it away for Oscar. When he called to give me his release date I assured him that everything would fall in order and the moment I hung up, I started brainstorming my next escape from Los Angeles.

That Saturday, Ray and I ended up at a wedding and met with our friend Alec, whose dad was a biker from the same crew I was getting my weed from. Alec was an all around good kid. He lived in New Hampshire, about forty minutes from Boston and he told me and Ray how well we could do selling cannabis there. I instantly agreed to relocate, knowing that the next couple of months were going to get real dicey here in Los Angeles. So Ray and I set our sights on New Hampshire. Cassidy and I were developing a close connection yet I had no intentions of taking her with me.

Finally the day had come for Ray and me to head north to pick up Oscar. He was being released from prison and we invited him to stay with us until he could get better established. Besides, it was the very least that I could do. When we picked him up it was really good to see him. We drove and smoked for a couple hours before we pulled off of the Interstate 5 to take a restroom break. I took Oscar aside, handed him five hundred dollars and explained my situation. He was not impressed a single bit and set down a date to have him paid off in full. I agreed and shook his hand. Of course, I had no intention of keeping my word. I just told him what he needed to hear.

The times were tight but I was hustling day and night to make enough money for the cross-country trip to the Shire. I was excited to be leaving but paranoid to get on the road because I was fronted several pounds of weed from the bikers to sell. They had no idea that I was leaving and I was burning the wrong guys for sure, but once I started I was one hundred percent committed. As the days passed and Cassidy and I were getting closer and closer, my feelings started to change. I caved in and asked her if she wanted to join me in New Hampshire. Ray was furious with me and I could not blame him, but the thought of being alone outweighed that. She told me that she would think about it.

As the trip grew closer, Oscar knew me well enough to know that I was up to something. Upon confronting me about my trip, Oscar took the personal pleasure of beating his frustrations and fury into me. He avoided landing any serious punches to the head but did succeed in breaking three ribs. I considered myself lucky. He followed up with the cliché comment about how it would be a lot worse if I did not get him his money and then he spit in my hands-protected face. I ended up in the hospital but there was little that they could do other than tape me up and prescribe me some Vicodin. I was really starting to feel the itch to get out of Los Angeles, immediately.

I still had Ray on board and I was able to stash away a fair amount of money. I found out that my parents were leaving town for a vacation roughly a week before my trip and I would be able to squat their house for a portion of the time that they were away. Of course they knew nothing about this. I was a week away from the eviction from the apartment that I had shared with Sadie and only needed a place to stay for a month before we left back east. So Cassidy, Ray and I moved into an old biker's house in Tujunga. His name was Dave and Dave was an awkward older guy. His intentions were obvious that he was more interested in sexual intercourse with Cassidy than actually helping us out, but I did not care what his intentions were, and Cassidy would not stray. She was a loyal woman and there was a roof over our heads.

Cassidy felt that it was appropriate for me to be introduced to her family and friends. Katie, Cassidy's mom, liked me from the get go. She was heavily into Alcoholics Anonymous which was foreign to me, but after twelve months without a drink she celebrated my one year anniversary which felt very encouraging. I could not believe that I had not had a drink in a year. This was the first time that I felt like I had accomplished something through my own will power. Ray did not drink so his determination and friendship was important to me as well.

Only weeks before our trip, Ray and I were in my car when we hydroplaned on the freeway and totaled it completely. Luckily, neither of us was injured, but had suddenly found ourselves in a strenuous situation and we were going to be forced to fly. Despite the hardship of not having a vehicle, I did nothing to change my plans. Plus, I was so deeply involved with these bikers for the weed that I was now laying low for fear of getting brutalized by these unforgiving guys. To keep me distracted from my stressors, I turned to Cassidy. I started spending more time with Cassidy and her friends and less time with the people that I grew up with. I met some great people and they all had a strong connection to each other. I knew this was the positive crowd that I needed.

We decided to throw a goodbye party at my parents' house instantly after their departure. We were able to convince Cassandra to let us in and stay while they were on vacation. Cassandra and I had not seen each other for quite some time. The last time we partied together, she had planted a bottle of beer over my head and I vowed to never drink with her again. She was the female version of me, especially when drunk, and it was always a crazy scene. The only difference was that this time I was sober and we needed somewhere to stay. Everyone came to the party, all of Cassidy's friends, some of my old friends, yet no one more important than Martin and Heidi. Martin had been taking care of his father, Ivan, who was dying from lung cancer and Heidi was becoming very sick from the HIV. This was an experience that I would never forget.

The three of us joined together in the master bedroom alone, away from the noise and the crowd of people. This was a golden opportunity for us to just sit down and converse. Martin was very distraught over his dad and had been shooting morphine to ease his mind. Heidi and I expressed dearly to him our fears for his well-being. But Martin being Martin, he only worried about us. We cried over the loss of Joseph and Heidi maintained her strength. They were enthusiastic for me that I was leaving even though they both were feeling abandoned on the inside. Martin definitely wanted to go with me and figured he should accompany me, not Ray. I told him that he could join me as soon as things settled out with his dad, whichever way that might be. Heidi loved me so much that it broke her heart seeing me pursue things with Cassidy, but she told me that she wanted the best for me and to be happy. This was a memory I kept in my heart and soul for the rest of my life because after that day, nothing would be that perfect again. This was the last time Los Angeles would ever be considered my home. Times were changing quickly and all that I could do was keep running from my problems. As Martin, Heidi and I stood up we embraced each other, creating an intertwined circle of love. This moment existed outside of time and space, forever frozen in the last time we would all be together.

Four days after that magical night, Ray and I were on a plane to Boston. I had no clue what I was doing or what I was leaving behind, simply a journey into the unknown. I did not have the nerve to say goodbye to Angel and Daniel, I just figured that they had a better life without my interference. Everything I needed was right in front of me and I was convinced that I had to go three-thousand miles to find happiness. I was careless with my treasures and blind to what the sole basis of my life was. A life, that by leaving, I would never know again.

GYPSY LOVE

*U*pon our arrival in Boston, we were greeted by Alec and his friend, Jerry. Alec was a proud young straight-A student, with involved parents, an incredible home and an insatiable appetite for drugs. I admired Alec and his scholarly ways in the art of deception, but only time would tell before I would find out exactly how well. He was able to convince Jerry to drive the one hour trip from Dover purely on the fact that we were in possession of California's finest marijuana, which was motivation enough. Once we were all piled into Jerry's car, we rolled up a series of overflowing joints and proceeded to get blazed out of our skulls. With my newly enhanced senses, I reclined my seat and soaked in the scenery. Massachusetts is indeed a beautiful state, far too enthralling to harbor a horde of Red Sox fans. Hell, I guess every state has its rough parts though.

Three toll booths and four joints later we arrived at Alec's parents' house. Betty and Chris seemed very inviting as far as parents go and they had an awesome old century brick house. Even though they held a slightly skeptical look towards Ray and me, they did their best to make their way past that and welcomed us with open arms. We assured them that we would find a separate residence within a week and we just needed a temporary home to establish ourselves. Dover was a great place with a unique colonial vibe. I also liked that I could walk along the streets without looking over my shoulder. In no way was it about anyone in particular, I just knew that things were different now and I could finally enjoy it.

The only solid contact I kept on the West Coast that I did care for was my aunt Karen, who I would call weekly to check in on. She had been going through a rough time ever since Bobby went to prison. Apparently Bobby had earned himself three to five years for burglary. All of that speed that went up the arm only provided him with plenty of time to think. I was hurt at first to hear that about him since we were as close as brothers, but then again, I was glad that it was not me. I could never have done that length of time. He always thought my traveling was crazy, about as much as I thought his drugs were and maybe we were both right. I do know that we were both in search of perfection, but we clearly had different means of achieving it.

When in Dover, I did not have to worry and my mind was free to be clear. The only hardship that fell upon me was my constant yearning to be with Cassidy. I liked her more than I realized. I did my best to convince her into relocating to Dover and to my surprise she actually sounded interested. Cassidy simply asked me to secure a job and a place to live and she would come. Without hesitation, I agreed and told her that I would jump right on it. Cassidy became my positive motivation to get things done. Within a day, Ray and I were able to both obtain jobs picking apples on an orchard. Along with the full-time job, we were also able to find a place for rent on the third story level of an old Victorian home. Everything was on the upswing and three weeks later Cassidy joined me in New Hampshire. Hallelujah, I was no longer alone and life was amazing with her there.

Our days consisted simply of expressing our feelings every hour on the hour, spare a few minutes and this was the style of new love that I liked. As with any recreational dedication, if an individual commits long enough to it, then greater results will be achieved. Well this phenomenon happened perfectly in sync with my life, and without a thought of concern Cassidy informed me that she was pregnant. I can honestly say that I was thrilled because this time things were going to be different. After all, I already had two kids that I did not take care of and now I had the opportunity to support my child with a paying job, even if it was only picking apples. I did not care, I loved Cassidy and I was going to do everything right, classic textbook fathering.

Ray and I were able to earn some extra cash doing temporary work plus held a consistent schedule at the farm. With all of this honest hard work, we were doing fairly well. Along with that, Cassidy's mom had provided her with enough money for us to buy a car and some basic necessities.

Little time passed before Alec showed up to inform us that his parents had thrown him out and he needed a couch to sleep on. Normally, roommates can be quite cumbersome, but I figured that I owed him and welcomed him in with the same open arms that his parents showed me. Besides, Alec always seemed to have the very best acid and that was a plus. Here I was, a father to be and still gobbling down acid. Addiction has no boundaries and addiction certainly has no morals.

One morning Alec gave us some intense acid just as Ray and I were leaving the house to go to work. Without thinking things through thoroughly, the two of us dropped two hits apiece and trotted off to work. Strictly on the basis that we worked out in the fields by ourselves, I never really could foreshadow this being anything but an awesome experience. Well things were going well and we were having a jolly good day, until the owner of the farm sent for us. As we drove back to the barn we put all of our focus into composing ourselves. By the time we arrived, she mentioned that her barn manager had been delayed and that she had no one else to conduct the third grade field trip on the process of making apple cider. Without any chance to make a rebuttal, she placed us in that position and scurried us along. We both laughed hysterically, but she was not amused and obviously too overwhelmed to see the humor in this. Somehow, by the grace of God, we managed to pull this whole charade off. Our presentation even earned us a round of applause from the students.

As proud as we were, it still turned my stomach, being surrounded by all of these children. I was reminded that I was about to be a father again, but here I was having fun with these kids and not my own bundles of joy. That is how quickly a high can turn on the user. My only way out was to pretend to be sick and have Cassidy come pick me up. On the way home, I cried to her about my guilt over Angel and Daniel. She remained quiet, showing complete empathy towards my thoughts and feelings. I felt relieved to be able to vent my frustrations, but as always, sobriety took my thoughts right back towards myself.

The next day Dean, a guy we worked with at the farm, told us about a job offer for us. He had an acquaintance up in Boston who needed help moving out of his house and we could make five hundred dollars cash each. The only catch was that this guy was a drug dealer and was guaranteed to be under surveillance. As sketchy as it sounded, I did not care and neither did Ray. So we did the job, however instead of five hundred dollars in cash we were given a half of an ounce of cocaine. I was outraged since I was completely anti-coke and speed and did not have a clue how to sell it. My only option was Alec, who after a brief negotiation settled for six hundred dollars, all in crisp five-dollar bills. The transaction definitely seemed odd, but all that I wanted to do was spoil Cassidy with my quick riches.

My perfect evening consisted of a night on the town up in Portsmouth. We did the whole romantic getaway right: horse drawn carriage, candlelight dinner and true romance. Cassidy and I were in love. She was my little Gypsy, as I called her. The evening rolled along flawlessly. That night as we got back from our excursion of love, Alec arrived soon after us with an eerily pale face. The first thing that crossed my mind was that our old Victorian house was haunted and that the cliché was true, but I was far off. Alec and some friends had been busted with an assortment of drugs: acid, weed, heroin and the coke that I sold him. Panic shot through my bones. He confidently said that I was in no part of the conversation between him and the officer. I explained that I was more nervous about them knowing our address because it was guaranteed to bring them knocking. I sternly gave him his three days notice to find a new place to live. I felt bad but had to do what was best for my new family. Besides, other than some occasional drug use, I wanted and was willing to change.

My little Gypsy was my inspiration in so many ways. She made me feel excited to be a dad to all three of my children, as far away as they may be. The first step of responsibility was to quickly get rid of all of our paraphernalia and prepare ourselves for the raid that we all knew was coming. After a few days and still no cops, I started to ease up a bit and drop the restless paranoia. Then, like thunder in a canyon, on the fourth day they came and they came hard. I was awakened early Saturday morning to what at first I thought were Alec and Ray wrestling in the other room. By the time I opened my eyes I had a shotgun pressed against my forehead. Another cop had stuck a gun to Cassidy's head, which at that point made her hysterical. She was then ripped from the bed like a child does with a rag doll. I started screaming, "She's fuckin' pregnant," but by the time I finished my sentence I was thrown from the bed and hog tied. The odd thing about all of this was that these rodeo cowboys were involved with the Federal Bureau of Investigation and Drug Enforcement Administration. This whole scenario seemed awfully out of place for a basic drug bust.

I kept screaming profanity at them, knowing that we had done nothing wrong. Once I ran short on breath, they started to question us about Alec, asking if he owed us any money. I told them no. They then asked me where I got all of the money that was sitting on my dresser. I replied that I worked for it, all five-dollar bills. I said that my customers were consistent. My answers were very short and sarcastic, with the occasional "Pig" thrown in. Outbursts like that, though as good as they felt, would get me several swift kicks to the ribs or "accidentally" stepped on. After an hour of interrogation, they hauled Alec away and asked us to leave while they finished with their investigation. So we walked down to the nearest restaurant to grab a small bite to eat and collect ourselves. Nothing could really be said, we were all just too stunned to form any logical thoughts. Then out of the blue, Cassidy broke the silence with an interesting fact. Alec had robbed a bank.

Good Friends We Have, Good Friends We Lost

As expected, the fallout of Alec's arrest proved to be costly for Cassidy and me, along with Ray who caught the first plane back to California. The raid had made front page news, which the owner of the property had read, thus giving us our thirty day notice. Along with that, I was not welcomed back on the farm either. To our surprise, Alec's parents were deeply remorseful for what had transpired and felt personally responsible. Their positive, Good Samaritan attitude was our lifesaver, even though it was not their obligation at all. We were absolutely delighted when his parents offered us their condominium. They had recently relocated to a house of theirs up in Massachusetts and we gladly accepted the offer. Alec's parents were astonishing people and this was the first time in my life that I did not want to take advantage of someone's kindness.

With the holidays upon us once again, Cassidy's family and best friend were en route to visit. To say the least, I was terrified to meet them. Cassidy, her mom and her brother were a close knit family, which made me feel meek and insignificant. I buried these thoughts and emotions deep inside and showed my best face. I wanted to feel welcomed in her family. Cassidy's brother, Max, was scheduled to be released from jail after being trapped up in a burglary charge. Approximately nine months passed before the judges realized that they had the wrong guy. For being the governing factor in our nation's law enforcement, the court system sure tends to take their time in the release of innocent individuals. This is a very blatant flaw.

The time had come for Cassidy and me to head up to Boston to pick up her family from the airport. Once we arrived, I could not believe how excited she was to see her brother. I never knew that a brother and sister could have such a close bond and I was instantly jealous of what they had. I also felt a strong connection with Max from the moment that I met him. He was nineteen years old with jet black hair that stretched halfway down his back and the thick style of beard that demanded respect. He epitomized the look that I wanted but could not have due to the hardships of still going through a late puberty. To top it off, Max also had an immaculate style of dressing, far more in tune with the current trends and fashions than I was. In a lot of ways, Max reminded me of Bobby. Like I said, I connected with him right away.

Cassidy's mom, Katie, was a godsend. Katie was a recovering alcoholic who loved cannabis and popping prescription pills. She was without a doubt the most generous and magnetic person that I have ever met. Cassidy's best friend, Shawnette, who was absolutely beautiful and had grown up with Bobby and Collette, completed Cassidy's visiting entourage. They were all pure souls who immediately welcomed me with love and attention. I felt honored to be part of something as special and unique as their bond. With Christmas around the corner and the company of new friends and family, I was on top of the world. We spent the frigid December days decorating the condominium and eating as a family. Then, to make things even more incredible, I awoke at the dawn of Christmas day to a blanket of fresh snow in our yard. That year, Christmas was postcard perfect.

The opportunity that I spent getting to know Cassidy's family was a blast. At nineteen, Max had lived a tough life. He had been involved with a gang for countless years and had witnessed too many of his friends slain. Tragically, he had already attended six funerals. This was a side of life that I knew nothing about and I was several years his elder. Despite all of his trials, Max was and continues to be debatably one of the funniest individuals that I have ever met, comparable to Bobby. His material was always centered on me and he could still make me roar with laughter. He constantly taunted me about the way that I dressed and he was right, I looked like a regurgitated Poison video. With his unique style of criticism constantly flowing through my brain, I slowly but surely began transforming my wardrobe. Much to my disappointment, it did not stop Max. Every time that I was around him, I had to be on my toes. Max had an extensive knowledge of movies, almost up to par with mine. We could keep everyone entertained for hours just by using quotes from movies to talk smack about each other.

To this day, it was without a doubt one of the best Christmas seasons that I have ever experienced. There was not a lot of emphasis on the exchange of presents but more about the presence of great family. The holidays were always the best time of year growing up, Melinda made sure of that. Then Desiree came along and after the trauma of our falling apart, I had not enjoyed the holidays for numerous years. Blessedly, Cassidy and her family changed that and I will never forget that. The true spirit of Christmas was back in my heart, a heart that I did not believe I still had anymore.

Upon their departure, Cassidy was heartbroken and became instantly homesick. We agreed to start making plans to get back to the West Coast, but I told her that there was no way I was ever going back to Los Angeles. This turned into a problem since all of her friends and family were in Los Angeles and all of my enemies were there too. I was in no condition or motivation to face my demons. Luckily, Cassidy had a friend who lived down in San Clemente and they got the ball rolling with options for that. Once again, it was Cassidy's mom who funded the whole process. I sighed with relief, since for once, everything was falling into place.

Cassidy was due to give birth in May, so we made plans to leave the first week of February. We decided that it was cheaper and easier to take a bus back, despite the generous offer from her mom to pay for a plane flight. Our intent was to spend some time in New York where Gerard had some cousins whom I could catch up with and I was ecstatic. As far back as I can remember, my dream was to go to New York. Then it hit me, it was the off-season and I would not be able to see the Yankees play. Fuck! At the time, the Yankees were one of the worst teams in Major League Baseball and it took a lot of faith and a thick backbone to follow them. That was fine by me though because being a Yankees fan was the only thing that was ever a constant in my life.

I managed to get in touch with Martin and explained my current situation and my fears of coming back, knowing that Oscar was looking for me. Martin assured me that everything would be alright and he too was interested in spending time down in San Clemente, claiming that he was going nowhere in Los Angeles and needed to escape. His main reason was focused around his overdependence on morphine since his father passed away a few months prior. Martin was twenty-two and jaded of his lifestyle. With a smile he could feel through the phone, I promised him that he had a home with me. Martin was the kind of guy that I wanted in my corner. So with my new family, Cassidy and I were going to make it.

Cassidy wanted Angel and Daniel to be involved in our lives as much as I did. I missed them immensely and anticipated my next meeting with them. Over eight months had passed and I was going to have to deliver some bona fide promises to persuade Desiree into letting me see my children. There was some tremendous tension between us that showed no signs of giving way. Desiree already had a son with Benny and they were on their own road. I knew that I was on the right road now too, yet I still held a deep resentment towards them. My heart would ache at the sight of them together, but with Cassidy by my side, I had the strength I needed to tackle my endeavors.

Our final week in New Hampshire had arrived and we were busy setting up the last minute plans. A house was secured for us in San Clemente and my cousin was able to pick us up from New York. I called Cassidy at work to let her know that I had the bus tickets and she squealed with excitement. Making her happy made my whole body feel good. She stated that she was almost off of work and she desperately wanted to be with me. With a smile that could not leave my face, I hung up the phone and continued to pack my belongings.

Within seconds the phone rang and I merely assumed that Cassidy had something more to say. Instead, it was Melinda, who I had not spoken with since she was robbed last September. She called to ask me what I knew about the whole incident. I had to remind her I was three thousand miles away yet due to my reputation I was being seen as suspect number one. I knew who did it but refused to reveal that information. I figured it did not matter now since Gerard had insurance and I would never snitch on family. *Yeah, it was an inside job.* I could tell Melinda was upset, so I instantly dropped my antagonistic attitude and asked her what was wrong. Out of nowhere, Melinda hit me with some intense information. She cried out, "Martin is dead." I asked her, no, I screamed, "What the fuck are you saying?" My body started to convulse, struggling to take in what she had just said. She went on to mention that Martin had overdosed while in custody at the Foothill Division. With a brash voice, I let Melinda know that I had to go and abruptly broke into hysteria, wrecking havoc on everything in the room while crying profusely. *How could this be? Why would he of all people overdose?* Martin knew what he was doing when it came to his drug use. I had just talked to him and we had plans to recover together in San Clemente. I promised him that we would be away from Los Angeles and get sober off of everything. I bolted from the house and kept running until my body could not push another step.

Taking refuge under a bridge, I sat alone, crying and freezing in the frigid, dark air. *Anybody but Martin, why him?* Martin was the chivalrous guy, the kind of person who would go out of his way to make another individual's life easier. I idolized him in so many ways. There was nothing fake about Martin. He had honor, loyalty and charisma that radiated towards all of those around him. As youths, we often talked about the notion of death and whether or not we would live to reach thirty. I suppose all teenagers think that way. Well that should not be the case because when an individual is twenty-two years old, thirty is not that far away and Martin had his whole life in front of him.

Unable to tolerate the cold any longer, I walked the two miles back to the condominium, still steaming in my blood with utter hatred. When I arrived back at home, I had several missed calls from Picasso. I called him and upon answering the phone I noticed that he was frantic with emotion. He filled me in on what had happened and that Martin had still been dealing drugs. With the death of his father, he had been hitting morphine three to four times a day and on top of that, had caught his girlfriend with one of his friends. Martin's heart broke as solidly as the dude's nose. Martin went into a drunken drug rage and started discharging his gun into some liquor store signs. He then put the gun down and waited for Johnny Law to arrive. While in custody, he went into cardiac arrest. Picasso and I both agreed that it sounded bogus and I was convinced that the cops had a part in his death. My brother was stronger than that. Whether I was right or wrong, the results were still the same. He was five weeks shy of his twenty-third birthday and I should have been there for him, to be his strength and motivation.

Six weeks later I was given some equally harsh news that broke me down even further, Tony Boyte had died from Leukemia. Apparently, in only a brief six months, the illness had taken a drastic turn for the worse and his body could not cope with its rapid deterioration. The reality of his death vented through my knuckles as I punched numerous holes into the wall next to me.

Tony had always resembled the older brother that I never had and throughout my life had been a spirit of inspiration. If there was ever anyone who was truly great in this world, it was Tony. Somehow, his loss felt like a thinning of my kin and I could not let it go. Tony was plucked from this Earth and I never had the opportunity to share any last words with him.

I was shocked yet melancholy, followed by absolute hatred at myself for not being around for either one. I never got a chance to formally say my goodbyes, so I would like to do so now.

Martin and Tony,

I miss you both with every bit of my soul, and not a day or night passes that I neglect to think of you and what each of you have done for me. I know that some of my actions have confused you from above, but rest assured that I persevere daily to make you both proud. My time on this Earth is limited and I anticipate standing in your company again. I will never forget either one of you. There is no replacement for your love and friendship, just a promise to remind the world that the both of you lived and touched my soul forever. I love you Martin Doran. I love you Tony Boyte.

Your friend and brother,

Anthony

THE CHALLENGE TO GROW

With the birth of our baby only three months away, I became the source for everyone's problems and as always I had the answers, or at least I convinced myself that I still did. I resumed selling weed, along with taking advantage of the welfare system and hustling money any way that I could. I had developed a deep resentment for life, the system, the law, anything and everything. The loss of my friends, Heidi's condition and Joseph's death all made me lose grip of my own sanity. Surprisingly enough, I was still sober, having achieved over nineteen months without a single drink. Maybe I was just tired like Martin, but at least I was not to the point where I was sick like Tony and I needed to keep it that way. I should have had a better appreciation for the riches in my life since I had a great girlfriend with a baby in development and her friends and family who were very supportive throughout the whole pregnancy. Katie provided us with all the bells and whistles: a new crib, diapers, baby monitors and etcetera. She also was picking up the bill for everything. We established ourselves in a beautiful home with a friendly roommate, Jenene, who had the most fantastic personality. Jenene, who was like a sister to Cassidy, had set us up with our new place less than a quarter of a mile from the beach. For once, everything in my life was perfect.

Cassidy and I were able to start seeing Angel and Daniel, thanks to Desiree giving me yet another chance at being a father to my kids. I can see why she had her doubts in me, I had doubts in myself. *How many other kids have kids? Why have kids if we never intend to raise them? Why expect everyone else to pay for them? Do any of us even understand what we are doing?* The individuals who get degrees and work hard, they are the ones who should be having children. Having a child should be considered an honor, one that I was not worthy of. Countless children this day and age go their whole lives without the positive influence of a parental structure in their lives. Those children are being raised by the addicts and the free-loaders of our societies. I played this game twice before and now I too was to blame, involved in the same game that I had just escaped. All that I could show for myself was my dedication to the continual abuse of the system.

I attempted half-heartedly to co-mingle with the people around me, but I had a bad temper and usually reacted without a second thought. I started to feel the need to drink, but managed to stay strong one day at a time. I never tried to join any program, I had seen it work thousands of times for others but never imagined it for myself. With our baby's birth only a week away, Cassidy did not want me selling weed anymore. Without hesitation, I complied and acted so righteous about it despite the fact that I was just doing what I should have been doing the whole time. We went to see Cassidy's doctor, who gave us a date and time for us to go to the hospital for the delivery. Much had changed in the seven years since Angel was born.

I became overwhelmed with excitement towards the upcoming event. I wanted to do something special for Cassidy, so I had Max and another friend help me put a magical evening into action. The set-up was absolutely spectacular, a table on the sand illuminated by the romantic glow of Tiki Torches and a delectable dinner that Max took the honor of serving to us. I also wrote a poem which Cassidy read aloud and her face glistened with tears of joy. Then in a moments notice, I blindfolded her and carried her down to the beach. My timing was flawless and just as I pulled off her blindfold, we were lucky enough to see the green flash that the sun makes as it sets into the ocean on a crystal clear evening. Everything was perfect.

Cassidy was a wonderful woman and I knew in every inch of my being she was going to be a great mom, the complete opposite of my fathering abilities. My heart was riddled with guilt over Angel and Daniel, and I still did nothing to change. The time had finally come to make a difference, an opportunity to grow as an individual and as a father. On May 30, 1992, another miracle arrived into my life and her name was Nicole Sparzo. Nicole was down right the most beautiful female that I had ever laid eyes on, just like her mother. As I looked across the room, I noticed the same pride and joy coming from Max. He loved his sister so much and was insanely proud to be an uncle. I was honored to call him my family, to call all of them my family. Cassidy's family was the kind of persons that I wanted to surround myself with. My only problem was that I was too pessimistic to be consistently positive like everyone else.

Within the week, my parents came down to San Clemente to see their new granddaughter. I had an ongoing struggle of a relationship with them and deliberately went out of my way to make them feel alienated. I believe that they wanted to do more for my children, yet I neglected to include them. As a stress release, I occupied myself by writing poetry, something that I had dabbled with since I was fifteen. However, despite how hard I focused on optimistic words, everything channeled right back into extreme hate.

I started making a regular habit of visiting Bobby in prison and I would always be full of adrenaline whenever I was due to see him. We would spend hours laughing, recalling the nostalgic stories of our childhood. My visits were the only pleasurable moments for Bobby. He swore over and over that he would never wind up back in prison and I knew that he was being truthful. He finally had learned his lesson. After each visit, I would be heavily depressed for leaving him behind. Despite what any DNA test would say, Bobby was every bit my little brother, not H-04214, a prison number. I loved him immensely and his incarceration turned me bitter in a heartbeat, so the only way to soothe my demons was to be in the presence of my family.

Cassidy and I balanced the household duties extremely well. At times, it did prove to be very strenuous, but then there were the moments in the middle of the night when it was just my daughter and I and everything seemed perfectly in place. I finally felt love and loyalty towards somebody other than myself. The new me was the man that I should have become long ago. This fresh outlook on life was a concept I knew I could hold, yet in the back of my mind, I still could not shake the fact that I was a professional quitter. Only time would tell.

I took Nicole to meet Heidi in hopes that it would lighten her spirits. I had not seen Heidi in nearly three months and when I did her change hit me like a sledgehammer. She was in horrible condition, yet unsurprisingly her attitude was far more superior to mine. Like I said countless times, she was one of the strongest individuals that I have ever met. Never once did the words, "Why me?" slip past her lips. She only spoke with a comfort towards death and even let a slight smile cross her face at the thought of soon being able to be back with her son. The concept of death scared me, yet to Heidi, it inspired her. I admired Heidi so much. I had lived most of my life convinced that I would die before thirty and I had always dreaded that final day of judgment. She just winked and said that the dying part was easy but it was us that she was worried about. I could not believe that amidst all of her inner anguish she was worried about us.

Stricken with tremendous guilt, I began contemplating the reality of the situation. Heidi in no way deserved this, I should have been lying there dying, not her. Heidi was only a kid who had a life full of adventure and wonderment to live. Instead, the AIDS contaminated her body, yet in doing so could still never contaminate her soul. Everything that I knew about AIDS was wrong, it did not discriminate. AIDS was and still is the people's disease. Heidi was an average person and this dreaded disease was taking her from me. I failed to understand the ruthless reality of AIDS and struggled to acknowledge how the disease could so swiftly take its toll. This is why I place a heavy emphasis on taking our time to enjoy our loved ones at every minute of every day. For soon enough our death bells will ring and that time to conjoin will be lost forever. We need to leave no loving thoughts unspoken, leave no embraces untouched and utter the words "I love you", even when it hurts. With a little extra effort and care, one's spirit will be warm and complete.

With our new home in place, Cassidy and I set out on a quest to befriend some new roommates. We ended up meeting three English chaps: Nigel, Currin and Philip. Despite being of English decent, they were the epitome of what I wanted for roommates. They were loud, obnoxious drinkers that I was making seventy-five dollars per head off of and all that I had to do was party with them. Also, around the same time Dino wondered if we had any space for him as well. He had taken a real hard fall from the heroin and ran out of places to go. I had no problem lending out my hand and giving him a place to stay. I had only known Dino for a lesser period of time but I stuck up for him anyways. He was a low maintenance kind of guy and I wanted to be a part of helping him recover.

However, despite how hard I tried to be the Good Samaritan, having all these people in the house began to irritate Cassidy and we would often escape up to Los Angeles to avoid all of the added stress. Nine times out of ten we ended up at her mother's house, but I preferred the beach and every so often I got my way. This was the way we lived for several months and our lives panned out to us living like nomads. Eventually Katie's patience hit the wall and she told us to leave, giving us five thousand dollars as a motivator to get up and go. With little hesitation I jumped out of my seat and proceeded to pack my belongings. Cassidy felt insulted and started screaming at her mom, "I don't want your goddamn money." Breaking from my silence, I respond, "Are you fucking nuts? Just go along with it and let's get outta here." Coldly, she muttered for me to "Fuck off."

From time to time Cassidy and I would get on each others last nerves, but I never once turned our battles into anything physical. I, in many ways, had definitely upgraded from my relationship style with Desiree, who I am ashamed to admit that I laid my hands upon more than once. I took far too long to learn that the last thing anyone should ever do is physically abuse a woman. There is no excuse for it, ever. So after enough lip service, I was able to convince Cassidy to accept the cash and move on.

With our tails between our legs, we headed back to San Clemente. As for our roommates, Dino was rehabbing quite well off of heroin and was offered a residence in Houston. He jumped at the opportunity with full force. Like me, he had grown tired of Los Angeles and was itching for a solid relocation. Amazingly enough, Dino stuck by his guns and developed into a sobriety success, overcoming heroin once and for all. I saw him as a sobriety guru and became enthusiastic towards my own upswing. Dino had the strengths and dreams necessary to succeed and watching him start a new life gave me the hope that now it was my turn.

Cassidy and I bid our farewells to Jenene and the English trio and found ourselves a new home. This was exactly what I needed in my life to make everything feel as it should. Our home became the classic television cliché. Cassidy made dinner every night, I brought home the paychecks, our weekends were spent shopping for knick-knacks and our post-dinner engagements consisted of twilight walks on the beach. Our lives became so damn normal that it did not take long before I felt uneasy and claustrophobic. I failed to recognize that every time I was presented with the opportunity to grow, I neglected to follow through. I genuinely believed that the fundamentals of a normal life were impossible for me to follow. I was plagued by the constant need to wallow in my own miseries. In reality, I had no idea how hard things really could be. I just tended to build my world out of the fragmented chapters of my life, and I seldom cared about whom I took with me or whom I left behind.

TELL ME YOU ARE THERE

The thoughts of failure and the everyday vigor of normalcy drove my insecure self right back to alcohol. I had failed to stay strong for even two years. The easier route always seemed to be found at the bottom of the bottle. I was already a twelve-pack and two forty ounce bottles deep while at the beach with Jenene when Max finally showed up to give me a lift. Upon realizing that I was intoxicated, Max felt obligated to have a drink as well. Our first drink together would prove to be a costly move. Our plans were to drive up to Anaheim to catch a band at a club and then stay with a group of friends at some random hotel. None of Cassidy's friends had ever met the drunken Tony so it was going to be an interesting event to say the least.

Max and I purchased a fifth of Cuervo tequila and a twelve pack of Budweiser, and then went along our way up to Anaheim. By the time we reached the Disneyland exit we were easily past our limits. Two guys in the next lane over harmlessly cut in front of us in a last minute attempt to catch the exit, but neither of us would just let this happen so what better thing to do than run them off of the road while throwing bottles at their car. They submissively pulled over right in front of Disneyland. We instantly jumped out of the car and proceeded to act like buffoons. I took the half full bottle of tequila and threw it at them, smashing it all over their car and into the street. Making the wisest decision possible, they stayed in their car and drove away. Max and I laughed the whole situation off and continued on our way to the club.

Once inside, it was obvious that the two of us were by far the most intoxicated individuals in the club. Cassidy was floored by my Mr. Hyde persona since she had never seen me this wasted. I was my usual obnoxious self, louder and more intense than everyone else around me. I held no fear towards anyone or any chance of me earning a true beating, which usually happens when an individual goes looking for trouble. We partied well into the early morning, which ultimately led to me waking up in my own urine-soaked bed. I was disgusted with myself and the night before was a total blackout. I now had to play detective to piece together the missing links from my night of debauchery. Cassidy took mercy on me and covered up my little accident. Most alcoholics would have quit drinking right then, but instead I simply shot-gunned the closest beer to me and bid my hangover goodbye.

For me, once I lost my sobriety, I was back on the bottle for awhile. I felt that I could instantly quit again, just not that day. So I began drinking heavily and as I drank, images of Martin, Tony and the inevitable Heidi dying crept into my skull and I became the essence of hatred. I felt as though I had no heart, only an empty black spot and within a couple of months I was drinking everyday. Before I could pop another top, I was back in jail again.

On one occasion, I went into such a drunken rage that Cassidy and Nicole took refuge in the back bedroom while I thrashed the living room apart, destroying all of my belongings. I knew that I wanted to be stopped by someone, anyone, since I was incapable of stopping myself. So on this night, I called the cops on myself with the intent on going to jail where I belonged. Although, by the time the law arrived, my attitude had changed and I felt like I was in a better state of mind. That was not satisfactory enough for them and they asked me to step outside with them. I refused. For a second time they asked. I told them to "Go fuck yourselves Bacon Bits." One cop went to check on Cassidy and Nicole while the other cop kept his flashlight pointed directly in my face. Reluctantly, I remained seated on the couch. The other cop returned and told me that I needed to leave with them. I assured him that I was fine and wanted to stay with my family. He explained to me that staying at home was not an option, so again, I told him to "Fuck off." Along with those words, in one fluid movement I jumped up from the couch and flipped the coffee table over. Both of the cops sprayed mace in my face and then tackled me into the couch. I went down like one of those pigs' straw house. They got their swings in, cuffed me and then dragged me from the apartment, making sure that I hit every piece of furniture along the way.

They eventually threw me down across the street in the neighbor's lawn, sought out the garden hose and proceeded to soak me down. In the process, one of the cops took some mace in the eyes from the spray-back off of my shirt and I erupted with laughter, prompting him to kick me a few more times. Once the cops were finished watering the lawn, they threw me in the squad car and made haste for the station. I was charged with assault and battery on a police officer. Five hours later they released me and astonishingly enough, I actually made it home in time to go to work. My boss had no idea about the previous night's incident and I felt as though I could finally exhale. However, Cassidy told me that she had dealt with too many of my shenanigans and wanted to break up. After a few days and a million empty promises, I convinced her to keep me. My life had come full circle and all the pain of my youth was surfacing again.

Within a month, I was drinking in front of Cassidy again and she simply just looked the other way. At this moment, it became evident that our relationship was not intended to last and my alcoholism was a huge reason why. I skipped my court date, feeling that they were going to lock me up anyways so fuck it, let them find me. Plus, I did not want to lose my job so I managed to lay low. To say the least, the law had me under their thumbs for the time being.

The best part of my day was spent loving my beautiful Nicole, yet I had trouble staying in one spot and was constantly looking for any reason to leave. My travels were ridiculous. One time without any notice or forewarning to my family, I went completely out of my way to take a pound of weed to upstate New York aboard a Greyhound bus. I should have been home the whole time, living my life and thinking things through. However, I wanted to dodge my responsibilities, and thus took too many chances with my freedom. On occasion, I would smuggle weed into prison for Bobby. To me, it was entertaining and I felt as though I was in some criminal movie with complete immunity from the law. Well I was not and the law tended to prove me wrong when I was least expecting it.

Nicole and I were playing "Hide and Go Seek" when a knock came at the door. I was hiding behind the entertainment center right by the front door, so I motioned through the screen to the three Jehovah's witnesses to remain silent. Then I jumped out and surprised Nicole. She screamed and then we both laughed with love and smiles in our hearts. I scooped up Nicole and went over to the door. Still chuckling from our little fun, I asked them, "What's up guys?" They inquired what my name was and I justly said, "Oh come on, I'm about to have dinner." They told me to hand Nicole over to Cassidy and to step outside. Then it hit me, these were not Jehovah's witnesses at all, they were undercover cops. They placed me under arrest with a warrant linked to the assault on a police officer charge. With a smug look of disgust, I went with them. Aside from missing out on dinner, I really did not give a damn.

I remained in custody and four days later I was in the court room. They were leaning towards a sentencing of one year in jail. When the judge asked me if I had anything to say, I nodded, put on my best face and lied. I told the judge about my car accident, along with the horrendous trauma in my head and its lasting effects. I delivered this Oscar winning performance with a massive stutter. *How could the judge not believe that I was mentally impaired?* He sympathized with me and reduced my sentence to a year of counseling. Five hours later, I walked out of jail laughing proudly at how I had swindled the system. Unable to commit to the counseling, I wrote my own progress reports using a fake doctor's stamp and after a year of falsehood, I received my certificate of completion. Looking back, the classes could have proven to be beneficial and would have saved me from a lot of pain and hardships, because in the end, I honestly got away with nothing even though I had just pulled off the ultimate scam.

Heidi's light was fading dim, so we as a family drove up to Los Angeles to say our goodbyes. We arrived early Saturday morning and I called her to schedule our visit to Cedar Sinai Medical Center. She stressed upon me not to come because she did not want us to see her in her current condition. I explained that we did not care about her appearance and that we would be there Sunday morning at ten o'clock sharp. Just like in the olden days, I was still able to make her laugh and without hesitation she told me she loved me. I expressed right back that I loved her too and she was going to win this battle.

Well I lied to her, because fifteen hours later Heidi died in her hospital bed. Once again, I was not there for her when I should have been. *I honestly know that I should have been there next to you Heidi. I should have been holding your hand and soothing your heart. My solitary excuse was that I was scared of the disease and despite what the tests said, I still thought I too was infected.* I thought I was bad already, but after Heidi died, I became straight evil. I held only one mindset, fuck the world and everyone on it. I was in devastating pain but it gave me no right to treat the people that loved me in such a wicked way. I was slipping and at the same time would not allow anyone to catch me. My life was falling apart quickly and I showed no signs of resistance.

I never realized it before, but after completely wrecking a yard sale, I knew that I was a lost soul. Cassidy and I needed some extra cash, so I gathered all of our old belongings and set them up to be sold. We sold a number of items right off the bat and by eleven o'clock in the morning, I was taking our profits and achieving a drunken status with lightning speed. By two in the afternoon, our beer supply was running low, so my friends and I decided a beer run was in our best interests. They made off on their way while I stuck around to make some more sales. As fast as they were gone, the police rolled in and were interested in taking me with them. I abruptly started in on them, which only led to me being cuffed up and taken to jail.

By the time I was allowed to make a phone call, I was sobering up and the guilt came crashing down. Despite all of my misfortunes, there is little worse than sobering up in jail. I strongly discourage anyone from testing this argument. I called the house and Max picked up. I asked him where Cassidy was. He told me she was sent to jail after recently receiving a Driving Under the Influence charge. I was astonished and at the same time infuriated, yet had no right to judge anybody considering my current location. I should have been there staying in control of the household business but I neglected to do so. Max informed me that he was going to pick her up and that I should call back in around two hours.

So there I sat, swearing this would be the last time that I was ever confined within these concrete walls. I positioned myself next to the window of my cell when who comes strolling by but Max in handcuffs. I coldly stared him down. He blankly shrugged his shoulders as they put him in the cell next to mine. Now I felt worse than before since because of my mouth, all three of us were in to jail. I did not need a reason to quit drinking. I was already living proof that alcohol does nothing to enhance my character. While under the influence, I was a complete failure.

I decided to take a short break from drinking to concentrate on writing Heidi's eulogy. Her funeral had been put off to allow her mother some time to heal. However, I know that she never did, she had lost her grandson and her daughter in less than a year. *How does one go on?* Her mom definitely had the same strength that Heidi had. I knew life to be very unfair and I put all of my focus into making my words perfect.

The day of Heidi's funeral, her mom took me aside and handed me a brown paper bag with a few of Heidi's belongings inside. One item in particular that Heidi wanted me to have was a Black Sabbath t-shirt, which still to this day is one of my most treasured possessions, and a letter. I paced a few steps away and sat down to read her words. In all honesty, Heidi finally poured her entire heart out to me. She wrote about of her incurable love for me. How her life was utopian because she had me amongst her presence. She wrote to me how upset she was that I had never seen that the best woman for me was her and that Nicole should have been her daughter. She told me that I was the love of her life and that the only thing that scared her about dying was the fact that we would never get to be as one. A reservoir of tears cascaded down my cheeks as her final words were absorbed into my soul. The letter crushed whatever feelings still existed within me. I wanted to die right then and there so that I could say to her that I loved her back, but the timing was too late for me. My life was always too late for me.

All of us gathered to say goodbye to Heidi. She would have been amazed to see how over two hundred and fifty people were there in remembrance of her. A gentleman by the name of Rudy played guitar and the entire congregation of mourners enjoyed an extravagant potluck at Heidi's request. Upon completion of the dinner, I approached the podium to deliver the eulogy. I highly doubt there was a single soul that day that did not feel her love. Her mom approached me and said the words that I wrote comforted her. So I knew the best thing that I could do was give her the poem.

The dismal reality of the service ripped a solid chunk out of my soul and the drive back to San Clemente was very withdrawn and silent. I felt an extreme desire to be invisible to the world so that I could feel my feelings freely without any judgment or reservation. With a drunken stumble I settled myself out on the balcony, crying and screaming to the sky, begging God to bring Heidi back. I screamed to Heidi, "Tell me you are there". At that moment, not one, but two shooting stars raced from the purple depths of space and into the ocean. My soul froze in its tracks as my eyes basked in pure beauty. I knew that Heidi heard me, she had arrived. I promised her at that very spot that one day we would meet again and that I could then give her the love that I had denied her in this life. I have never recovered from her death and I pray to God that I get a chance to keep my word to her.

I love you eternally, Heidi Murphy.

Shortly after Heidi's goodbye, Cassidy and I fell into using speed. I, of all people, hated the drug after its destruction of Bobby but I would do anything to avoid feeling anything, so speed was a cheap alternative. I was incapable of snorting it so I just threw it in my beer and would tweek for days. Soon after, Bobby and I had stopped talking. He had hooked up with Shawnette and had no interest in her other than using her. I told her that he was no good for her and she turned around and told him what I had said. Bobby promised that he was going to destroy every bone in my body upon his release. I was crushed, but soon just tuned him out of my life.

By my third year in San Clemente, my life was a complete disaster. I took Max to court for his third DUI and the judge was not amused. We thought a couple of weeks were all that he was going to get, but instead Max was sentence to eight months. I realized then that times were changing and the light juvenile delinquent sentencing that I was used to was a thing of the past. The time had finally come when every time I stepped outside of my house, a cop was standing there. Every time that I came out of the store, there was a cop and it was the same cop who busted me at the yard sale. He told me point blank to get out of San Clemente. I replied jokingly, "Are you sayin' I gotta get outta town by sundown, Sheriff?" He was not entertained and told me that I had worn out my welcome in San Clemente.

Upon arriving back home, I told Cassidy about the strange encounter and I asked her if she was still going to be there for me. Despite all of her efforts, Cassidy was tired of the life that we had. Max was in jail, Katie was going bankrupt from supporting us off and on for years, and Katie's boyfriend, Carl, who had decided to go walk-off his drunkenness one evening, died in a fluke accident. Supposedly, Carl was out hiking while still overly intoxicated and after catching some bad footing, plummeted several hundred feet off the side of a cliff. He had been sober for over fourteen years, but apparently during the preceding three months had picked the bottle back up. Four months passed before his body was finally discovered and identified strictly by his dentures. His alcoholism prevailed and had cost him his very life.

So with all of this intensity surrounding her, Cassidy needed to escape. I then convinced her that Las Vegas was the perfect solution, deciding that we could both leave California and live together simply as friends. My mindset was farfetched at the time but we were out of options. We, no, I had abused yet another place, another woman and another chance at a better life.

ADDICTION

The constant desire for me to live a nomadic life had finally worn thin on Cassidy, so she demanded that I found a solid residence suitable to raise Nicole in. Las Vegas was a fresh option and with mutual interest she agreed, especially since her mother lived there. My enthusiasm rose equally as high as hers, for Nevada offered the perfect escape to all of my legal issues that were mounting in California. I could not help it; life just always seemed easier when running from my problems, problems like Angel and Daniel.

With the new move intact, I made the time to say goodbye to Angel on her ninth birthday. The moment passed by so smoothly that I failed to realize that it would be roughly five years before I would see her or Daniel again. However, I did not care. I was on a selfish trip to care only for myself and pretend that I actually cared for Cassidy and Nicole. My outward affection towards them was merely an act. Deep down inside, it was still all about me. I held little regard for anyone that loved and cared for me, the only thing on my mind was Las Vegas.

Las Vegas became my new sanctuary, a place where I could indulge myself in twenty-four hours of drinking and gambling, an overbearing amount of scandal and enough unadulterated sex to convert even a preacher to the lustful side. Las Vegas was the perfect recipe for a smooth cocktail of debauchery and dereliction. Plus, the benefit of dealing drugs allowed me to flourish without the burden of a job. The best part was that I felt no sense of remorse since in my mind I was doing nothing wrong.

The only downfall to the Las Vegas move was that Cassidy and I were strictly roommates and the tension that it created was unreal. Our time spent together was brief, and the love to annoyance ratio shifted in a heartbeat. With sexual tension shooting through the roof, alcohol became the only formidable solution. One evening, after an endless night of drinking and no fighting, the inevitable set in and we slept together for the last time. As the old proverbs say, the last time is always the most memorable and after one thing led to another, the miracle of pregnancy was upon us once again. In no way was I convinced that the baby could be mine, but then again, I knew that Cassidy had never strayed. Cassidy was by far the purest of souls when it came to fidelity. I, on the other hand, was a complete basket case when it came to controlling my libido. With failed results, I struggled to talk her into an abortion. I figured it made sense with our relationship already being over, but after one appointment Cassidy could not go through with it and walked out vowing to continue being a mother.

The stresses of a new baby led me to take an interview with a temporary work service about possible career opportunities. They inquired if I had any unique skills or specializations and I responded that they should train me in the field of radio broadcasting. The life of a radio personality intrigued me and I felt that it was a brilliant idea since I possessed that smooth jazz voice that all of the female listeners would love. They offered me a position in another location and upon reading my acceptance letter I set my sights on Lake Tahoe. All that I had to do was stay patient.

Despite how easy waiting sounded, it actually proved to be quite brutal due to my everlasting addiction to gambling.

Surprisingly enough, even alcohol took a backseat to my need for video poker. My slavery to gambling had sprouted its roots only a few months earlier when Cassidy and I had come to Las Vegas to celebrate New Years. A few thousand dollars later in victory cash and I was hooked. There was no escaping the serenade of a winning machine. As hard as I would try to fight the urge, I awoke each morning knowing that this could most certainly be the day that I lost the rent. My life was at the mercy of chance and luck, both of which skimmed right past me.

Though long overdue, I eventually hit a progressive jackpot and ended up with enough chunk change to escape Las Vegas. With little hesitation, I provided Cassidy with several thousand dollars and off I was. Yet before I could even reach the Greyhound station, two grand was hastily donated into a gas station poker machine. Blindingly delirious from my stupor, I ransacked Cassidy's house, retrieved the money that I had just given her, called up Dino and was off to Houston. I had burned Cassidy immensely and never thought twice. All that I knew was that I was states away from the burdens she imposed upon me and therefore nothing else mattered.

Being in the presence of Dino again was soothing for my conscience. Dino had recently overcome his addiction to heroin and had developed a great life in Texas with some genuine friends and a supportive girlfriend. I was proud of his accomplishments and equally ashamed at what little I had done to better myself. The only comfort that I found was through knowing that I was far away from the illustrious gambling of Las Vegas. However, where that void from gambling was left, alcohol and ecstasy quickly stepped in. As the silhouette of me drinking reflected in Dino's eyes, I could see the disgust and torment that lurked within. He hated my alcoholism even more than I hated his heroin addiction.

After what was only a few short weeks, Dino told me that I had overstayed my welcome and he sponsored the bus fare for my trip back to Las Vegas. Not a single thing had changed in my absence except that Cassidy was growing closer to having our baby. I felt like I was shoulders deep in quicksand with concrete shoes. Fleeing my responsibilities was no longer an option. My only ray of sunlight occurred when I received an unexpected call from Bobby who was finally released from prison. After three and a half painstaking years my brother was a free man and I immediately made plans to see him. I was thrilled to be back in Los Angeles where he was anxiously awaiting my arrival. Seeing Bobby outside was everything that I could hope for and I was ecstatic for him. He was in amazing shape and his intellect was sharper than I had seen in a long time. I had missed my brother dearly. Our first day together was joyfully spent drinking and laughing over nostalgic memories from our childhood.

The drunken glaze in Bobby's complexion took me back to the time when he, our buddy Steve and I were beyond tanked up and decided to do a dine-n-dash at a Bob's Big Boy Restaurant. Brother Bobby could never hang with the alcohol and three quarters of the way through our fifty dollar dinner, Bobby made a swift movement towards the restroom. Within five off-balanced steps into his journey, he covered his mouth and projected his portion of the meal all over the lobby and hostess. To call the situation hilarious would be an understatement. Nevertheless, it did not matter and we were busted. Now here we were, ten years later and still equally as immature. Bobby was two weeks shy of his twenty-fourth birthday and I was only two days away from my twenty-fifth. We were no longer kids yet still neither of us had any direction in our lives, two off-centered cuts from the same cloth. Bobby was the closest thing that I had in my life to a legitimate brother and he swore his prison days were forever behind him. I valued every word that he spoke and likewise, he valued mine.

Two days later was Friday, August 5, and my twenty-fifth birthday gave me the confidence that I needed to make some brash new changes in my life. I had a buddy of mine named Carlos who was tattooing people at his house for free and I was all for it. Without any hesitation, I pulled a leaf from Carlos' cannabis plant and placed it on the outside of my right calf. "Plant this plant right fuckin' here." Although slightly disgruntled from my intense nature, he agreed and within an hour I was forever branded with the green bud in black ink. As I grew older, I would often tell individuals that I had the ink done when I was fourteen. Somehow, it made more sense to me that this was something only a naive teen would do, thus I hid my insecurities behind a child's innocence.

Soon after, Bobby called me from his house to find out where I was and let me know that Lana was waiting there to see me. I acted all cool and sly, telling him I would be there whenever I could. Truth is, the moment I hung up the phone I proceeded to act like a school boy with his first crush. Nothing more than the rhythms of her name made my heart explode with emotion. An hour flew by and I still could not achieve the perfect look that she deserved. I have always taken great pride in my appearance but this time my only focus was to impress Lana. Fashionably late, I strolled into Bobby's and was greeted by Lana with some sarcastic comment that instantly set me back a step. However, once my eyes met with hers, I was so awestruck by her beauty that whatever she had muttered just seconds before was vanquished. She then ran and jumped into my hug, wrapping her legs around my torso. I absolutely loved it when she hugged me that way. Roughly two years had passed since I had held her last and letting her go was the last thing on my mind.

Supposedly Lana had reduced herself to living in her car and had an astronomical tolerance when it came to smoking speed. Along with that, many of the locals talked all kinds of nonsense about the lifestyle that she chose. "Whatever," I responded. Their words were wasted air because to me she was still a knockout. Anytime that Lana was near me, my whole world was at peace. Lana and I became inseparable, spending more and more of each day together. I could sense a mutual attraction and I almost fainted with joy. I had wanted her for what seemed like an eternity and now I knew that she wanted me too. Our bond became so close that she confided in me about her failing struggles to gain control of her sobriety. Lana had always been a pot smoker yet despised all other drugs. However, after the loss of her grandfather, grief sent her into a downward spiral and right into the clutches of hardcore drugs. Crack-cocaine became her staple diet, all of which came to her free of charge. All that she had to provide in return was her soul and everything that went along with it. I found myself at a loss for opinion. I could not judge her for her honestly yet I could not help her with her pain either. I attempted to give her some words of encouragement but when I opened my mouth all that could be heard was silence. Sadly, our night only ended with us agreeing to stay in touch and I dropped her off at home, her '79 Grand Prix parked in a dimly lit cul-de-sac down the street from her mom's house.

I discovered later that night that my friends were throwing a social gathering at a club in Alta Dena for my birthday. By the time that I arrived at the club I was far beyond a 0.30 Blood Alcohol Content level. After a few stiff rounds, I decided that it was time to call Lana. She was plaguing my every thought and nothing could keep me from thinking of her. Much to my relief, she wanted to see me as well, so I assured her that I would be there promptly. First things first though, I had to evade Cassidy, who had become a six-month-pregnant shackle around my ankle. My only option was to act overly dramatic, so I started a huge scene at the bar, bashed in the windshield of my car as a bonus and then off I sped to Lana's.

Now Northridge to Ontario was easily an hour long trip and my B.A.C. was escalating to what had to have been at least a 0.40, yet somehow by God's grace I made it to her mom's house. After a brief attempt at pointless idle chit-chat, we ditched the charade and ripped into each other like it was our last day on Earth. Life was grand, although I truly wish I could have experienced that moment in a more sober state of mind. I had waited a lifetime to be with her and so much of that night I fail to remember. The following three days were spent locked in a hotel room getting to know each other better, in both body and mind. Our bond was so magnetic that we both agreed that this had to continue. The one solitary issue we had was Cassidy. Even though we as a couple were non-existent, Cassidy was still pregnant and I felt immensely guilty. Guilt was an emotion that I was previously unfamiliar with but now could not avoid. Ultimately, the trip to Los Angeles left everyone just a little emptier than before.

Lana went back to her car and her speed, I went back to Las Vegas and my gambling and Bobby went back to the needle and prison. The poor guy could not even last two months in established society. We were all lost, we were all out of control and we were all addicted. The lives we thought we had lived so rough already were only the precursor to what the future had in store for us, mere pawns on our first moves to battle.

My Souls Unconditional Mate

*F*or the first time ever, the concept of true love became a conceivable reality in my life. The lustful relationship that I had started with Lana swiftly evolved into an insatiable yearning just to be in her presence. Our lifestyles had pushed us to the outskirts of mainstream society, leaving us alone and abandoned, together. Neither of us knew how to control our stressors, but unlike me, Lana at least put forth the effort. Between the gambling and the alcohol my emotions were on a constant rollercoaster, pushing me further and further into a frenzy and Lana paid the price. The verbal abuse that I used to subject Desiree to was now present in my relationship with Lana. In no way was verbally abusing her intended, she was just always there and sadly enough, she continued to be. Upon realizing my errors, my gut wrenched at the thought of why she still put up with me when she deserved someone so much better. I had spent my whole life waiting for the girl of my dreams and almost instantly took her for granted.

Lana soon joined me in Las Vegas where settling in became a heavy struggle, so to make ends meet she found a job cleaning houses and I took work in a warehouse. That was exactly the place an individual winds up without the beneficial support of an education. Although despite my grim workplace, I was constantly making optimistic plans for the future and every wise elder I spoke with said that I was still young and had plenty of time to flourish. As much as I tried to take heed of their advice, my tortured mentality would overrule the situation and each word that they spoke became a joke to me. In no way was this true, that time is a luxury that we all possess and is influenced by our will. Far too many friends, more youthful and innocent than I was were never given this chance. I was caught in an internal whirlpool and had no control over where I was going.

So there I remained spinning, until a miracle occurred and my life was given a twinkle of light. On November 18, 1994 a glimmer of hope was born and his name was Juliano Sparzo. Another child was brought to this world by an incompetent fool who had no right being a father. A father is a real man who stands up before adversity and faces his responsibilities and I was nowhere near being a real man. For the first six months of Juliano's life I was completely hit or miss, equally as much as my relationship with Lana. The curses of alcohol and gambling had made me unreliable and violent. Everyday I made repentance for my ways and my sins would be forgiven, but before the false words could even pass through my tongue, I was right back to my addictive routine. Gambling can have a nasty hold on an individual.

Soon I became one hundred percent dependant on Lana since the battle against her vices had emerged her victoriously. I admired her perseverance and found myself wanting to imitate her every move and decision. I was falling madly in love with Lana and that suddenly switched me into my flight mode. The idea of love was inconceivable and it confused me on a level that I had never experienced. Knowing that I would do anything for her, Lana demanded that I sought help for my gambling and drinking. I wanted to adopt a better lifestyle but I just had no ability to turn the desire off. The only solution that was a constant in my mind was escaping to Lake Tahoe before all hope was lost. As much as

I could taste that dream, it was still not a reality, so Las Vegas would have to suffice.

We continued to live frugally and after residing in some fifteen dollar per night hotels, Lana and I managed to scrape up enough cash to move into a decent weekly unit. With this newly inspired upswing, I made the effort to see the kids multiple times throughout the month and even provide them with some child support. The only downfall was that it was usually Lana who covered it. Lana truly lived selflessly for me. Cassidy and I, on the other hand, were incessantly at each other's throats and the relentless stress of raising two kids by herself was pushing Cassidy to her final nerve.

On one particular Saturday, it was my responsibility to watch the kids since Cassidy had to pick up a shift at work. All was well, until Lana's car refused to start and my entire nervous system kicked into panic mode. By random chance, a mutual friend named Sheba came to my rescue and offered to help. She mentioned that her boyfriend was available to assist me and that he could be over to my house in no time. My panic swiftly turned to skepticism since after all, this was Las Vegas. Much to my relief, within minutes this model-American poster boy comes walking up and introduces himself. His name was Ken and Ken said with a gleeful grin, "C'mon buddy, let's go get your kids." I eagerly obliged and jumped into his car. For the next five minutes, everything was perfectly normal until he decided to treat me like Barbara Walters and proceeded to tell me his entire life's story. Ken went on and on about how he is on trial with something like fifty felonies and blah blah blah. All that I kept thinking to myself was what a head trip this character was. I had no place to talk or judge anyone but I could not help it, Ken had it bad.

Somehow I endured his confessionals just long enough to arrive at Cassidy's house where I anxiously bolted from the car to the front doorstep. Cassidy erupted out of her house with Nicole and Juliano, screaming at me about how my sluggish ways were going to make her late. Then it happened. As I was tuning her out,

I locked eyes with my son who had a permanent smile the whole time. Suddenly, my whole world lit up like a Christmas tree. I felt protected, I felt euphoria, I felt rehabilitation, I felt God and for the first time since I was a youth, I felt love. A feeling of warmth rushed through my body as Cassidy handed him to me. The peacefulness that I experienced was immeasurable. Regardless of how miserable my life panned out to be, I now had a justification to straighten up my act.

Yet with all the joys associated with my newly discovered son, my relationship with Lana was rapidly deteriorating. She decided to move out of our weekly unit and in with her employer, leaving me cold and lonely on my only true home, the streets. Cassidy's house was not an option and during my brief encounter with Ken, whose benevolence outweighed his insanity, he had told me that if I ever needed anything at all to look him up.

So as the clock rounded past two in the morning, I arrived knocking at his door and much to my surprise he welcomed me in with no hesitation. I was astonished at his generosity. Ken was merely an acquaintance and here he was providing me with a roof over my head. We spent the remainder of the night drinking and bonding. Most of our conversations revolved around our prior experiences with the law and we soon discovered our evenly matched corruption. On one instance, I tried to swindle him out of some rent that was due and without the slightest delay he called my bluff. From that day on, we were the best of friends. Countless times he was there for me, like a tweaked out sidekick who only wanted to see the best for others. His only demon was his insatiable thirst for methamphetamines. By this point in my life, I had personally watched drugs kill and ruin more lives than I should have, and thus I had a very slim tolerance for drugs.

Settling into Ken's house was a breeze and amazingly my positive attitude brought Lana closer to me again. Ken even went as far as to securing me a job with a promising future. Thinking about the future was usually only a temporary event but it started happening more and more. However when my mind was not on the future, it was focused on what shred of a relationship I still had with Lana. My depression led to booze and before I knew it, Lana was subjected to my frightening verbal abuse once again. My screams carried far into the neighborhood and it was not long before the cops were summoned and I was off to jail, but this time with Lana alongside me. My confusion grew into brute anger at the thought of her going to jail, after already being verbally bashed, for some unpaid traffic tickets. I kicked the backseat of the squad car and spit on the officer driving. He remained quiet and focused. I held no regard for what happened to me since it was Lana that I was worried about. However, by this point there was nothing that I could do.

Once in jail, I started sweating over my job and became desperate to find any way to get out. The only solution that I knew would work was to call Melinda, so at eleven thirty at night I broke my two year absence. Reluctantly, she wired the money to Ken who was swiftly there to bail me out. Sadly though, that was the only time I would speak to her for another two years. I was a disgrace to the Sparzo name and still they never gave up on me. Words can never express the gratitude that I have towards their enduring patience.

Eighteen painstaking days passed before Lana was finally released and she came out of jail with a new mentality, no more Las Vegas and no more Tony. Her only alternative was to move back to Los Angeles where I knew her banished habits would resurface. Everyday without her was a pin in my heart, but at least I had my job and my infallible brother Ken. He would often console me whenever I was in a downward spiral and jointly I stopped blaming others for my misery. Ken introduced me to the Tony within myself, the one that I always knew existed but could never find. His positive influence completely blinded me to his crooked ways of drugs and identity theft. I believed that a young gentleman with the head-turning looks and polish that he possessed could get him away with anything. I considered myself honored to have such a genuine friend, a person as lost as me who would never let me down. I owed him the world.

While my friendship with Ken was blooming, the remainder of my close loved ones had all but vanished. Lana and I were strictly on friendly terms and Cassidy and I were not even that. Cassidy was breaching the point of insanity and there was no denying that it was due to my lack of participation in my children's lives. I felt an eerie shadow of Angel and Daniel every time I thought about my negligence towards Nicole and Juliano.

Very little could hide that the main culprit to this behavior was my addiction to gambling. Almost religiously I would work sixteen hours a day for five days a week, earn twelve-hundred dollars and within seven hours of my paycheck have it all embedded into the one-armed bandit. My lifestyle was maddening and Las Vegas was filled with the sole prescription, payday loan centers. Not all remedies are pharmaceutical and Las Vegas could cure all of life's woes for a nominal percentage. Alcoholism was no longer my only lifelong disease.

The moment that I realized I was a chronic gambler actually occurred on my twenty-seventh birthday, which also was a payday on my day off. A great day was turned into tragedy before the sun even reached the high noon sky. Broke and intoxicated, I stumbled the three miles back to Ken's and passed out. I vaguely remember dreaming of Lana in all of her splendor and instantly after waking I had to call her. However, instead of Lana, Bobby answered. He had recently been released from prison after serving only nine months for violation of parole. After a brief discussion over my love for gambling, Bobby immediately insisted that I bailed from Las Vegas and came back to my true home. I always thought that Bobby had the most unique and convincing outlook on life, so without a moments rest I started packing. I managed to persuade a gentleman I worked with to shuttle me to the Interstate 15 where I could hitchhike back to Los Angeles. The only hassle was that I had to wait for four hours.

Within those four hours everything changed. Lana called me

and was furious that I was skipping out on my job. I cried to her about how I could not stop the gambling and she sternly responded that I was acting weak and immature. The call ended abruptly as I smashed the phone on the ringer. Moments later Ken came bursting through the door, disgusted at my lack of motivation and focus. Ironically, he did not react like I was expecting him to by engulfing me in a guilt lecture, instead he ushered me down to his car to enjoy a birthday beer. Once the tab was cracked, I started ranting on my self-pity trip and he snapped, threatening to take me over to Johnny Taco's Gym and beat some sense into me. With a sudden sense of phobia towards Ken, I guzzled down my beer and pressingly cracked another. Alcohol mellowed things out, and after a few more beers Ken swayed me into pursuing the life that I had started in Las Vegas. So I put all of my focus into making gambling non-existent and my relationship my new priority. Choosing to stay in Las Vegas was well received by Lana, who made it clearly obvious that she wanted to be back with me. I tried to express how dearly I missed her but every time I spoke my tongue tripped on the words. The only phrase that I could mutter was how terrible I felt since I had nothing to offer.

As for Cassidy, she and I were getting along but I could tell Cassidy was breaking down mentally and once again I was swarmed with guilt. I was shocked by guilt's everlasting presence in my life and it confused me beyond words, but every mistake and palter started to weigh heavily on me. *Was I actually evolving into a real human being with sentiment and fault?* On one occasion, Cassidy called me more hysterical than her usual self and I immediately sensed the storm to follow. She bore into a rant about how she was overwhelmed by the kids and that if I refused to take them then they were going to be sent into the Foster Care Program. Cassidy demanded that she was to remain completely uninterrupted and that all of the responsibility was mine now. Without hesitation, I agreed to supervise them and quickly called Lana to fill her in on our new blessing. This was our golden opportunity to be together as a couple and as a family. Lana was ecstatic at the news and made plans to be in Las Vegas by the next morning.

That next day was payday and I had earned enough to get us into another lower end apartment. Alas, we had established our first notable place together that did not have a vacancy sign illuminating the front window. With little more than some clothes and personal belongings, our future was now on track. Cassidy was benevolent enough to bring the kids and their beds for us. October 9, 1996 became the day my life finally made a turn for the better and something that seemed so simple took me twenty-nine years to accomplish. To further note, when the good times start to roll, they do so with contagious momentum. Two weeks later, the Yankees were the World Champions for the first time since 1978 and I wailed like a newborn baby freshly slapped on the butt. Lana was baffled at how I could be so emotional over baseball. I corrected her, "It's not baseball, it's the Yankees." Seeing the conviction in my eyes, Lana forever vowed her devotion for the Yankees and pride cascaded through my soul. We became inseparable, the utmost of friends. Lana was my world and like a meteorite in the crisp autumn sky, I fell very hard for her.

One evening, we were rambling about nonsense like our birthdays and we realized that we were born exactly three years three months and three days apart. Furthermore, when she was brought home from the hospital, our families had been living in the same apartment complex. There was no denying that we were soul mates destined to be together. My heart was drowning with delight. Lana introduced me to wonderful feelings I had never experienced. Despite the immense amounts of baggage that encased both of our lives, for the first time we were tackling them as a team. Our peers were skeptical towards our bond and often blurted out pessimistic nonsense, but I was hardly fazed since Lana was my crowning achievement.

Deep inside, my heart was broken at the thought that Lana was incapable of having children of her own, but the relentless love she exhibited daily towards Nicole and Juliano was beyond what I could ask for. I never could have made all of this happen without her. Multiple months passed and it was clearly evident that Cassidy was not capable of taking the kids back, which was completely advocated by Lana and me. We were an established family and to make it official, Lana and I were married on January 4, 1997. Overwhelmed with excitement, we called our parents with the wonderful news and were surprisingly greeted with harsh negativity. Maybe it was deserved considering our pasts but nonetheless it hurt us both deeply.

Although my life was proving to be promising, I still had a gambling problem that could not be controlled. Lana put all of her efforts into helping me, but that did not stop the fact that I was buried deeper into my vices than either of us could imagine. Despite all of the adversity that she faced, Lana never once lost faith in me. Through the struggles of her own addiction, she had learned that the key to success was patience and perseverance. Lana was amazing, the perfect woman. So with the feelings of getting out of Las Vegas growing stronger, our mutual desire to leave and raise the kids in Lake Tahoe became our main priority. We shared a dream to live a normal life without addiction and we were committed to it. Regardless of stress or difficulty, any task could be accomplished simply by knowing that we had each other and a steadfast obligation to the kids.

During this period of rectification, I had made a bold move to reestablish my connection with Benny. Along with Desiree, Angel and Daniel, he had moved to Texas a few years prior and this was the first time since then that I vowed to stay in touch. Benny had always treated me with the utmost of respect, part of which was seemingly spawned by a sense of guilt. However, he had nothing to feel guilty about since he had taken his responsibility to the extreme and was a bona fide father. His success through his actions was the extinguisher to the execrable inferno that I had created. This brought me great pain but it was a reality that I had no choice but to accept.

Apparently, Benny had grown tired of Texas and inquired

about a life in Las Vegas. I could only say the truth, "Great place to visit, terrible place to raise kids." Perhaps if I had abstained from gambling my perspectives might have been different. So after we solidified some options for their move, Benny finally turned the phone over to my children. I was astonished at how quickly five years had turned my meddling children into autarchic teenagers. Pride overtook my every emotion, but deeper down I felt like I had become a blank page in the story of their lives. Nevertheless, the anticipation of seeing them outweighed any thoughts of self-pity that I had briefly adopted.

Yet unfortunately, along with the dusk must trail the darkness. While sitting absently at my desk job in the Pyramid Casino, I received a manic call from Lana. Jumping from my seat, I pleaded with her to calm down and breathe. After a fraction of an inhale, she blurted out, "You're uncle Ted died." I had not spoken to my parents since the last time they bailed me out of jail so this struck me by complete surprise. After realizing the actuality of Ted, my heart grew immensely weak and every joint within me gave loose, collapsing me to the floor. Uncle Ted was not just an uncle but an irreplaceable friend. Without fail, he was always the one who pretended to be my boss whenever a potential job opportunity came up and I needed a credible reference. Ted, himself, was personally responsible for the position that I had acquired at the Pyramid Casino.

Before I could even absorb the harsh reality, my thoughts were interrupted by the phone once again. This time it was Gerard, insisting that I returned home to be with the rest of the family. I complied and made arrangements to leave at once. All that I had to do first was make my way home to bring my beautiful Lana along with me. I divulged to her about how angry I was over heroin's death-claw grip on my uncle. Never once did she speak her thoughts, but instead maintained her status as a silent mute and I worshipped her for it. I made one last stop to a pay phone at the Interstate 15 leaving Las Vegas. I called my aunt Karen to notify her of my visit. She was an absolute wreck, for Ted was not only her brother but her best friend. To make matters even worse, Karen then informed me that Bobby had been busted just two nights earlier for yet another ludicrous violation.

By his third prison stint I found that I had stopped caring, yet still never stopped loving. I was in no place to judge Bobby for his actions, all that I did was reached the point where I realized that the only person who could right his course was himself. All that I could tell my aunt was to pray for serenity and that I would be there in no time. Upon hanging up, I dropped to my knees and tears rolled down my face. Aunt Karen was my symbol of strength and devotion and any pain that she experienced made my very soul ache with empathy. She had persevered through all of her trials for so long and now she was slammed with a double whammy. I collected myself, sulked my way back to the car and off we drove for Los Angeles.

Seeing my parents was surprisingly comfortable despite how dismal the nature of the visit. Gerard broke the whole scenario down to me about Ted's final days. Apparently, after his seventh attempt at rehabilitation, my grandparents decided to take a second mortgage out of their home and fly Ted to New York for a blood transfusion. This was a final effort to clear the heroin from his system. Ted went through with the procedure and was greeted back in Los Angeles with astonishing support. Friends and family alike agreed that it was the best that he had ever looked, but what they could not cure was the mental state of his addiction. That is one thing doctors can not fix. So while on a new blood bender, Ted boosted my grandpa's car, wrapped it like a stripper around a neighborhood light post and then fled off into the bushes. The event had pressed my grandpa's last nerve and without a wince of remorse, he kicked Ted out to the curb. Ted was officially stranded with no options. Three days later, his body was discovered underneath my grandpa's house. His feet had been slightly protruding from within the crawl space, combined with the cologne of rotting flesh. The end of Uncle Ted's life came alone and addicted.

My grief quickly turned to fury. *How could a man I loved so much do this? Why was the final barrier of self-preservation broken?* Sadly, my grandma who was struggling against both dementia and Alzheimer's was never made aware that her Teddy was gone. The news would have crushed her will to live. My grandpa, who had just lost his son, did not want to risk losing the gem of his heart too. So the mourning stayed muffled for the next fourteen months until my grandpa finally gave in and followed his Ted. To me, his house became an evil place and I chose to never pass through its doors again. As a kid, it was a wonderful, lively home, now it was just a mausoleum.

No more than two months later the news continued to grow worse. Instead of simply putting in his mandatory ten months, Bobby was given a life sentence with parole possibilities after thirty-five years. His laugh was chillingly empty as he explained his third strike story and I was stunned at what I was hearing. What had started as a level one trespassing violation turned into an outrageous life sentence. No domestic violence or burglary even took place. Poor Bobby, while high on PCP, simply walked into the wrong house. For this brief lapse in physical awareness Bobby received thirty-five years, about thirty more than a child molester and about ten years longer than a murderer. The system has some unjust rationale behind many of its rulings.

Bobby told me that he loved me and delivered his goodbyes. With a life sentence hanging over it his head, Bobby knew he was not going to make it. I acknowledged his sincerity and expressed my love for him. With a void space in my heart, I hung up the phone and prepared myself for a life without my brother. I missed him dearly. Through all of these hardships, Lana remained as my foundation and she filled my life with optimism and love. We shared our pain through loving words and I never spent a single moment alone. Lana's presence cured any angst that dwelled within me.

My world became brighter once again and a month later, I was reunited with Angel and Daniel. They were both so articulate and beautiful. Desiree and Benny had done the perfect job as parents. Connecting with them was a lot more difficult and different than what I had originally imagined. I wish I could have seen the whole experience from their viewpoints. After all, I was the one who had neglected to be involved with their lives. I should have made the effort to be there since day one. I hated to hear the words "Deadbeat Dad" but that was exactly what I was. A child without the benefits of a father is a severely growing issue in our society.

Despite all of the positive efforts that I was doing for Nicole and Juliano, the guilt was deadweight on my shoulders and Lana did anything she could to ease my depression. Many of my peers started to see her steadfast strength and often questioned why she still chose to be with me. With the sweet voice of an angel, she would reply with a smile, "Tony is my everything!" Pride for my Lana radiated from within me. We had a love that would last forever, a forever that I was now starting to see. All of this was possible, thanks to my priceless Lana.

STEPPING STONES OF LOVE

My love for Lana proved to be the best thing that I could ever ask for. The stutter steps that we had been taking all of these years had finally turned into full-fledged strides. In less than three years, Lana and I had gone from sixty dollars a week, living on a burger without cheese each day to a great duplex home, a new car and a bank account. Not only that, but we still had Nicole and Juliano as well. To say the least, I finally had a family. Lana taught me how to be a dad and not just any dad, but an everyday dad. I actually enjoyed coming home to my loving wife and kids. The past year had seen endless heartbreak and we still managed to see things through. With every passing day our relationship grew stronger. The way that Lana loved Nicole and Juliano was, to put it in the simplest words, raw beauty. The more I saw in her the more change I sought in myself, but regrettably the maturity level between Lana and me was easily a ten year difference.

Lana was the one who wore the tool belt in the household and could fix anything. I, on the opposite end, was the one who read the manual, tried my hardest to finish the job but would ultimately get overly frustrated and storm away. Then my flawless wife would come to save the day and all would be well. This sequence became more than a routine. Lana was an old soul and a wise woman whom I respected deeply. My immaturity and delinquent behavior often wore her patience very thin, but she shrugged it off and made running the home effortless. Her pure love was the sole reason for the success of our home and marriage, a safety that I had never allowed for myself until now.

My irresponsible lifestyle soon led to me losing of my job due to gambling while on the clock. The situation had put us into hard spot and Lana was forced to call upon her mom, Phyllis, for financial assistance. Phyllis came to our rescue multiple times throughout the past, but this time she was serious about promises being kept. I agreed, failing to realize that she was taking the money from her retirement fund. In a pathetic attempt to muster what little dignity I still had, I made the final decision to break free from Las Vegas before it devoured the last of my soul. A week later, bankrupt and silent, we left for Los Angeles and the reliability of my parents' house.

The move proved to be very hard on the whole family. With school halfway through, Cassidy decided to keep Nicole, and we took Juliano, who at this point I could not be without. Nicole and Cassidy shared a unique bond and I felt that it was an appropriate gesture of peace between us. Las Vegas did not wreck me, I wrecked myself in Las Vegas and I believed the only way to break the spell of gambling was to leave. My weakness had ruined my credit, placing me right back at square one with my parents. Pride became the newest emotion to stumble in my life and losing it made me feel weak and invisible. The only way to get it back was to keep my sights on Lake Tahoe and the mindset that Los Angeles was just a temporary side-step.

Lana rejoiced over my enthusiastic nature regarding Lake Tahoe and every word that she spoke was the perfect motivation for me. The phrase that stuck with me the most was when she would remind me that we were lightheartedly hopping on the stepping stones to a better life. I now started to believe in what she saw and together we made Lake Tahoe our main goal. All that we had to do in the time being was get away from the home that I no longer felt a connection to. I decided to make the most out of my time in Los Angeles, so I looked up some old friends to see what everyone had made of their lives. I soon found out that I had less in common with them than I had originally thought, and most of it had to do with alcohol. Over the past year, I had limited my drinking and thusly was not impressed with many of my brothers, who were still living misguided lifestyles. So I moved on.

Due to a false sense of entitlement, I found securing a job to be an obstacle that I had not foreseen. I was under the impression that I deserved top dollar for my services in a respected position. I had that job while at the Pyramid, but in Los Angeles, it amounted to ten dollars an hour as a delivery driver. Lana reminded me that these were the stepping stones she was speaking of and that I needed to keep the faith. The whole stepping stones analogy was a gimmick to me, but she stood solid by her words and was thoroughly convinced that we could accomplish our goals. I was surprised that our Lake Tahoe dream was responded to with such criticism, yet their negativity only motivated me to prove them wrong even more.

One of the only individuals who remained supportive of me was my brother Brad, who by this time was making a huge success of himself. Brad had moved his way up into a position in home security for one of the most powerful politicians in California. He used to be my go-to guy whenever I wanted to destroy the town and now here he was, serving as a bullet-proof vest for the big man. I felt an immeasurable sense of pride for him. Happiness for someone else's accomplishments was new to me but I welcomed it, hoping that it would foreshadow the changes in store for me.

Brad's success made me feel that I too could create a future. I had grown jaded of my lifestyle. The guilt, the pain, the anger, the addiction, and living with my parents, it all needed to go. I was a thirty year old father with a family to support and Gerard reminded me of it daily. At this point I genuinely believed that we would never be able to have any form of a quality relationship.

All that I ever did was disappointed both Gerard and Melinda and I shunned him for his honesty. Truth is, I had no right living with them, and it was my irresponsible ways that had landed me there in the first place. I put up with about two more months of their regime-style household before enough was enough snapped and I moved my family over to an available room in Martin's mother's house.

From the moment we stepped in, the memory of Martin sprung him back into life. The house was arranged as though Martin had never left us. The love that his mother, Rose, had for him, sent sympathy tingling through my veins. Rose had never recovered from Martin's death, none of us did at that, but her steadfast remembrance of his life gave the house indescribable warmth. Nevertheless, we were together and her love for Lana and Juliano was more than I could have imagined. Lana, Juliano and I had an inseparable bond and no matter how hectic the times were, we kept each other inspired.

Most of my hours spent at home were consumed with brainstorming options for a cleaning service in Lake Tahoe, much to the mockery of those around me. Granted a cleaning service might appear to be a low-shot goal, but in our eyes, we saw it as the road map to a meaningful life for Nicole and Juliano. Lake Tahoe was a safer place where we could start our lives over with a fresh, clean slate. This decision was concrete and any fears of running or bailing out shot right off into oblivion. As much as we put our efforts into the future, the present brought many challenges and the number one culprit was Lana's health, which would knock her down several pegs over the next few years.

Within an eight month period, she was hospitalized twice and through it all, she constantly wore her signature smile. Every incident built her stronger than before, turning her into the amazing woman that everybody desired to be near in hopes that her radiance would pass onto them. Nothing ever brought her down except for my negativity, which usually crept up when things were not going my way. I had an obnoxious attitude towards the world and still felt like I was deserving of all of its splendors. This was the egotistical way that I had perceived life, which was completely contrary to the way the world really is. My little tirades were usually short lived and Lana would often set me straight, sometimes even from her hospital bed. I would turn on a dime and man up, but just not for a continuous amount of time. With faith and determination, Lana endured through her surgeries and extended hospital stays and our goal of Lake Tahoe was still within our grasp.

Soon after Lana's last release, we moved back into my parents' house as our stay with Rose had panned out to be more detrimental on her mental condition than anticipated. We all felt extremely bad for her, but knew that we could not stay in that house for too much longer. Moving out was easy, but I must have been high on something to think that Gerard and I could actually co-exist under the same roof. We made it through approximately two months of bare knuckle to the chin tension before total havoc broke loose. By the time Lana reached the house late in the afternoon, I was pacing in the street and everything, including the screen door, was in the street alongside me. Gerard stood fuming on the doorstep, exhausted of anything else to throw at me in his attempts to shut me up. Once again my boisterous mouth and asinine opinions had earned me the curb, yet this time I brought my wife and son along with me. Limited on options, Lana called Phyllis once again to come to our rescue and with arms wide open, she welcomed us in.

Phyllis already had a blossoming relationship with Juliano, and with her baby girl finally back home it balanced out the strain that accompanied me. Phyllis was a Brooklyn girl, and a lot like Gerard, could sense and thus call me out on any funny-business instantly. She was a pure bred Dodgers fan and the insults we exchanged daily would make ever a sailor's jaw drop. Phyllis had a coy way of delivering her taunts in a classy manner that absolutely enraged me. I despised the Dodgers and any of the seventh-inning cardboard cutout fans who hissed their name. Besides, the Yankees were three time World Series champions.

As frustrating as that woman was, I still loved her immensely for the devotion and involvement that she showed in Juliano's life. She gave Juliano the world and never stopped to scold or punish. Phyllis was Juliano's safety blanket and staying at her place brought out the best in my son. Living with her was a blessing and made the final months in Los Angeles rather pleasurable. Life with my family was perfect whenever we were all together.

Roughly a month later, Lana had to make a return visit to the hospital and this time the stay was prolonged. The impending threat of her health was agitating me for all of the wrong reasons and it destroyed Lana inside. I foolishly spent more time focusing on the money aspect, or lack thereof, and was completely blind to the porcelain angel forlorn for my love. I struggled to ditch my selfish mentality and open up in the way a loving husband is supposed to feel when his fragile wife is in agony. This crass behavior was in no way acceptable and admitting this blatant disregard for my wife's well-being is a personal step that I need to make. I have regretted this for countless days, a regret towards my selfish actions amidst the presence of the most impacting woman of my life. Lana was the type of woman who passionately gave all of herself and asked for nothing in return.

From the depths of my heart Lana, I am sorry. I apologize for the hurt that I subjected you to by my utter disregard for your health and well-being. I love you dearly and cherish your presence in my life.

Lana's recovery happened just in time as we were approaching the final days of our residency in Los Angeles, which infuriated Phyllis who was under the delusion that we were intending to stay. In no way was that on my agenda, even as amazing as she was. The last memory that I have of our time in Los Angeles was spent watching Juliano next to Phyllis as she placed her trembling knuckles squarely into our family portrait. There is no denying that it was my face that she was focused on. She had accepted the burden of my homeless family without hesitation and here I was ripping her daughter and grandson out of her life. All of this time I was so oblivious to the impact that my desire to escape Los Angeles had had upon her. Phyllis was responsible for many of the blessings associated with our revival. Everything that was wonderful in Lana was present in her and I broke that love. I will never forget the sacrifices that Phyllis made, sacrifices which ultimately allowed us to make that special move to Lake Tahoe.

Arriving at Lake Tahoe was beyond our wildest expectations. The sapphire blue of the lake shimmered with the light of the setting sun as crimson clouds hung suspended over tremendous snow-covered peaks. All of this beauty left a tear of joy in my eye. This place was God's personal sanctuary. I was finally home.

The new millennium was knocking at the door and with it came the confidence to make a life worth being proud of. My mistakes were happily sealed in the twentieth century's tomb, never to be released until the ink of these pages. Our arrival in Lake Tahoe assured the both of us that no dream was unachievable as long as were worked as a team. Every blessed word that passed through my beautiful Lana's lips was correct. The stepping stones that we followed had indeed brought us to a better life, the type of life where I prevailed as a supporting father and the purity of the lake could cleanse my wasteful ways. The door had opened and with clasped hands, we both stepped through it together.

Taking the Higher Ground

*O*ur new beginning in Lake Tahoe was everything we expected it to be and this was a total shock from the lives that we had been living up until now. The differences in our lives were like night and day. The city life had aged us far too quickly and Lake Tahoe became our fountain of youth. However with every piece of Heaven must come a little Hell and it lurked in the disguise of Stateline, Nevada, where the alluring glow of lobster buffets and two dollar blackjack tested my strength without relent.

All that I convinced myself would keep me at bay was immersing myself in the presence of Lana, which only worked for about a week. Lana was amazing at first impression interviews and was able to land a job with a cleaning service. Her personality was so charismatic there was no way a potential employer could resist. With a steady forty-plus hour per week job for Lana and my random stints to get quick cash, we were finally able to get our dream underway.

Starting the cleaning business kept me busy and away from the casinos. With gambling out of my mind, I found owning a business to be equally stressful and discouraging. The temptation to quit was constantly whispering in my ear, but with Juliano and

Nicole coming up in six weeks, I really had to make things work. Cassidy had taken Juliano back from Phyllis just a week after we left and almost immediately grew tired of them both. I could not blame her, since after all they had my genetics in them.

We managed to lease out an apartment so small that I could have sworn I was back in Los Angeles, minus the ghetto birds. The Lake Tahoe dream of our first place was demolished when I took in hand the keys to a slum that would turn even a hobo back to his Maytag refrigerator box. No joke, there were crack stains on the tiles, multiple holes in the walls, ranging from bullet to knuckle size, and the deadliest looking clan of cockroaches I had ever seen. Seriously, those little buggers were the Hell's Angels of our carpet and walls. Now that was the way that I saw things. In Lana's eyes, this was just another stepping stone and she had no objection towards living there.

Her optimism was strong and in many ways I felt that it had a strong link to her newfound love for Sylvia Brown. Lana would quote Brown's philosophy as her own and I used to give her great levels of opposition. I held no interest in psychics or their outlandish beliefs, but what Lana believed in so passionately eventually dug its roots into me. Even though I still remained hesitant and skeptical, I admired Lana's free thought and commitment to her ideals.

All in all, my life was at the point where I really could not complain and I began to improve my attitude. Then the phone rang and in that one instance, everything changed. Cassidy was on the other end, hysterically crying that her younger brother, Mikah, had died in a car accident. I attempted to inquire about all of the details but her constant crying drowned out my words. After several minutes, she finally calmed down long enough to fill me in on the whole situation. Apparently, while his friend was driving him and a few others back from a concert, the car had swerved off of the road and the only person injured was Mikah. Her words were immediately followed by an outburst of tears and the clicking of the phone.

While waiting for a return call, I started to think of my first experience with meeting Mikah and the wild story that he was involved in. He was introduced to them by his father while Cassidy, Katie and Max were in a coffee shop. Without any hesitation, they accepted and embraced him into their household. There he had lived for the next ten years and then all of the sudden this tragedy hit. The phone rang again, interrupting my thoughts, and when Cassidy spoke this time, she was a lot more collected. However, there was something different in her voice, it lacked the backing of her heart, and the thought of her and her family's pain crushed my own heart to rubble. I then contemplated how I was going to explain this unforeseen passing of their uncle Mikah to Nicole and Juliano.

The feeling of calling to tell them that their beautiful twenty-one year old uncle was raised to the Heavens felt so absurd and out of place. They did not need this in their lives, but a drug-related car accident brought it with a concrete reality. Nicole reacted a lot more intensely than I had expected and I yearned with all of my soul to be able to absorb her pain. However, this moment of understanding and acceptance was her own lesson and my gorgeous little girl showed strength. She did so by whispering a private goodbye and then explaining the loss to Juliano in a way that he could understand. Tears formed in my eyes as I listened to him accept what he could not control and grow as a strong little man. Uncle Mikah would be proud of them, as proud as I am to praise Mikah's name and that even though his time was short, his life was vividly influential.

Mikah, you left a lifetime of love to your sister, brother, parents and your many friends. We will always remember you, just because you were Mikah, dammit!

Roughly around this time, I met two young guys, Tom and Don, who I simply came to refer to as "The Michigan Boys". They lived in the same complex as us and after seeing the cannabis leaf on my calf, felt the need to inquire me about some smoke. I mentioned that I was fresher into town than they were but I would see what I could do. We all laughed and shared an immediate bond, despite the slight embarrassment that I felt for being called out on my tattoo. The Michigan Boys were the first friends that I made in Lake Tahoe and thus another piece fell into place of my dream picture. I was creating companionships with other locals. Several weeks later their close friend Wes came to live with them and this kid was an absolute animal. I loved his "fuck-the-world" attitude and saw a younger version of myself in him. The Michigan Trio made my transition to Lake Tahoe seamless and outrageously entertaining. To boot, they had a flawless knowledge of sports and since their Detroit Tigers were hanging from the bottom rung of the baseball league, our friendship could develop nicely.

With patience and faith, our slowly rolling business received its first job offer and a sense of euphoria rushed down my spine. The dream that I had envisioned for so many years had alas taken form. Although I had no clue what we had in store for us, both Lana and I sped with great urgency to our first bid. The client was a gentleman by the name of Rich and Rich would soon prove to be one of the most beneficial individuals in not only my business, but my life as well, by seeing the value in my potential. At first, I felt like a conman when I quoted our prices, yet without hesitation the price was agreed to and before we knew it, our first job was done. Doing business with Lana was incredible since she had an immaculate work ethic and left that place looking pristine.

The job was well accepted and before we could blink, the word of our stellar cleaning abilities spread like a brushfire. Lake Tahoe is the type of small community that puts a great deal of worth into its local proprietors. If a business does a quality job, then their name will be shared amongst the locals and the business will have an opportunity to thrive. Our cleaning business was capable of providing this quality service and our clientele reminded us constantly at how privileged we were to be making a life happen in such an unblemished landscape. I can honestly say that it is the locals that make Lake Tahoe what it is and it was their responsibility to maintain the easygoing mountain charm.

The optimism and good vibrations of the locals flowed upon us and when the kids arrived, everything was perfect. Both Nicole and Juliano loved Lake Tahoe at once and made us vow to never leave. Lana and I laughed joyfully at how raw and light-hearted they were. Only two months had passed since I had seen them last, but the delight of having them in our new home was unreal. The stepping stones of our lives continued to lead us further into a successful future.

I was astonished at how much I could accomplish with a solid amount of legal, hard work. The concept of a business became less of a fairytale and more of an everyday routine. My life had seen far too many years before I genuinely understood the value of an honest job. However unlike Lana, I continued to strive for more and never settled for a set number of clients. In a town like Lake Tahoe an individual is either well-off and living comfortably, or working like a fiend to make it year-round in an eight month workplace. Rescue Cleaning, as I soon named it, became a twenty-four/seven business and I was great at what I did, never squandering any time except for Juliano's baseball.

Signing Juliano up for his first season of baseball was such an intense rush, it stayed with me for weeks. I was overly proud to be his father. At one point, I was approached and offered a position as one of the volunteer coaches to assist during practices and scrimmage games and faster than a virgin in a Playmate, I agreed. Then came the blindside haymaker to the temple, a mandatory criminal background check. I swiftly talked my way out of what was probably the best opportunity for my son's life and I sulked silently into the shadows with shame. Backing off took a great deal of nerve, but I did it for Juliano, so that none of these individuals would judge my son because of my past. Nonetheless, everything worked out for the better.

Watching him play was two beautiful hours of absolute happiness. Juliano was a flawless player. He never failed to find himself easily and instantly listed on the All-Stars roster. He was the first Sparzo to ever grace the tabloids with a positive caption. Everything that I loved about baseball was present in him and I praised him for it. I was a steadfast supporter in his skill and never missed a single game, aside from the occasional weather hold. For me, baseball season was the best time of every year that I spent at the lake.

The events of one average day at his practice took me back to a poem that I had written as a youth. The poem had revolved around a father who was never at the ballgame and when the teammates questioned the boy about it in the dug out, he would lie to protect his father's name. So on this day practicing with my son and his team, one of the kids asked, "What's wrong with your dad's leg?" I had been using a large white Ace bandage to cover the pot leaf tattoo in respects towards my son and his team. Before I could muster up a dimwitted response, Juliano jumped in with this story about how I slid my Harley Davidson into a ditch after avoiding a three hundred pound bear in the dead of the night. All of the kids surrounded us with amazement. My son had lied to protect his father's name. Juliano looked back at me and was so proud that he had his dad's back. The sensation of teary eyes overwhelmed me. Pride had collided with guilt and triumphed as the dominant mentality. The divine line between Judas and me was now growing remarkably stronger and I found that my karma was in total equilibrium. Then again, one way or another I managed to slide backwards and gambling was no exception.

My only solace was my dear Lana. Our love continued to flourish at an exponential rate and with her thirtieth birthday less than a week away, I was committed to throwing her a surprise birthday to remember. We had recently met a couple, Anthony and Becky, and Anthony was a walking talent show. He possessed an uncanny gift for strumming the guitar and delivering a sweet sounding harmony that enchanted any ear within its range. So for her thirtieth birthday surprise, I hired Anthony to perform for her the Creed song "Higher". The man was a complete genius and had the entire song, chords and lyrics, dialed in just three days. To say the least, Lana was absolutely astonished. Tears streamed down her blushing cheeks as she squealed with excitement. For Lana, this song representing everything that was promising about the life we were developing in Lake Tahoe. The more happiness that I brought to my Lana, the better I felt about my place in the world.

This positive outlook on life was more than enough to inspire new goals and dreams for my life. The concept of starting an AIDS Foundation in memory of Heidi and Joseph Murphy became a distant light of hope for me. All that I had to do was find the means to make this idea a reality. My only rational source for these means was through the art of gambling. In no way was this legitimate as a method for increased income because two out of three times the house wins, my house loses and the lies grow more frequent.

One night after vanishing for five hours and stumbling home broke and equally drunk, I barged into the house with a story to tell. Like a thespian at a casting shoot, I delivered some long-winded nonsense about how I was helping out homeless people and Lana just listened. As soon as I was convinced that she bought it, Lana softly asked, "So what happened to your knees then?" Taken aback, I looked down and realized that I had the indentations from the coin slots pressed distinctly right above my knees. I stood there vacantly, looking dumber than a yokel on a trivia game show and the always great and wise Tony had nothing to say. Lana erupted with laughter, slapped me on the back of my head, then my butt and briskly walked upstairs. *Damn I love her.*

Caught slightly off guard, I thought about how odd it was that I had lied and gotten away with it. All that I lost was a little bit of respect from Lana. So since she was not officially "mad" at me, it allowed me to let myself off the hook and back to yet another day at the casinos. I had spent years battling the same demons that still haunted me day in and day out, demons lurking incognito as gambling and alcohol. Far too much time was spent battling and losing my self-respect, credibility and loved ones' faith. I would catch my conscience always a second too late and comfort my woes with immediate spending. While I was up in the count and winning hands, I would use my spoils to buy Lana's forgiveness back with shopping sprees. Disgustingly though, I secretly kept the receipts in case I needed the money back the next day.

A few weeks passed before I received a call from Cassandra telling me that my grandmother had recently died. In an attempt to refrain from crying, I acted out in a frigidly cold manner towards my sister. I had abstained from speaking to my parents for over a year and thus had thrown her right in there with them. To be honest, she never acted out maliciously towards me or demonstrated anything other than love and kindness, but I did not care, she was one of them and that was all that I saw.

I chose not to attend my grandmother's service, feeling as though I had already lost her many years earlier when she first started showing symptoms of her illness. Oddly enough, it seemed to me that everyone shared my mindset except for one person, my aunt Karen. Her life was now completely bare, stripped of all of the individuals who were influential to her. With my grandparents out of the picture, I pressed her to sell their house and move to Lake Tahoe. Aunt Karen's life was in sheer turmoil amidst raising Collette's three kids and her own prison grade son. With Bobby incarcerated for life and Collette's eternal addiction, I thought I could help her despite the fact that I already needed Lana to manage my own life. Karen said she would consider it as an option and that was how her status remained.

Over the next three years, we hop scotched around town, on the constant search for that elusive neighborhood where everyone is gregarious and barbecues together. In Lake Tahoe, finding that ideal neighborhood is more of a phantom than a reality since ninety percent of the population lives there seasonally and are constantly coming and going. All that we desired from the depths of our hearts was to belong and fit in, to be known as locals.

Alas, our search for the Holy Grail was finally over and we

found our sanctuary in a rural neighborhood with a breathtaking view of the majestic Mount Tallac. The untamed wilderness was my fenceless backyard and the panoramic outlook from the balcony would give even Ansel Adams goose bumps. With enough business to comfortably supplement our income and gambling slowly fading off into the distance, my life was at its apex. I was on airs, engrossed in a life that was perfect to the tenth degree. Nothing could ruin this, not even me.

Hello and Goodbye

*L*ike a ten year old on Christmas morning, I awoke far too early, beating both the sun and the birds, and rushed outside just to stare wide-eyed at our wonderful home. Too many years had passed before I was capable of feeling pride in myself. My life had finally happened and no longer was I a step behind the rest of the world. Everyday proved to be more promising and the people that we befriended were pure and just.

One such friend we met was a young punk rocker girl from Southern California by the name of Victoria. Victoria was an amazingly beautiful sprite with multiple colors in her hair and vibrant make-up. I loved her look and equally loved her aspirations for Hollywood. I genuinely believed in her dreams and a sense of desire to see them turn into a reality captivated me. Through hard work and dedication to her goals, she actually saw her dreams come true and to this day she is sober and successful amongst the Hollywood circuit. Victoria has grown to be one of the dearest friends that I have ever gained. The spirituality that surrounded her pure soul made the Lake Tahoe merger flow that much smoother. The natural high was unreal, which usually lasted until I sparked up a joint or cracked open another beer. Then, anything spiritual that I felt quickly vanished.

My inability to stay sober bore deep into my conscience. The strength that I thought I had possessed often proved to be non-existent. A week long stretch of sobriety from liquor was constantly rivaled by my sheer love for cannabis. I was an eternal slave to controlling substances and it pained me. I truly had forgotten how to survive without the assistance of a drink or drug. I was stuck without any options, and any chance that I had of finding the answers to my troubles became even tougher as I grew closer to my new neighbors.

Our neighbors consisted of John and Sherry who resided across the street from us and Jay and Anne who were living next-door. Our common grounds were easy to find since we all had kids, we all held productive working lives and we all loved to drink. The fit in our circle was perfect. However, my perception of everyone was equally as clogged as my drug-riddled system. When individuals have that many similarities, they are bound to share some of the same problems and we surely did. The only way to refrain from despising everybody was to focus solely on their positive attributes.

Jay and Anne were the youngest of the couples and had recently arrived from Southern California just like us. Anne was a highly driven woman who always spoke with an optimistic mindset and I frequently found myself hanging on her words of inspiration and focus. She opened my eyes to my world and pushed me towards a more productive lifestyle.

After spending some time reflecting inward, I realized that my health was starting to show serious signs of deterioration. Most of it was due to the fact that I was severely overweight, smoked heavily and despised any form of physical activity. I could easily categorize myself as a prospective heart attack victim. Almost daily, a friend and co-worker of mine, David, would call to my attention the hap hazards of my lifestyle and the impending doom that was in store for me. Since his father had been lost to lung cancer, the constant reminder of Juliano and Nicole being fatherless plagued my thoughts. David's continuous input annoyed me, but not before it actually got through to me. The image of me putting down this vicious addiction started to play on loop in my head. I made a commitment to myself that when the New Year rolled through I would banish smoking forever. Cigarettes had occupied twenty of the thirty-five years of my life and the reality of my addiction made me sick to my stomach. My body was burned out and desperately needed a second chance.

Less than a week later, my aunt Barbara and cousin Teri came up from Los Angeles and I was thrilled to see them. They were the first family members who took the time to visit us since our move to Lake Tahoe. Aunt Barbara was on my case immediately in lieu of my utter disregard towards my parents and their existence. Not caring a single bit about what she had to say, I tried to subtly change the topic but good luck with that, Barbara was a hardcore New Yorker who always put family first. Teri, on the other hand, was a pleasure to be with. As youths, we shared many adventures together but the trials of life had separated us for countless years.

She opened up to me about her new love interest and the solace she was finding through God, both of which I responded to with great skepticism. Instead of embracing her happiness and showing my support, I only called light to the negative. *What right did I have to be the silencer of encouragement and faith? Is it that difficult to simply join another individual's dream instead of smashing it?* Today, I am honored to say that Teri discredited all doubts and is blissfully married to the man of her dreams while enjoying a guilt-free sober life filled with spiritual healing. She is living proof of the splendors that await all of us as long as we stay committed to the righteous path.

My aunt and cousin left not too long after their arrival, but not before Barbara gave me her final two-cents and the numbers to some family that I had not spoken with in roughly fifteen years. I was intrigued at how quickly that many years could pass and made a conscious effort to change my ways. I started by calling my cousin Barbara, who coincidentally had the same name as my aunt. Italians have a unique way of keeping the name list short within the family tree.

I have always taken a great pride in my sense of humor, so I decided to catch her off-guard by pretending to be Internal Revenue Service agent Gus Rockford. I thoroughly enjoy how quickly an individual will get serious when they hear the words Internal Revenue Service and the nervous laughter that follows when I reveal myself. Surprisingly, the conversation went well until she muttered some comment about Gerard and Melinda. Her whole demeanor shifted as she bombarded me for not having the decency to let them know that I was alive and well. I protested with hollow words but she checked my attitude immediately. Cornered and lacking momentum, I conceded to think it over. However, once the call ended, my next move was straight to the liquor store to obtain some liquid courage.

By the time the midnight's toll rang throughout the house, I was well into a twelve-pack and ready to converse with my folks. After two and a half years of emptiness, Melinda was ecstatic to hear my voice. My voice quivered with drunken tears and hopeful promises that I would call her the next morning when my mental state was more stable. Once disconnected, I passed into a deep, almost comatose slumber.

I awoke the next morning still in my casuals with a searing pain in my skull, boiling regret in my stomach and half of a beer dispersed across my lap. Alcohol always guarantees the proudest moments. Collecting my head took more effort than necessary and after a brief run down from Lana on the previous night's activities, I was back to myself again. Sometimes blacking out spares me from the embarrassment that I am intended to feel, but it still never brings me peace.

Within twenty minutes, my old man was on the phone and we were joyfully discussing the Yankees, once again our only neutral zone. Had it not been for baseball and the Yankees, I believe that Gerard and I may never have been able to partake in a quality conversation. Every bit of advice he ever decided to express was delivered like a parental lecture, which would ultimately fall upon deaf ears. I wish that I had the patience to hear his words in the way he had intended, but that was just not in my nature. Aside from all of my pride issues, Gerard invited us to spend Thanksgiving back in Los Angeles and I gladly accepted. With that all of that settled, around the same time I received a call from Ken who had just waltzed out of prison and was living down in Orange County. After announcing that I was already heading down there, I insisted that he joined Lana and me for Thanksgiving and he eagerly agreed.

A few months passed and before we knew it Thanksgiving was upon us and we were all together at my parents'. Ken had brought a beautiful Russian girl with dark wavy hair and prominent blue eyes by the name of Kate. Melinda showed instant irritancy towards the additional guests, but bit her lip and proceeded with the delightful dinner. I felt that she was being selfish by wanting this to only be a family event since after all it was Thanksgiving, and the more the merrier. Besides, being there with just them made me feel strangely uncomfortable.

The dinner conversations stayed appropriate and at one point, Lana spoke to Gerard about how nothing could halter us now since we were bonded as a family. I believe that that Thanksgiving Day was the pivotal moment when my parents realized that Lana was the very best thing that ever happened to me. They adored her from there on out, embracing her as one of their own. That dinner together was a flawless experience and we left with smiles, promising to stay in touch more regularly.

The four of us then made our way over to Phyllis' house to spend time with her and Lana's step-father, Tug. We arrived to a seemingly vacant house with the lights turned down low. With a skip in her step, Lana headed in before us and within seconds came bursting back out of the house screaming hysterically. I raced in and immediately froze in my tracks when I saw Tug lying motionless on the floor. I checked for a pulse and after realizing that he still had one, I helped him back onto his feet and over to a nearby chair. The situation was so intense that my heart was racing like a cocaine addict.

Tug had symbolized more than a parental figure to me. He was the old-fashioned style of gentleman who demanded respect through his good nature. He was the only man that I had ever called sir and refrained from swearing in the presence of. This day had grown too real too quickly and the fear of losing him shook both Lana and I to our very core. Growing up, Tug used to be that sarcastic man who we would steal beer from and his only response would be, "Damn kids." I held a great level of respect for him and now here he was in a frail situation.

Ken and Kate felt the need to escape all of the excitement and I just stood there, silent and in shock. Lana was a complete wreck, enraged by Tug's situation. She ran to the phone and demanded answers from her sister, Jamie, then slammed down the phone and insisted that we drove to her house. Somehow, over the next few hours, Lana's rage shifted from Jamie to me. The consumption of alcohol, in relation to her father's predicament, had fueled a bad temper in Lana. I really should have been more understanding but that was not me, especially while under the influence.

By the time the next morning sprung into existence, the prior nights events were nothing but a distorted memory. Then it dawned on me that many things were different, Tug was involved in a losing battle and thirteen months later Harold Frandsen, husband of Phyllis, Daddy to two and role model for many passed away. Witnessing Lana go through the loss was heartbreaking. She was an ideal daughter to her parents and now here she was, just a little more empty than she deserved to be. Who she was as an offspring to her parents made me feel shameful for how I acted towards mine. She genuinely loved her daddy so much and was a model example of the way that a child is supposed to care for their parents, yet another thing that I knew nothing about. The dismal passing of Tug had brought our own family closer together and we worked through the pain of goodbye as a team.

A strange feeling punctured my soul as I realized I had finally found my Yoko. John Lennon and Yoko Ono's love was the epitome of what real love should be and I now saw in Lana what John saw in Yoko. Lana and I were inseparable, with a love that not only could survive through the harsh times, but managed to flourish. Suddenly, like a light switch in my mind, I felt the pure desire to be a husband and a father, an exemplar of greatness to my family. Then again, life did not always go the way that I wanted it to, especially just because I had a brief moment of clairvoyance.

When the call came collect I was stunned, it was Brother Bobby, live from Corcoran! Five years had drifted by since our last conversation and he was not calling to catch up. Bobby informed me that his mom was very ill and that I needed to contact her at once. Bobby was quick in his delivery and it was obvious that the prison time had made him a stern and centered man. The brother that I knew for so many years was gone and buried, replaced by a man who the system of rehabilitation had made as solid as the concrete that imprisoned him. The world works in strange, peculiar ways.

I agreed to call my aunt and upon hearing her feeble voice, I instantly started to cry. Karen calmed me down, telling me to get a grip and to continue the conversation with a controlled demeanor. She explained that Bobby was exaggerating but that she still needed me to come as soon as possible to help her with the kids. I told her that helping her would not be a problem and everything would work out. Lana, who was hovering silently over my shoulder, gave me a warm hug and softly whispered how amazing she thought that I was to Bobby and Karen. I kissed her gently and then made my way upstairs to pack a few things. The opportunity had finally arrived where I could do something positive for someone else. My aunt was counting on me and there was no way that I was going to let her down.

We left town bright and early the next morning and arrived in Los Angeles by noon. The moment that I saw my aunt I knew she was not doing fine like she had made herself out to be. The chemo therapy had stripped her hair down to mere fuzz. She looked gray and gaunt to me. Karen was always the most radiant woman with beautifully flowing auburn hair. Fear for her overtook my every emotion. With the same roseate nature that she was known for, she assured me that she was on the upswing and that all of the chemo therapy was working wonderfully. I pondered why she did not call me sooner and she simply stated that she had no intentions of worrying me. So after a great visit and some words of encouragement, we left to look in on the kids.

As we arrived at my grandmother's house, my jaw dropped with shock combined with absolute disgust. There was zero resemblance in this run-down shack to the house that I had grown up in. Busted shutters sunk halfway into the dead, leafless bushes, graffiti created a mural of hate and slander on all of the outside walls and pale Bermuda grass entangled every step that we took across the once concrete walkway. Inside, the condition of the house was twice as bad. The ceiling took up more of the floor than it did the actual ceiling and a calico array of mold was the dominant paint job. One deep breath in this house made my nose burn like I was inhaling in vast amounts of smelling salt. There was no way that this tainted abode was still habitable. Then my younger cousin, Aldo, emerged from his door-less room and I exploded with rage. He just stood there, looking dumber than a mule on a railroad track. Then Marie, Collette's oldest daughter who was the same age as Aldo, walked in and I turned all of my anger over to her. Their sheer disregard for the maintenance of this once immaculate house was unacceptable.

Lana finally pulled me back, threw her palm over my mouth and then assertively asked where the little toddlers were. I had been so preoccupied with the semblance of the house that I had completely forgotten why we were there in the first place. Marie then made note that they were down the street playing at the park. Here it was, past nine o'clock in the evening and two toddlers were roaming around in one of the worst neighborhoods in the district. I immediately sprinted straight to the park, where much to my relief they were safe and together. After a brisk walk back home, I sat everyone down and established some ground rules.

As earnest as I tried to convince them of my sincerity, each solitary word was met with an overwhelming level of contempt. That is, from everybody except for the three year old Melissa, who stared up at me from her toys with her sparkling green eyes and smiled. This was the first time that I had met Melissa and her resemblance to Collette was astounding. Her smile brought comfort to my heart and I suddenly felt a safe connection with her.

As the night came rolling to an end, I took a break and stepped outside to collect my thoughts and piece together this whole situation. For some beautiful reason, gazing into the celestial sky brought me a quaint sense of peace. However, my moment of reverence was short lived as Lana moved slowly up next to me and rested her head on my shoulder. My words came out quivered and weak as I expressed my hesitations towards our new obligations. Lana gently responded that this was the responsibility my aunt entrusted upon us and we were going to see this through. Her steadfast optimism never failed to amaze me.

The next morning we arrived anxiously at the hospital to pick up my aunt and she was delighted to see us. I made sure she knew that both Lana and I were completely at her disposal and that she would not even have to lift a single finger until she recovered. The endless love and bliss that she emitted made every cell within me feel warm. Keeping up with our word was easier than I had thought and caretaking for my aunt proved to be very beneficial for her health. Once Karen was capable of managing enough of her everyday tasks, we made a break for Lake Tahoe to grab the kids and immediately turned back for Highland Park.

Much to my dismay, the kids took complete advantage of my aunt's ailment and my anger rose quicker than a thermometer in a volcano. *How dare they have the audacity to cause additional turmoil to an elderly woman with their playground antics?* Then it occurred to me that these were my offspring and all of my malicious characteristics were embedded in them. My parental control was useless and their fear and confusion placed me as the enemy. I was forever deemed the scapegoat in their eyes and every word that was directed towards me was spoken with a negative tone. I had shattered their world and I deserved every bit of it. Aside from my kids, telling Aldo and Marie that they would have to live with us in Lake Tahoe until Karen recovered built even more resentment towards me. I could not blame Aldo, so much of his life included unnecessary stress from living in the same house that Ted, Grandpa and Grandma had passed away in within a four year period and now Mama Karen too. I could not fathom the level of pain that this kid, way too strong for his own good, was going through. I figure God only gives us what we can handle, and Aldo sure got his fair share of misery.

Not too long after, Collette arrived to meet with all of us and I was amazed at how much she changed. Her metamorphosis from beauty to beast was astronomical and it was all due to hardcore drugs. However, I still loved her and we spent the next hour catching up on the past four years, hugging and crying along the way. She spoke of her fears towards life without her mother and the abandonment from the rest of the family that was sure to follow. I comforted her, explaining that Lana and I would never ostracize her and that Karen herself said that she was going to recover fully. Collette shot back with great disbelief, claiming that she had done all sorts of research on cancer and that her mom's hourglass was running low on sand. Even though I felt that it was just the heroin speaking, I agreed to contact my aunt's doctor and check in on all of the details.

Much to my relief, Lana and I could not miss out on any more of the cleaning business so we had to make our way back up to Lake Tahoe. Before leaving, we arranged the house to be as simple as possible for my aunt and then convinced one of the neighbors to act as a temporary caretaker. Everything was looking positive for Karen, who was also watching Aaron and Melissa as well. We took Aldo and Marie up with us to Lake Tahoe where we were able to have them enrolled in school by the following Monday. By Tuesday I had received the much anticipated call from the doctor and he was straight to the point, stating that my aunt Karen had approximately nine months to live. I attempted to argue in her defense but was abruptly interrupted by the doctor, who explained the severity of the tumors in her lungs with thorough detail. I was jarred at how real the circumstances of her life were getting. *Why Aunt Karen? She never clogged her system with the pollutants of the alleys or those of the over-the-counter world. She was a pure soul with an unjust outcome.* My aunt became the final turning point in my war with cigarettes, which after already a year without use I knew that I could conquer forever. Her sacrifice would not go unnoticed.

Without delay, I called my aunt to express all of my sentiment and sorrows. Solidly, she told me that the doctors were clueless to her willpower and did not know what they were saying. Then it struck me, she was in complete denial and her passing was inevitable. After a brief consultation with Lana, I told my aunt to sell the house and then we could use the money to get a place where all of us could live. Much to our fortune, I had a client who was more like a father that was able to help us cover all of the costs, which estimated to be around ten thousand dollars. The feelings of having someone help make our life that much easier was incredible.

Lana and I spent the next six weeks going back and forth between all of the lawyers, realtors and doctors, and what it created was absolute pandemonium. Then include the kids, whose shock from being stripped from their home and friends only fueled their hate for me. Above all of this immediate insanity though, I think the most haunting thought in my mind was how I was going to tell Bobby that his mother's life expectancy was only a matter of months. Almost twenty years earlier, it was me that told him the truth about his dad and now it was time for his mom. Through the phone I could sense the internal battle that he was facing between pure rage and an ambush of tears. Bobby said that he loved me and then cut the call short. No words could have changed the mood of that conversation. I simply prayed for his strength and prepared myself for the storm to come.

On the last week of May, Lana and I went down to Highland Park and picked up my aunt Karen. I stepped down from my pride bucket and called Melinda, asking her to come see Karen off. She complied and was accompanied by my aunt Dina, who I had not seen in over two decades. Bringing the three of them together was a miracle in itself because Dina and Melinda had not spoken to Karen since the death of their mother. Death can have a grave impact on a family's bond. I realized that I was in way over my head but nevertheless I had to keep my word. We brought her to Lake Tahoe and the wonder that bestowed those somnolent eyes made her glow with joy. Once again, Lake Tahoe is the land of miracles, a real-life fountain of youth. Karen was delighted to see Aldo and Marie, and all of us made a comfortable existence together. The challenge presented itself and we were all willing to persevere through it. I genuinely believed that we could do it.

Then the fatigue set in and I started to wear down from the combination of the noise and the kids. To top it off, I had not drank in almost a year and by the time we made our third trip to Los Angeles, my discipline level had diminished and I was back to drinking daily. The custody battle with the Foster Care Program over Aaron and Melissa was like fighting with great white sharks for a mackerel and it took some extreme patience just to bring them home. Both Aaron and Melissa were born heavily addicted to heroin and showed some of the early signs of emotional instability.

Everyday I questioned what I was doing and Lana reassured me that it was the right thing. No one else believed that but her. She put up a strong front against all of our selected friends and family who felt we were deranged for committing to such an immense undertaking. Their lack of faith infuriated me, but we carried on thanks to the help of more positive friends and supportive clients. Lana and I stepped up to our burden and settled all of our obligations.

After a strenuous twelve-hour shift of cleaning, I arrived home to the nerve-racking glow of red and white as an ambulance sat idling in my driveway. I rushed in to the image of paramedics hovering over my aunt. Lana pulled me aside and told me that Karen was losing her life faster than expected. We followed directly behind the ambulance as it raced towards the hospital, not knowing that we had rushed our way to the worst news possible. The doctor informed us with the grim fact that my aunt Karen was looking at her final seven days of life. I argued that she was without a doubt going to live until November and that it was only June. He said that his information was concrete and that she could die either there at the hospital or at home with her family. Incapable of mustering any words, I just stared daggers at the doctor and left with my aunt.

On the car ride home, my aunt became highly upset at us for calling the ambulance and again explained that the doctors knew nothing. I shrugged my shoulders and slid my hand over her cold, frail hands. Once we arrived at home, we settled her into her bed, which was a pullout couch in the entertainment room and made our own way upstairs.

After a restless three hours, I went downstairs to check in on her. She was sitting up against the backing of the couch looking eerily silent but awake. Wanting to help the situation, I asked her if there was anything that I could get for her. With a raspy breath and unmoving, unblinking eyes, she just waved me off. Completely ignorant to what was occurring right before my very eyes I closed the door, poured myself a glass of water and went back upstairs.

No more than an hour later, Lana woke me up with a frantic pitch in her voice and rushed me downstairs. I opened the door to a room that I immediately noticed had an unnatural vibe to it. Karen still remained in an upright position but this time everything was different. Her eyes lacked a certain backing, just soulless orbs shadowing a life eons away. My aunt Karen had taken the mysterious step into the unknown. So many thoughts cascaded my brain. *Why the hell did I go back upstairs? I should have stayed with her throughout the night and kept her warm.* I believed her when she said that she was going to live, but I guess I believed her too much and now she was gone. Her final moments were spent alone in the dark on a couch in the entertainment room.

I sat there with Lana and my aunt's vacant body, so distraught that I continued talking to Karen, asking her what we should do. Lana finally stopped my nonsensical babbling and gave me strict orders to send the older kids down to say their goodbyes while I was to remain upstairs with Aaron and Melissa. I did exactly what she told me to do. A short time later, we called the police who showed up swiftly and carted my aunt into the cadaver transport. That was it, she was gone.

Three to four hours passed and the sun was barely resting on the horizon when a phone call disrupted the heavy silence, it was Bobby. With a whisper only he could here and barely at that, I delivered the news about his mother. Oddly, his only response in diction form was, "Wow, so that's it?!" His voice cracked with emotion, and was abruptly followed by an onslaught of painfully muffled tears.

Buying My Soul Back

The dark days that followed my aunt's passing were spent in solitude, reflecting on what my life had amounted to and what I could do to salvage what little I still had left. To make matters worse, Aldo and Marie both insisted that we moved them back to Southern California immediately and I could not blame them. The intensity of Aaron and Melissa was pressing everybody to the edge of their sanity. Even Nicole and Juliano were feeling the agony of neglect. The passing of my aunt had flipped my Utopian world upside down.

As the school year ended for the summer, Nicole made south to Las Vegas to live with Cassidy, and Juliano stayed with us to finish off his successful baseball season. Baseball once again distracted me from the inevitable reality that was swarming around me. Lana and I put the very best into our situation and made an effort to rebuild our reputation and solidify our dreams.

Our first order of business was getting Aldo and Marie back to Los Angeles where much to my surprise they were welcomed with little warmth. Sadly, everyone acted far more interested in the house and it's appraisal than the actual kids who used to live in it. Bobby made a regular habit of contacting me every evening from prison with advice for what to do about the house. His opinion was the only one that I accepted and made an effort to stay focused on. However, the constant barrage of demands had worn thin on me and anxiety attacks were becoming more prevalent, pushing me to a constantly nervous, and always needing to drink mindset. We sought to take loans from the same clients that we did work for and amazingly Rich, our first and truest client, kindly obliged without any wince of hesitation.

We continued our grueling trips to Los Angeles and finally made solid plans for Karen's funeral. A breath of sweet relaxation was non-existent when juggling the property in Los Angeles, the business in Lake Tahoe and the kids in both locations. We were deep into debt and our only salvation resided in selling the house. Several months passed and alas the house was sold.

I had no issue about splitting half of it with Bobby since after all he had a long history with that catacomb. He deserved his fair share to counter-balance the countless hardships that plagued his life. So with more than enough cash in our midst, we made our way back up to Lake Tahoe with rejuvenated hopes. The thing with money though, is that as soon as an individual gains it, it finds ways to spend itself just as quickly. Splurging via a spending spree was amazingly easy and before I could even get my wallet back in my pocket, I had in my name some new furniture, a new entertainment system and a better car. Each of these material possessions was a tool I used to mask the insecurities that dwelled within me. I accounted for that by spoiling the kids, mainly Juliano, who I surprised with a brand new set of baseball equipment. I also wired several thousand dollars to Collette, who was persistently demanding half. I gave her what I could but had to make sure that I saved enough to keep my word to my aunt and buy my family a house.

Lana would often ask me what was on my mind and after expressing my worries, she gently reminded me that this was all going to work out and that I still had great potential. As wonderfully supportive as she was, I failed to see the Tony that she saw and found myself spiraling aimlessly into a nervous breakdown. Every minute of every day was spent in a tense state of anxiety, dreading the next moment that I was going to scream until my face turned blue or drop to the floor in a fetal position, scared and crying. I was edgy all of the time and jumpy towards anything that was out of the ordinary, which in my eyes was everything. I was petrified of the world and the world was petrified of me.

In my brief periods of mental stability, I was able to see the fear and confusion that my actions were having on Lana and the kids. Juliano started to look at me differently, like he was searching for his dad when he looked into my eyes but could never find him. So whenever the feeling of guilt stepped in, a present magically appeared to keep them distracted from seeing me as the let down that I really was.

As I lost control in my life from all of the burdens that I had accumulated, my sanity was quick to follow. Lana was terrified for me and begged me to see a professional and get myself on some medications. I followed through with her request and after a brief consultation with a doctor I was prescribed Paxil for the anxiety. I took roughly a month's worth, if that, of the proper dosage and felt exactly the same as I did before. I decided that I was over prescription drugs and kicked the pills to the curb. In no way did I want to be a slave to a pill for the rest of my life, and soon after that brash decision the outbursts escalated.

Maintaining employees on the payroll was next to impossible since none of them wanted to work for a boss who was a complete basket case. I was always screaming erratically while at job sites and demanded seven-days-a-week availability. The turmoil in my head had brought misery to others and I had no way of staying in control.

The only person who was nil fazed by my neurotic outbursts was my incredible Lana, who stood firm in her beliefs that I was not a lost cause just yet. She pleaded for me to re-visit the doctor, who changed my meds and then advised me to seriously reconsider the way that I lived my life. I accepted his advice and put all of my initial focus into gaining control of my alcohol dependency. I could still make my life worth living and alcohol was not going to help. I even for the first time in my life signed up for a membership at a gym, complete with a personal trainer and decided to fight for my existence.

The rivalry amongst Juliano, Aaron and Melissa was growing immensely and I could easily see things from all of their perspectives. Juliano had never shared Lana and me with anyone, not even Nicole, and now he had to be surrounded by kids who loved being hyper way too much. Losing Nicole was a shameful event in this period of my life, the way that my beautiful girl just fell off of the map after we had done so much to accommodate to her individual lifestyle. Regrettably, I never had the time for her that she deserved and when I did, it was only in the form of spending money and not simply loving. I realize the faults of my actions Nicole and I love you with all of my heart.

The karma that had lingered in my shadow for what had seemed like an eternity was now starting to take form. Whatever storm I had coming my way was brewing on the horizon and I was in for a harsh reality check. I started to think of all of the wrong that I had committed to so many of my friends and family, but at the same time I fully believed that what we were doing was right. Aaron and Melissa were not an obligation, they were a blessing and as the days passed, the light that they shined into our lives grew brighter and brighter. Aaron and Melissa became symbolic to the relationship that Lana and I had. They were the children that our love brought to our family, and the ones that we could never physically have together.

Consequences

According to all of my peers, the amount of business that I was taking on put me in way over my head, but I did not care since the money was outstanding. With our business picking up, I began putting more focus into the future and this was a sign that my goals were growing more realistic by the day. With funds from the business, along with the surplus money from the house, I was finally able to live a life where I could give rather than take. Something as simple as paying my bills on time became a crowning achievement to my day. Maintaining a solid work ethic also allowed me to spoil the kids with whatever their little hearts desired. We were surrounded by genuine friends and the people that we met gave me an idea of what life could be like if I just put forth that extra effort. Many of our friends marveled at the marriage that Lana and I had and I took great pride in our love. There was no doubt that our marriage would continued to bloom vibrantly with life. I loved being married and I loved being committed to my wife.

A couple that we knew by the name of Leeland and Grace were planning out their own wedding and inquired if there was any possibility for me to conduct the ceremony. Lana and I had recently watched an episode of *Friends* where Joey became an ordained minister and we decided that it would be an excellent gesture of love and good will. After what seemed like only some quick research and a brief questionnaire, I was certified as an ordained minister. The news traveled fast and was responded to with continuous mockery, simply at the notion that Anthony Sparzo was a minister. Nobody took me seriously, constantly hounding me to fess up that this was all some elaborate joke.

However, I disregarded all of their negative words and took the honor of officiating the wedding very seriously. To say that it was an absolutely phenomenal wedding would be an understatement. The ceremony was flawless and with tears in their eyes, both Leeland and Grace stood together as a beautifully married couple. The euphoric feeling that swarmed me when I saw how happy that I had made them made my heart swell with pride. My actions had made the world a better place for once and it made me smile.

Not too long after, Liza contacted me with the interest of having me conduct a marriage ceremony for her and her girlfriend, Tisha. Since same-sex marriage was not legal in California at the time, I was their only option. I instantly agreed without any biases or judgment. I would never ostracize any individual for feeling a pure love towards another individual, regardless of their gender. Love in a free emotion that should be shared amongst all of us, it is one of the most positive and beautiful feelings we can ever experience. No man has the right to halter another man's destiny. So with an openly clear mind, one which many thought was half-baked, I went forth with the ceremony.

My love for Liza and her happiness was all that mattered and the wonderful conjoining of these two beautiful girls was priceless. Their love was felt everywhere that day. My soul suddenly felt a new purpose and all that I wanted to do was preach about the wonders of love. Anyone that felt the same way about their significant other as I did about Lana deserved my blessings and no law was going to prevent me from keeping the sanctity of that truth alive. Love had kept Lana and me solid for six great years and I soon saw love as a splendid gift that we can all give to our hearts.

So with love glowing all around me, I reestablished my valuable connection with Bobby. We had spent the last two months talking multiple times a day and now I was finally going to get to see him after nearly eight years. I had developed an immense level of guilt for never reaching out to him sooner and actually making it to his prison for a more fulfilling experience. Looking back to his first incarceration, I used to visit him monthly without fail and if I could not make it down there that month, I would write him to let him know that he was not doing his three year stint alone. On several occasions, I would even smuggle Bobby in some small dime bags of weed, giving no regard towards my own freedom, just wanting to do something special for my brother. Now, eight years later I could finally be there for him, the way that my aunt would have wanted it. The adrenaline that flowed through my veins while I was driving down to Corcoran was unreal, a complete natural high. I experienced a level of euphoria that I thought to be all but extinct and now here I was, standing outside the gates of a concrete fortress with a joyful heart.

After the lengthy process of checking me in, I hastily moved my way over to Table Six as directed by the correctional officer. In a last ditch effort to make my visit better, I stopped by a vending machine and bought Bobby a plethora of his favorite candies. Having lived the life of a recovering junkie, Bobby had found a new vice in the sweet addiction of sugar. His sweet-tooth was worse than that of an obese kid's on Halloween. When he finally came into the busy room, I watched his eyes dash back and forth in search of me, so I kept my head ducked down low to tease him for as long as possible. Once he spotted me we just erupted in laughter. With tears of laughter overflowing our eyes, we gave each other a heartwarming hug and sat down to converse.

Seeing Bobby in the flesh was incredible. He was a thick, solid man with an illustrious variety of tattoos that covered all of his body from the neck down. Everything about my brother had changed except for his eyes, eyes which contained a lifetime of pain. There was despair in his eyes than I had only witnessed in a select few people. Not only was he doing thirty-five years, but now the only person who made him believe that he might one day get out was gone and he never had a chance to say goodbye. He asked me question after question about his mom and with every answer his demeanor grew more and more relaxed.

When the conversation was not revolved around his mother, we discussed the remainder of his prison time and the new law politicians were trying to get passed. Apparently, it would overturn the three strikes law which had put Bobby there in the first place. Never once did Bobby expect any pity for himself, he only expressed the lucid nightmare he could never wake up from. He had a record with no counts of violence against him, just a misled youth whose addictions had pushed him straight down the path of crime and consequence. So with the anticipations of a new law and the promise that I would never leave his side again, we said our goodbyes and the visit was over. The last look on his face was a disappointed smile since he knew that as soon as the guard walked him out, his grim reality set back in.

Once outside of the prison, I stumbled blindly to my car with a gut-wrenching pain throughout my body. Every breath of the arid, ninety degree air made the pain grow stronger. Leaving Bobby behind in that legal concentration camp did not feel right in any perspective that I looked at it. The least amount of time that he could serve was thirty-five years and this was for a man who did not steal a single item or physically harm a single soul. Murderers, molesters and rapist surrounded him and were serving less time. This is one flaw in our society that will never make sense to me, never.

Being back at home was not any better and became a very hectic place for me to live. Melissa and Aaron were next to impossible to control and Juliano was constantly upset that he was not the prized youngest child anymore. Whenever disappointment lingered in the air, I went back to my signature move and spent too much money on pointless stuff, but this time it did not work and I was dumbfounded. Money was always my failsafe solution for any problem and now it was getting me nowhere. So when things got too tense at the house, I would ditch my burdens and make haste towards the casinos.

Once there, I could sink shamefully into my favorite cursed video poker machine and bury my fear and worries in the form of twenty dollar bills. No matter how much truth and enlightenment I sought for in that machine, I soon came to the point where even winning left me feeling hollow and inapt. I knew damned well that I had a dangerous gambling problem, but I put all of my efforts into hiding it. The only person who could see through my charade was Lana and she was not entertained a single bit. However, her love for me overpowered any hostile feelings and I used this to my advantage. The guilt would often weigh down on me so greatly that I would force myself away from the casinos and spend all of my allocated gambling funds on whatever knick-knacks Lana and the kids desired. Deep down I knew this abstinence from gambling would not last and it distraught me to know that I was forever enslaved to a damn machine. I was truly pathetic.

With me being so self-absorbed in my own world, Lana did an amazing job at stepping up and giving Melissa and Aaron the love that they needed. I know my aunt was watching down from Heaven with pride over the amount of love they received, but I still struggled to accept them the way that I did Juliano. In no way were they bad children or unlovable, they simply confused me beyond hope. Melissa and Aaron were any parents' ideal children, but my lack of faith and biases pushed me right back into the loving arms of alcohol. Alcohol had a nasty grip on me that gave me a false sense of belief that I could still function normally in society, when in true reality I was putting twice the amount of work on Lana. Yet despite the amount of slack Lana had to pick up, she never lost her composure and saw every job through to the end. To make her grandeur even greater, she would fill my head with the reassuring thoughts that I was en route for an upswing and this darkness would soon be shined upon with a blessed light. Lana was my strength and my foundation, everything that I needed to keep my goals in focus.

Every morning I was awoken by a terrible feeling of guilt in my stomach, one that ceased to subside until I slept again. This guilt was caused by my moral conflict between keeping the kids in respects to Karen or the hopscotch of Foster Care homes that were in store for them. The voice in my head that reminded me that this was too much of a burden would constantly drown out the voice that praised me for the positive difference I was making in these kid's lives. I found the guilt to weigh too heavenly on me and when even the casinos neglected to satisfy, I made my way down south to visit Bobby. However, the high that I would experience through my visits with him was swiftly thwarted by the bottomless depression that overwhelmed me every time I left him behind, alone and abandoned.

I started to feel helpless at both ends of the spectrum with no glimmer of hope in sight and no control of my emotions. If I was not screaming my lungs out into the wind, then I was in a pathetic fetal position with a reservoir of tears in the cups of my hands. Furthermore, if I was not cemented to the third video poker machine from the left at the Horizon Casino, then I was either drunker than a freshman sorority girl or higher than the entire audience of a Willie Nelson concert. Inside my soul, I was every bit of a wreck that I deserved to be, yet on the surface, I never could have looked happier. Any outsider's perspective of us with all of our money and costly possessions would have thought nothing about our daily living.

Then again, behind closed doors we had everything we wanted in our lives except for happiness. Lana had finally reached the point where the twenty-four hour headache that I caused her was way too much and she demanded for me to re-visit with a doctor. The thought of seeing a specialist made me feel weak and vulnerable, but I agreed and was soon prescribed an anti-anxiety pill. So after a few short weeks of regular dosage, I actually started to feel focused and collected again, which even inspired me to try taking a few days off from alcohol. Much to my surprise, the absence of alcohol actually improved my social demeanor. I still deeply resented the fact that I had to take a pill to be happy, but it did prevent my sporadic outbursts and that boosted my drab mood. Being positive was all that mattered, well, that and the playoffs.

There was no possible way that I could be dismal and depressed when the Yankees were up by two games against the Red Sox and playing strong. This was one night when I could certainly take a break from not drinking. By the time that the Yankees' nineteenth run had scored, I was well into the double-digits of both beers and shots of tequila. Now it was time to go out on the town and party. Lana and I made it to a friend's house where apparently I had continued to celebrate via binge drinking. This night was truly perfect down to the last detail, which consisted of a completely free house to come home to since all of the kids were with a babysitter. Knowing they were under good supervision gave me the green light to drink myself into oblivion. As I have written countless times before, I am a bona fide alcoholic, always have been and always will be.

So the party continued and by six o'clock in the morning, I awoke alone and desperate with a searing headache in a well lit room on a cement bench with a thirty-five hundred dollar bail for domestic abuse attached to my name. With great effort, I sat up and began to reassemble the puzzle of the previous night's events in my head. Unfortunately, the only image that I could recall was the pain, confusion and disappointment that resided in Lana's eyes as I knocked her to the ground while tearing the living room apart in one of my sporadic rage sessions. *What the fuck had I done?*

My future with Lana was smoldered into ashes. My actions had finally come full circle and I had to shamefully accept the consequences. There was no chance whatsoever that she would forgive me and I could not blame her. All of this time I knew that she was better off without me, but I ignored the signs and continued with my malicious habits. I was a coward amongst men. No real man would ever use physical force against his wife, intended or not, let alone any woman at that. I was no man at all and I knew that alcohol was the main culprit for my disrespectful ways. I had always known this in the back of my mind, but after seeing the way that it affected others I willingly decided it was time to change. What I needed to do was put all of my energy and efforts into regaining Lana's trust and love. I wanted her to forgive and forget because I wanted to be forgiven and forget the horrific atrocity that I had committed.

So after posting the thirty-five hundred dollar bail, I had to appear in front of a judge before I was finally able to go. The judge spared little time in heavily ridiculing me over my past and stated that one more severe offense of any nature would land me in jail for some serious time. After a lengthy lecture, the judge settled my case with twelve months of anger management classes, some hefty fines and a slap on the wrist. To be honest, considering that I had not harmed Lana on any serious levels, just a brash turn and knock to the ground, I had been let off for once with what I deemed to be a suitable punishment from the judiciary system.

So I approached the anger management classes with a pompous arrogance that I knew all of the answers, even more than the counselor, Mark, who was in charge. Although after several classes, I began to see my issues from a more well-rounded perspective. Even though what Mark was saying made complete sense in multiple ways, I still felt as though he was casting an additional judgment on me because of my actions involving Lana. His self-righteous attitude made me feel like the scum of the Earth for how I had lived my life. I had no choice but to shut my mouth and open my ears, and once I did, I started to hear and understand my dark side. The fear, the violence and the anger all made sense as I listened more. I now clearly wanted to change and make right with my life like I should have been doing over the past thirty years. I was jaded of myself and starving for a new beginning.

I decided to be confident in my decisions and create a momentum shift for myself, so I started by kicking myself off of the medications cold-turkey without any advice from a professional. This proved to be a costly mistake and within a week I was once again a deranged lunatic. My erratic behavior was right back to where it used to be, and with a vengeance. I had no choice but to re-consult the doctor, who scolded me for disregarding his professional advice and put me back on some stronger medications. After several weeks of disciplined dosage, I was back to a stable state of mind and willing to let it bring out the best in me. I took a step back and analyzed what I was doing with my life. I was juggling the combination of managing a business, providing for my family and the never ending quest for the house I promised to buy.

I was well in over my head, but I kept my focus and integrity for fear that I would in some way let Karen and Bobby down. They had put all of their trust and faith in me to do the right thing with the house and the kids, and for me to abandon my duties would be the ultimate disgrace. The guilt was lurking in my shadow every moment of every day and the only way to keep it at bay was to dedicate all of my time to others. In my mind, the more that I did now in the present, the more that my deviances of the past would be erased. As optimistic of a concept as this seemed, my vision was distanced from the real reality and my world was far from salvageable. Lana was still in my life in physical form but her soul was no longer with it. My actions had left no trust in her heart and it left me feeling deserted and broken. Karma had tripped me into the waters of self-misery and I was drowning in the consequences of my actions.

My only outlet was in the unlikely presence of a childhood friend, Oscar, who I had been in contact with off and on over the years. His life had put him in the path of a life's sentence for being caught with a kilogram of methamphetamines in California and was looking to serve fifteen to twenty years in prison. After escaping into the underground society, Oscar had created a new life for himself in the suburbs of Chicago. Finding myself in a catch-twenty-two situation between guilt and duty, I reached out to him in a desperate attempt to find my answers. Most of the time, an individual would find it abstract to approach a felon as a counselor, but it was the straight-to-the-point characteristics of Oscar that I needed to bring me clarity. I invited him to come spend some time in Lake Tahoe and he was more than willing to accept.

Seeing Oscar again after so many years was exactly what I needed and for a brief period of time, I did not feel so alone. Even though Oscar had made a success out of himself, he still showed vast wonderment towards my life and all of the things that I had done. His genuine interest made me feel like my life was not as bad as I had made it out to be. He divulged to me his own struggles in letting go of the past and progressing forward. He then went on to explain that in his eyes, each of my efforts to resurrect my soul was all done in vain. The misdeeds of my past could not be abolished if I was still only thinking about myself. I spent no time developing a rebuttal, for it would only have been wasted energy. I brought Oscar here to give me the truth and he did just that.

As an illustration, knowing that the atmosphere was growing dreary, Oscar started recalling the times that we had as juveniles when we used to take refuge in the back of his El Camino. Our conversations would often revolve around the world outside of Los Angeles and the dream of a better life. He then stated that I had indeed discovered my dream and that I was so self-absorbed in hosting my pity party that I was blind to see it. He was absolutely right and the only real problem in my life was my own selfish behavior.

Everything that I had done from a delinquent teen until now was completely drenched in ethnocentrism. I had taken from my parents when I should have been giving, I mentally and physically abused the only two women who ever took the chance to love me and I neglected my children to the point where they would have preferred a life in an orphanage. I had hustled both friends and strangers, I had conned the system in everyway possible and when it was all said and done, all I wanted to do was give it all back. My material possessions no longer mattered, I only wanted my aunt back, my brother out of prison, my parents' trust and Lana's love. Above all else though, I just wanted to be forgiven. Despite how dramatic I made my repentance out to be, I could not shake who I was and all of the malevolent antics that I had committed. I had no option but to accept the realization that I could not go back in time and change things, all that I could do was be where I needed to be in the present and that was with my family.

All of this time the answers were in the salvation of my kids and Lana, who were in desperate need of a reciprocal love and likewise, their love was the release that I needed to escape from the murky dungeon that was my soul. With their support backing me, I was able to put all of my efforts into fulfilling my obligations. I made visiting my brother a quality experience and did so with regular schedule. Melissa and Aaron were getting my complete attention and the hyperactivity actually began to decrease. Quality time with them was very beneficial for all of us.

With Oscar gone but leaving me with that one hundred percent attitude only a motivational guru could provide, I took to the world with a more passive mentality. I approached my anger management classes with an inquisitive mind in an attempt to learn what rooted my manic behavior and the hatred that led it to the point of causing black and blue. I made a cognitive effort to correct my ways in lieu of channeling my disputes with Lana in manners other than physical abuse. I tried to debate the difference between physical abuse and physical defense and Mark would remind me that one more violent outburst would land me right back in jail with limited contact with my family. As an additional kick while I was down, he asked me who would protect my family from me if I could not even control myself.

Mark had broken down all of my invincible defenses with his brutal truth and no rebuttal existed. At that moment, I knew that the course of my life had changed and no longer was violence the means to an end. The guilt that I would carry if my actions put me in the same situation as Bobby would be tremendous. Many trials still stood in my future but I knew with confidence that I would never find resolution through misdirected hate and empowerment, or the white of my knuckles. I learned then and there that the one true way to bring peace was through the heart. Within every cell in my body, it shames me to know that it took me thirty-six years to learn the lessons that most individuals inherit naturally through common sense, but I had a lot to be thankful for and once again it came in the form of Lana and the kids. There was no denying that things were going to get better, after all, with all that we had went through, how could they not? Anger became an emotion of distant memories and with a suggested decrease in dosage I was relieved to be back to the non-medicated Tony.

With steady patience in both my classes and one-on-one visits with Mark, I accepted that my life was still going to push me to my limits, but as long as I only focused on the good in everything, I would always be progressing forward. I replaced fear with health and put my gym membership, which was lacking much attention, to great use. I decided that a healthy soul could only flourish in a healthy temple that was my physical. With my health in check, I had more time to reflect on my past and present and find regret in the fact that I listened to the wrong people for too many years. Instead of taking heed to the advice that Gerard provided, I accepted false prophet from the forty-year-old burnouts who told me that I had all of the time in the world. They were so very wrong. I should have taken the time when I was fifteen to make everything out of nothing, instead of nothing out of everything.

All of my sins started at the ripe age of fifteen and they dwelled within me until I felt as though my soul had ceased to exist, a mere zombie to the world. Too many consequences occurred before I understood that at any given point in my life

I had a chance to regain my soul. I was just too blinded by false lights to see it. A righteous soul is not something that can be bought but deceitfully can be sold. Regaining that lost soul back again is possible as long as an individual retraces his or her steps to the crossroads of life and marches full-heartedly in the right direction. I was extremely fortunate that I was presented with that opportunity to accept my faults and move triumphantly towards a life of satisfaction. So many beautiful and worthy individuals that I have known never got that second chance and I owe it to them. I owe it to my parents, I owe it to my children, I owe it to Lana, but most of all I owe it to myself. An individual can never learn to love the world until they can learn to love themselves first.

Ten Years Gone

With the feelings of fear and anger subdued and left behind me, I was finally free to put all of my attention into the future and its new possibilities. Lana's and my main priority became fulfilling our promise to my aunt and purchasing a respectable home to grow old in. Aunt Karen's only dream for us was to live the life of a normal American family and making her dream a reality would give me the chance to finally let her go, for her to forever rest in peace. I was offered quality advice from both family and friends, but the only words I chose to hear were those from a select few of my clients who had made a quick buck in buying and selling houses. I tried to follow their instructions which they made to sound ridiculously easy, yet if I had any form of an education whatsoever I would have realized just how difficult it was. So after a lazy attempt at introductory real estate, I quit that foolish dream and kept focusing on buying my own house.

Lake Tahoe was rapidly growing into a higher income community, so Lana and I decided that the best course of action was to make a trip up to Washington to purchase a home. In my beliefs, as long as I bought a home, my aunt would be satisfied, even if it was in another state. Our quest for a home came to any amazing end when we found the perfect three-bedroom house within our price range. I gave little regard to the fact that this ideal home was nearly a thousand miles away and that using it as a vacation rental until we could pay it off was not going to work. In my fantasy vision, this was the end to all of my struggles towards a much anticipated better life. Then, once again, reality set in and I was forced to pay notice to the two property leases that I already had back in Lake Tahoe with the house and the office.

I quickly realized that I did not have the discipline to make all of this work. To boot, my lack of intelligence and patience put me further into despair and I once again found my salvation at the bottom of a bottle. More than religion and family, alcohol was the one thing on this planet that I knew would always be there. A beer or three every morning assured me that no matter how intense my day got, I could still keep a lazy grin across my face and it was that grin which I felt was the key to boosting my morale.

With spirits lifted, I could actually tolerate work and family for a greater period of time, but the one thing that I always lacked was consistency. I failed to maintain a consistent work ethic yet still complained off-and-on that I was not getting what was due to me. I saw all of the luxuries my clients had, the comfort my parents had, the stability my sister had and I wanted the same for me and my family. However, what I was blind to see was that the one thing they all had was consistency and the ability to see things through. All that I had towards my credit was empty promises, a spurious smile and a weak handshake. Soon, many of my clients took pity on me and provided some financial assistance. I had stooped to the next level above panhandling in a last ditch effort to keep my life on pace.

Lana was utterly clueless that everything had just made a turn for the worse. She was so preoccupied with working double-digit hours each day and believing that I was taking care of all the business aspects that she failed to see the truth. The guilt corroded my heart and the burden of my lies had finally turned my dark soul black. Feeling the weight of the world crushing me ever so slowly, I sulked back in my chair and drank my troubles away. I soon found that waking up still drunk was the only way that I could function and this was a serious misconception. There was no conceivable resurrection from the freefall that I was in, my life was reaching terminal velocity and the Earth, as reality, was approaching with great celerity. The business was a disaster as long as I was drunk and involved. So I soon decided to add Vicodin in with my daily diet of alcohol in a desperate attempt to numb my mind from the world around me.

With bill collectors hot on our trail, our only solution was to change locations to a household more within our frugal budget. The constant change was detrimental on the kids, never giving them a stable residence to call home. To me, staying one step ahead of failure was more important than my kids' proper upbringing. The kids were constantly butting heads and the strain was rapidly taking its toll on Lana and me. After my arrest, Lana had taken pity on my abandoned self and took me back in, but the admiration and good nature were nowhere to be found. In her eyes, I was just a co-worker who helped her take care of the kids. All hours of the day were spent in absurdly uncomfortable silence and only the screams of the children could echo any life through our stagnant hallways.

Within six months we had relocated to yet another house and struggled to stabilize everything once again. However with four reckless young bachelors living next door who loved to party, snowboard and have bonfires every night, things were going to be interesting. I thought for sure that this was going to be a perfect fit until it occurred to me that these guys were all in their twenties and that I was now the forty-year-old burnout.

The guys consisted of Nick, Steve, Mike and Zac. Nick was a boisterous shit-talker from the God-forsaken city of Boston and our conversations would focus so intensely around our baseball rivalry that no hour of the day was safe from ridicule. Steve and Mike, the brothers, were a couple of transplants from the central coast of California who brought with them the casual and carefree beach attitude that was infectious to all of those around them. They also embodied that competitive brotherly attitude to push everything that they did to the limits, and it proved to be very entertaining. Zac was a Texas Hold 'Em prodigy from Washington and with him constantly online and at the casinos playing, it rejuvenated my love for poker that I had so recently banished. I considered myself lucky to have such a positive influence for my gambling living next door. When the times were good, the times were great.

On Saint Patrick's Day I had awoken early and made my way to my favorite video poker machine and within three hours I was three thousand dollars richer. I arrived back home to all of the guys outside shot-gunning beers and acting in a solemn, relatively depressed demeanor. Something had to be up because this was nothing close to how they normally behaved. I had them toss me a beer and then asked them why they were so troubled on such a special drinking holiday. They mentioned that they had plans to spend Saint Patrick's Day down in the Bay Area but their driver was too lazy and hung over and that none of them could drive. Without any hesitation, I told them that they had thirty minutes to grab their things because I was going to take them down there with all of the expenses paid, including the hotel. I felt euphoric at how a little benevolence towards others with my riches could make the world of difference and it proved to be one of those insane getaways that I will always remember.

When money was not being spent on frivolous excursions, I spent a lot of my time next door sitting around the fire pit and telling stories. I would feel ashamed inside as I regaled them with my exploits in crime and failure. However, my stories were well received and the younger brother, Mike, seemed to show a continual level of interest in what I had to say. He mentioned that I gave him a sense of who he did not want to be and that he could experience the rough side of life vicariously through my stories. Mike was constantly telling me that I should actually take the time to write my stories down in a journal and maybe I could even make a publication out of them someday. His idea was truly brilliant, but in all reality it made no sense. After all, I was a habitual liar and did not deserve anything in life of merit.

In order to be honest about my failures, my addictions, my pathetic behavior and my intolerance towards everybody, I was going to have to put all of my shame and humility outside of myself. Mike reasoned with me, explaining that my trials and errors could be a powerful tool in helping kids who are currently where I used to be and are in need of that extra motivation to choose the right path. I laughed at how crazy he sounded, but honestly, I loved his ambition and ability to turn a dream into a reality. This was not something that I was in any position for, nor did I want to go divulging my mishaps to the world. For me to write a novel was ridiculous, I was a lonely vagabond jumping on a train to nowhere.

Mike would not stop reminding me about what a great opportunity this was to get my skeletons out of the closet and live a guilt-free life without the nervous tension that shame creates. So for the sake of argument, I agreed to start writing. Truth is, I had tried to write several times in the past, but writing with intent to publish was an astronomical commitment, something that I knew nothing about. So with a new stressor in my life, I just did what I always did when I grew claustrophobic and made immediate plans to see the Michigan Trio who were back home in Michigan.

Lana had no objections towards me leaving town and it was a stake in my heart to know that our time together was crumbling before me. Instead of staying firm and doing everything within my power to keep my family united, I thought only about myself and a trip to Michigan was just what I needed to put my mind at ease. I promised Lana up and down that when I returned I would make everything back to the way it was when we were happy. I was the King of Fools, making promises that I knew damn well I could not keep. There was nothing Lana could do except for cry as she realized that she alone was now in charge of juggling all three of the kids and a twenty-four hour cleaning service.

I knew that my actions were wrong and hurtful, but a case of Bud Light allowed me to survive in complete denial. Once I reached that level of inebriation, it was impossible to escape without a solid level of focus and persistence. These were two things that I lacked completely. Drugs and alcohol had weakened my spirit to the point where I shut myself off to any and everybody. Nothing that was part of my life mattered, not my business, not my family, not my promises.

The night before I was scheduled to leave, I received a call that a friend of mine, Kimmy, had been found dead from a prescription drug overdose. My body went numb, emitting no vibes of either angst or acceptance, just a blank look and a collapsed soul. After several seconds of thought, I raced to my cabinet for Vicodin and then the refrigerator for beer. I was still alive and she was not, and that was the extent of my mourning.

Depressed and quiet, I chose to still take my flight and landed in Michigan where I wasted no time in abusing my body with pills and booze. Seeing Tom, Don and Wes was a great remedy for my woes. I assured them whole-heartedly that all was well in my life. My stories were so well rehearsed that in my state of intoxication even I was starting to believe them. Deep down I knew that I had no right to be there, but I continued to drown my conscience with a fermented downer.

The guys had a surprise for me and pulled out tickets for all four of us to catch a Yankees game in New York. They decided that one of them could drive and this allowed me to continue doing what I did best, consume mass quantities of beer. I can honestly say that my body has been drunk throughout all of the states that connect Michigan to New York and I have no recollection of any of them. Attending Yankee Stadium was one of the highest dreams on my checklist of life ever since I was a little kid, but this was not the way that I had envisioned it. I always had dreamed and visualized myself sitting in those sacred seats with either my father or my son, yet neither of the two were an option since Gerard was at work and Juliano was at school.

I suddenly understood the selfishness in my decision to take this self-reflecting vacation and I spent the majority of the game pondering my actions.

By the sixth inning, the guilt became too unbearable so I demanded that we left the stadium and headed back home. Reluctantly, my friends followed with me and the long drive to Detroit was spent getting even more wasted. I should have spent that endless amount of time focusing on how I could reverse the course of my misdirection, but instead I only found solace through empty bottles clanking back and forth against each other. The next morning, I caught the first flight out of Detroit and once I was home, no time was spared in recognizing the consequences of my mounting failures.

Abruptly, there was a knocking at the door and it was three men from the company that had financed my television. They said that they did not mean to impose and they just needed to take their television back. Without a choice, the four of us walked into the living room where Juliano was quietly enjoying his cartoons. He had no idea what was going on as the three men unplugged and walked away with the fifty-five inch television he was watching. I found myself speechless as my son stared at me with confusion over why I was letting all of this happen. I attempted to form my thoughts into acceptable words but did so with great failure, very suitable for my overall existence. I turned to Lana for advice but she could not even look me in the eyes. With sheer disgust for myself and everything associated with me, I marched upstairs, popped two pills, grabbed my keys and headed for the casinos.

All of my addictions had finally triumphed over me and had officially taken the last of what little good I still had left. The time had come when all of my favors had been exhausted and every last dime had been borrowed, so now all that I could do was start giving my possessions back. I was evicted from my office and the bank was about to repossess my car, when somehow I was able to finagle my way into leasing a great GMC truck. I was merely postponing the inevitable.

I took a trip with my new truck to visit with my folks and when Gerard first laid eyes on my truck, he was beyond amazed. He complimented me on how successful I must be doing and shook my hand with the most warm, comfortable grip that I had ever felt. Gerard then commented at how he could never afford a truck this luxurious. I sulked inside at how big of a fraud I was. Gerard had worked without relent for the past forty years, yet I was still the one with the new GMC. Hearing the praise that Gerard gave me, even though he was ignorant to the truth, forever destroyed any joy that I had with my truck. I was ashamed at the false success that I had made myself out to be.

All of my addictions had dug me into a hole so deep that not even light made a presence. My visits with Bobby were scarce and dismal. He had put so much raw faith in me and I failed to live up to my expectations. The only thing that he asked was that I continued to stick by his side. I swore to him with all sincerity that I would always, no matter how difficult times got, remain as his right-hand man. He still believed in me and that quaint little shimmer of trust was enough to make me believe in myself once again. Bobby was the stronger man, the brother that I could never lose pride for.

I would leave the prison with the same feeling a spiritual man has when he leaves his place of sanctuary. However, that sense of tranquility did not last once I arrived back in Lake Tahoe and back into the routine of legal mind-altering substances. Despite how numb my soul was, it still did not bypass the harsh reality that I was immersed in. Lana had successfully found a way to avoid me at all hours of the day and I knew that rekindling this love was like trying to light a match in a hurricane. Even though I was not allowed to see them, I knew that Lana's sparkling blue eyes were as cold as cemetery stone.

I was at work late one evening when I received a call from Lana, explaining to me that she was leaving me for good. If this were two years in the past, I would have been overly dramatic in some sense and either flipped out to the point of intimidating her, or even worse, physically convinced her to stay. Yet now I was the conservative Tony and my passive thoughts understood her reasoning, so I let her path take its course. She then changed the pace completely and informed me that Juliano had run away. I went into a class five panic mode and slammed the phone down without any exiting salutation.

I rushed home, grabbed Lana and brought her with me to help search through the neighborhood. With failed results, we returned home to a squad car parked in our driveway with Juliano in the back seat. I explained the situation to the police officers and thanked them for returning my son. This became a pivotal moment for me because I consciously chose to be cooperative and actually show respect towards the law.

I was relieved to know that Juliano was safe and as we sat down as a family, he exploded into a rant about his viewpoints towards all of the negligence. I was trapped with nowhere to run, no pills to pop or alcohol to binge, just a furious twelve year old. The one person that I loved more than anything in the world was blatantly expressing his disappointment in me. I wanted to argue my point but that would have only further proven him right, that I could not handle anyone calling me out on my flaws. Cornered and stunned, all that I could muster was a quivering but genuine promise to make the effort to right my wrongs. With the house finally dark and quiet, I made my way upstairs and cried myself to sleep.

I awoke the next morning with an empty feeling of fault blended with dishonor. I stumbled slowly downstairs where I saw Lana packing the last of her, Melissa's and Aaron's belongings into the car. I spoke not a single word to her and just continued to drink my glass of apple juice. I then glanced over at the calendar that she had left on the wall and it was circled with today's date, January 4. Today was our ten year anniversary. By the time I made it outside, all that I saw was an empty driveway. Ten years were gone, and so was she.

Lord Giveth and the
Lord Shall Taketh

*B*eing alone for the first time since I was fifteen gave me more than enough time to contemplate what I had done and the series of events that had brought me to where I was. With Lana gone, everyday felt as though I were in solitary confinement. The only two people that I had to look out for were Juliano and I, and that was very unsettling. I had taken Lana and her unfailing forgiveness for granted, so after much thought I caved in and gave her a call. Much to my relief, she answered, but she was standing firm in her decision and there was an obvious air of liberty in her voice. Being free of me was probably the happiest moment in her life. Lana was going to be able to put all of her focus towards Melissa and Aaron and give them the attention that they had always deserved. With me out of their lives, they were finally free to live without the fear of a drunken dad and his sporadic outbursts.

So with Lana and the kids on their own life's journeys, I was able to put one hundred percent of my spare time into staying busy with Juliano. My son brought me the peace and love that I needed to keep my focus throughout these dire times. The trials of my life were many, but Juliano held firm in his dedication to me by being the model son and I made an effort to be the model father as well. Material possessions and their lack of presence did not matter, as long as I still had Juliano by my side to keep me on the straight and narrow path of success. This was a great load of stress for a twelve year old, but he gave me something to believe in and I went with it.

When my time was not spent hanging out with Juliano, I was next door with the guys finding new ways to make jackasses out of themselves. Mike would always greet me the same way, with some sarcastic comment about when we were going to get this book started and finished so that he could get paid and not have to run an extension cord from their house to my garage just to keep their television, stereo and computer running. His randomness always entertained me. Mike knew of my current hardships and insisted that this was the prime opportunity for me to focus on my writing. I tried to argue that I was not smart enough to write a book since I had no education whatsoever, but he quickly shot back that writing had always came naturally to him and that he had found the perfect solution. He claimed that he could take the words that I wrote down through free association, the skeleton, and he could structure them into credible book form, thus adding the meat and the flesh to the bare skeleton and leaving a true work of art for the world to see. In awe of such brilliance, I gave Mike a solid handshake and told him that this might actually happen.

Mike's persistence had pushed me to the point where I was through with just thinking and talking about writing, and actually started doing it. I figured that my life could not get any worse, so I might as well put all of my efforts into this. I turned my alcohol and pill-popping free time into moments where I could reflect on my past and transcribe my thoughts onto paper. Everything seemed to flow out wonderfully, but as soon as I read over what I just had written, I grew exceedingly depressed and threw those pages into the garbage. There they would remain until I looked at Juliano and felt shameful for setting myself up for such failure.

I would look at him and feel that he deserved to hear the truth about his father. So to clear my mind of the clusterfuck that was my thoughts, I would take Juliano outside to play some catch.

Over the past year, Juliano had honed his baseball skills in so well that he had turned into an immaculate baseball player. Juliano even found himself on the front page of the sports section and this was one of the proudest moments of my life. Pride was one of those emotions that I could never really enjoy until I saw the happiness that my son's accomplishments brought him. Just by watching him going through the mechanics of baseball, I was able to see a dramatic change in his maturity. He was growing into the ideal young man that I myself never had the patience or ability to be.

With Juliano being the focus of my change, I soon found myself wanting to be a symbol of self-advancement in his eyes too. I wanted to make my next thirty-nine years as clean and healthy as possible so that I could someday play catch with him when he was my age. I was not going to fail him by abandoning my goals and this time I was determined to see things through. A vice-free existence could be just the key to winning back the trust of my parents, my clients and Lana, all of whom had aged greatly due to stress induced by me. I no longer desired the life of an addict who had to lie, cheat and steal in order to get ahead. I really wanted to have a life to be proud of, to be involved in something that others accepted and admired.

I had met a girl who I shall abstain from crediting with a name. Knowing that I would never see it again, I loaned her several thousand dollars to help with her rent in a desperate attempt to feel better about myself. The knieving nature of this girl made my eyes open wide to the ways of my past. Seeing how blind she was to her own actions made me find the breaking point in my own life. I could no longer live in denial of who I was. I was not a good father to any of my children. I never got to be an influence for Angel or Daniel, and Nicole was right in their shadow. The reality started to sink in and I knew that if I did not make an immediate effort to change, Nicole and Juliano would be as distant as Angel and Daniel.

My intentions to stay in touch with Angel were not always put aside. I did come in contact with her several times throughout the month and I truly could not believe that she was still excited to talk to me after our falling out during the previous year. I loved her endlessly, the same with Daniel, but could never be consistent with them. However, Angel never failed to keep giving me chances and the more I paid attention to the woman that she was becoming, the more I noticed how she had grown to be one of the funniest women I have ever met. Angel was her own original soul with an amazing personality and a huge heart. I was proud to be a part of her. She was the kind of girl that if I was a kid around her age, I would love to be one of her friends. Her attitude was infectious, leaving everyone who was blessed enough to be near her feeling positive and good. The only person who could break that perfect vibe was me. Every promise that I ever made just foreshadowed the inevitable let down and all that I could attribute it to was my addictions and the person they made me be. I pray that one day I can provide the consistency both Angel and Daniel have sought for in me for over the past two decades. They both are far too beautiful to lose.

So in an attempt to settle my worries, I had contacted Benny and sought guidance through the trials of his ways. Here he was, being pressed to give advice to the same man whose first two kids he had spent the past seventeen years raising. I was the epitome of the word pathetic. Benny was gracious enough to offer his words of encouragement to me on a daily basis, keeping me strong as I worked harder and harder to be an involved parent. I needed to prove that my involvement with my kids could be a positive thing and all of my efforts thus far were not for waste.

Benny went through his own share of struggles, but always managed to keep a positive demeanor in providing his family with the care that they needed. He and I had been so much alike as children and it amazed me at how different we were as adults.

Benny just had more willpower, and was able to eliminate drugs from his life by the time he was twenty. Even though drugs were never the first of my choices when it came to mind-altering substances, they always seemed to make a cameo appearance soon after I took my first drink. Alcohol was the number one culprit for ninety-nine point nine eight percent of my mistakes and the only prevalent reason to stop this abuse was the fact that alcohol was slowly but surely killing me.

Benny also called note to my pathological lying and linked my alcoholism to more than half of the false promises that passed through my slurring lips. His knowledge of me was flawless and I soon found myself anticipating his call everyday, which he always managed to do. Benny was a man of his word, everything that I strived to be. Far too many of my years were shrouded in hate towards Benny when all of this time he was an agent of love and respect. *How could I not cherish a man who has been the amazing father that I neglected to be?* Angel was dead right a long time ago when she expressed to me that I was that type of man that could never be trusted and that was a moment of true shame and humility when I heard those words from my own daughter. Disappointment was the one word most commonly used when referring to me as a person. From my grade school years until now, any individual that has ever given me faith and love was ultimately left vulnerable and disappointed.

So with a new sense of direction and focus from my close brother Benny, I had the strength to finally flush the pills from my system and concentrate on abolishing alcohol from my everyday existence. Putting the bottle down forever was the ultimate dream, but its cold, firm grip on me proved to be more than I could handle. I refused to accept counseling or Alcoholics Anonymous as an option since I felt that the accomplishment would not be fulfilling unless I did it all myself. I was the alcoholic who almost died twenty years earlier and it was up to me to overcome my adversity. My only sense of Zen in this time of darkness was the blind faith of knowing that there was a light in the distance and I was going to find it.

The first gleam of light came soon after when I met a positive, energetic man by the name of Stasha. Stasha went to the same gym that I had been attending and spared little time in approaching me to see if I needed a "spotter". Since I always went to the gym alone, I never had anyone to workout with. Stasha stood at six feet tall with a lean, muscular build that made him look more like thirty-five years old instead of the fifty that he actually was. I had no problem at all befriending him. I told him about how my fears over my age and weight were starting to wear my self-esteem thin, and that it was affecting my family as well. Stasha had an incredible outlook on life and mentioned that as soon as I was confident in myself, then I could be confident in the world around me. I loved his positive mentality and immediately looked up to him as my mentor. I found myself doing a lot less talking and a lot more listening. I respected everything about Stasha. He had a strong marriage and two well-behaved teenage boys, all of whom he loved endearingly. The respect and grace that he showed for me was that of an honest man, a strong man and a wise man, and these were all characteristics that I desired for in myself.

I have taken a lot of what Stasha has taught me and integrated it into my efforts to love and be there for my children. Juliano has grown to test every nerve in my body, and I can clearly see the conflict in myself between leaving who I was and becoming who I am meant to be. I can then look at Juliano and see how much of me is now a part of him, which truly scares me half to death. I pray that he never has to repeat my sins and experience the sorrows that have been forced upon me. My beautiful son is way better than that. These prayers to God were extremely difficult for me and my focus was often tested by insecure thoughts of vulnerability, but I wanted nothing more than peace for my children. I prayed for a life of happiness, love, success and longevity. These were and still are part of my daily prayers.

I would talk with Stasha about my improving thoughts and

he listened and corrected me without humility. I took all of his advice and seeing his success with his family gave me a whole new picture of how mine could be. The impact he has had on me was a Godsend and ours is a friendship that I will forever hold dear. My thoughts were changing so quickly and I was seeing how immature my life had been up until now. Partying at my age was not where my priorities needed to be. Besides, I never knew how to party, just rage, and a respectful night of minimum drinking was never an option. This life of outlandish behavior was growing exceedingly flat and I wanted to change so that I could see how much of a positive influence I could still be for my children. The one thing that I needed to engrave into my brain was consistency.

So with eyes wide open, I began to see the light that was all around me and I basked in its radiance. Melissa and Aaron, for one, were two beautiful souls that I was long deprived of. Being away from them made me yearn to be in their presence even more, and from the way that Juliano was acting in regards to them, I could tell that he felt the same. Lana was benevolent enough to let us spend limited time together and we made the best out of it, even if it was for only one hour per week. Seeing Lana again was not as detrimental to my sanity as I had expected and I was actually okay with just watching her sit there, self-absorbed in her own thoughts. I always knew that she deserved so much better than me and with the ghost of Lana's love no longer haunting me, I was starting to appreciate who I was for the first time since I was a kid.

I committed myself to doing the sober things in life that used to excite me as a youth and before I knew it, I was writing everyday throughout the day. The concept of writing a novel was slowly forming into a reality and I really wanted to see it through. There were no promises of success or fortune and that was fine by me, this book was my chance to do something good with my life and that was more than enough to sustain my motivation. I pondered on a daily basis at how long I could stay sober and I managed to stay sober during the day, but as soon as the sun nestled into the wilderness, the bottles were out again. With the temptations of alcohol looming over my shoulder, I decided my only sanctity was via a much needed vacation and for the first time ever, I actually chose to visit my parents, alone. With Juliano down in Las Vegas for Spring Break and Lana on a separate trip with her mom and the kids to Disneyland, I was free to do as I wished.

Seeing my parents was ten times better than I could have imagined. They astonishingly treated me less like a delinquent son and were pleased to welcome me into the family. Gerard decided that the best way for us to bond was over a series of beers down at his favorite dive bar and within the next two hours, we were well inebriated. With a loose and sanguine conscience, I comfortably told Gerard about my new interest in writing a novel regarding my derelictions and it was received with immense negativity. As the night progressed and the more that I spoke of my writings, the angrier Gerard became. By the end of the night, I was out on the street and banished from my parents' home for the heresy committed towards my family's name. Too many days passed before I could finally let that night go, but the more I wrote the more I realized that his reasoning for being irate was just. So with a humble heart, I accepted Gerard's advice and wrote with brutal honesty. I confessed all of my sins, all of my deceits and failures for the world to see with the hope that one day it could be for a greater good, a way to tell Gerard how much I love and appreciate him.

So while still down in Los Angeles and fuming over my squanders with Gerard, I called up my old friend Carmen to see if she was interested in spending some quality time together. She pleasantly obliged and we decided to make a break for Las Vegas. Along the way, Carmen began moaning and groaning, complaining about multiple symptoms ranging from her aching stomach to sporadic neck and back pains. I patiently begged for her to bear with it and that the luminous glow of Las Vegas would rejuvenate her. I soon discovered that she was not fooling around and three days into the trip I was rushing her back home. She was later admitted to the hospital with severe medical complications. Her conditions were diminishing so rapidly that her life expectancy was only thirty-six hours. I had never considered myself to be a superstitious man, but after all of the illness and death that I had experienced, I was starting to see myself as some sort of a walking jinx. Luckily, she was strong enough to recover fully from her illness. However, I did not enjoy how my vacation was going in the least bit, so I cut out in the middle of the night and returned to the solace that Lake Tahoe brought me. Somehow, Lake Tahoe seemed minute in its stressors when compared to the hustle and bustle of Los Angeles.

Lana, Phyllis and the kids arrived back in town a few days later with all smiles and I was ecstatic at how well their vacation had turned out. Sensing my honest intent, Lana offered to take Juliano and me down to see the Oakland Athletics, who were hosting the New York Yankees. Full of excitement, I quickly agreed to her amicable gesture and felt no tension towards treating Lana solely as a friend. A great sense of peace and tranquility overcame me as just the three of us sat there and enjoyed a wonderful evening at the ballpark, not to mention the Yankees won seven to two.

We awoke early the next morning and headed back to the fresh air of Lake Tahoe. A majority of the trip was spent listening to Lana talk about Phyllis and her lack of presence in my life, so she invited me to join the two of them for lunch and I agreed. We dropped Juliano off at Lana's house and then headed over to Phyllis' apartment which was only a few blocks away. In no way was the love rekindling between us, but being her friend was still more comfortable than being alone.

As we arrived, Lana ran inside to get her mom and I opted to just stay put and listen to Jim Morrison sing "Spanish Caravan". I turned the stereo up loud and reclined my seat back. Then, in the peripheral of my right eye, I caught a bolting shadow and a figure collapsing to the ground. I jumped out of my truck with urgency as I realized that it was Lana in a hysteric craze, crying incessantly and ripping handfuls of grass from the yard. As I tuned my hearing in on the foreign tongue that was being blurted amongst the sobbing, I heard the words "my beautiful mommy". Neighbors stood on their doorsteps and watched as I cradled Lana in my arms. After several minutes of a tear-drenched hug, I let Lana go and ran inside her mother's apartment.

I searched around the front room and kitchen before heading into the bedroom where my attention was immediately drawn towards the bathroom and a running shower. Three steps were all that it took for me to get a clear view of Phyllis' body halfway out of the shower. The horrific image barely made me flinch and all that I could mutter was "Why like this, Phyllis?" Aware of Lana's presence behind me, I darted directly to the shower curtain and ripped it down to cover Phyllis' exposed remnants. Lana screamed hysterically that she needed to try and wake her Mommy up, but I firmly held her back. I had seen enough souls pass before me to know the look that death leaves in an eye.

As I turned around and stared into Lana's eyes, I saw a degree of pain that I had not seen since the way Gerard reacted to his brother Joe. For the first time in years, I connected with someone else's sorrows. I wrapped my arms around Lana, feeling the intensity of her breaking heart beat heavily against mine.

After several hours of illustrating the day's events to the paramedics and police, I was finally able to get Lana away from that dark, cryptic atmosphere. By the time that we reached her house, she was remarkably mellow and collected, and she earnestly desired to reveal the unfortunate outcome of their grandmother to Juliano, Melissa and Aaron. She sat the kids down before telling them the dreaded news and the looks on their faces as each of them individually processed the information made my heart melt with empathy.

The pain in Juliano's eyes though was highly unbearable since out of all of the grandparents that he had, Phyllis was the one that he admired the most. She was the ideal grandmother in his eyes and he soon lashed out his frustration and abhorrence on

Melissa and Aaron. I was pained to intervene but I had to let Juliano know that venting his anguish through malicious violence towards others was not the answer. He was confused and angry at my abstract parental involvement and I was completely at a loss.

I turned to Lana for some ad hoc advice but she was in no condition to be my support. What she was in the condition for was a stiff drink to temporarily put her nightmare away. I could not take the hypocritical role and say "No", so I simply complied and did whatever she needed. Over the last year, her world had been flipped upside down numerous times and I condoned any means that she felt could bring her harmony.

When I was not involved, family and friends were, and Tracey, who had been with Rescue Cleaning for several years, stepped up to the plate with great enthusiasm and took over Lana's share of the work. Her momentum ran strong for several days, but after a ten day work week of covering Lana's shifts, Tracey needed to request some personal time off too. After a brief inquisition of her sudden change in availability, she announced vociferously that her fiancé, Francisco, had committed suicide. He had let the pressures of his life push him too far and he settled his score by hanging himself while high on crystal meth. His demons had won the battle for his soul. Never did the fact that a daughter and a girlfriend would be left with a corpse and no outlet of hope cross his mind, only the haunting sense of failure. A moment of clairvoyance hit me that the way I was living my life had me on the same death path that Francisco had found. I needed to change and I needed to do it immediately.

I put a lot of focus into the negative outlook good people had to experience because of the selfish actions of their pessimistic counterparts. Tracey, for one, was an unwed mother whose perseverance to provide for her daughter allowed her to stand firm in the face of adversity. Lana saw her children still as her main priority and bypassed any vain feelings of abandon. I chose alcohol and watched the seemingly pointless life of mine crumble around me. I should have been wise enough to see past the false glamour of alcohol, but with Lana still so distraught, all ambitious change was lost. I sat alongside Lana as she allowed alcohol to destroy every last thing that was good in her. I was the one who deserved to be dealt the worst cards in the deck, not her. She was always the one who accepted her losses with patience and grace, thus allowing her to let go and move on. Yet this time it was different and her mental instability had gone too far.

On Father's Day, while unable to cope with her mother's death, Lana attempted to find an eternal sleep by putting a bottle of Crown Royal and half of her prescription pills straight into her system. Lana wanted to die and God alone chose not to accept her into his realm of Heaven yet. I randomly walked in to the "office", which was a room in my house, where I saw Lana lying sideways on the floor with a buffet of halfway dissolved pills and vile dispersed all around her. Luckily, she was still breathing and I quickly rushed her to the shower in a desperate attempt to hydrate her. Within two minutes, she was coherent and responsive and I walked her to my room where we slept side-by-side, strictly as friends.

The following week proved to be equally as upsetting as Melissa and Aaron's aunt and uncle decided to pull them from our custody and raise them in a sober household. If I ever had a question or doubt about how much I truly loved them, it became apparent when they were taken from my life with no opportunity to ever contact them again. I was torn by the fact that all of my efforts fell short and there was nothing that I could do to get them back. To boot, just when I thought that things could not get any worse, Juliano called from Las Vegas to announce that he would not be coming back to Lake Tahoe. Suddenly, everything became way too real for me, but I had nothing left to argue. I did not want to see him go through any more pain from a life associated with me. His mom had a way better grip on life than I did and he would finally have an opportunity to flourish.

I tried to remain positive but the alcohol and drugs I had fallen back to had once again destroyed any hope that resided within me. If I thought being without Lana was alone, a life without Juliano was like being a hermit atop a mountain. My family and friends grew distant in a heartbeat and I could not blame them, I was incapable of tolerating me, why should they? The lifetime of sin and heartache that I had forced upon others was now rebounding towards me and I deserved every single bit of it. So many individuals have gone through the same trials and hardships that I have, but at least in their case they continued to seek guidance through a supreme being. This is where religion usually steps into place, but for me, the faith in a higher deity was non-existent. I had neither strength nor religion as an accomplice. Long ago, I had abandoned the Lord, and thus was completely blind to the importance and relevance that he had in my life.

When it rains, it monsoons, and my rock bottom had arrived when Max called me from Las Vegas to inform me that Dino had passed away. *What the fuck?* Dino and I had experienced a short falling out two years earlier after he had grown overly exhausted with my selfish ways. Apparently, Dino had been diagnosed with a medical condition that ultimately led to a Vicodin prescription. The pills had poisoned his system, causing a complete failure of his liver, kidneys and pancreas. Dino had already conquered the horrors of heroin fifteen years earlier and had created a quality new life for himself. He decided to take his second chance at life with pure faith and integrity. Although his intent was strong, the underlying reality of his addiction simply made the Vicodin too easy for him to abuse. So within a short period of time, complications associated with the medication had taken him from us. The first memories that crossed my mind were Dino's flawless smile, coupled with his infectious laugh and it was all abruptly silenced by a doctor recommended drug.

I felt that it was imperative that I said my goodbyes to Dino, so I contacted a mutual friend, Vinny, and we made the trip to Houston to be in attendance at his service. The ride over to Texas gave me an ample amount of time to overly think my own life, and the shame that sprung into the limelight was horrendous.

By the time that we reached Houston, I was astonished at the amount of love Dino had developed in the course of his rebirth. Seeing him in that open casket was an absolute nightmare and the only thing that crossed my mind was alcohol. I confided in Liza, telling her about my vulnerable mindset, and she reminded me that Dino absolutely detested my drinking and that if he had been there to see this behavior, he would have knocked me senseless. My emotions came to a halting stop and did a complete turn the opposite way. She was completely right. I cared immensely about both Dino and his sister and looking like a letdown in their eyes was very heartbreaking. I could not continue to live my life hurting any and everyone that mattered to me.

On the ride home, I had even more time to reflect on Dino's existence and wondered why it was him, instead of me, who was stepping into the unknown realm of death. I would have gladly changed places with him in a nanosecond and I do believe that the outcome would have resulted in fewer mourning souls. Hell, there might even have been a parade. Dino had more to live for than I could ever accrue in even five existences combined. Vinny, who had remained rather silent throughout the entire drive, must have sensed my mental anguish and chimed in, claiming that from the looks of me, in no way did alcohol fit my personality. I had heard this same comment a thousand times before, but coming from him somehow felt as though maybe it was Dino telling me to stop.

A sudden moment of truth flashed before my eyes and I realized that if I continued my addicted, liquor-riddled excuse for a life, I was going to be dead in a New York minute. My whole life had panned out to me always seeing myself as the victim when in all reality I was the one who victimized everyone else around me. Alcohol and drugs had abolished everything in my world that made a difference and God granted me a countless number of chances to set the record straight, but all that I did was squandered them too. I had multiple opportunities to have a loving and devoted family to call my own and all that I did was cast them aside. Some individuals live their entire lives to the fullest and still never once get a chance to raise a family.

I had nothing left in the world to claim to fame, just a road of wreckage trailing behind me and the foreshadowing cloud of failure looming ahead. The only glitter of salvation was in the tantalizing glow of sobriety. Alcohol is merely a poison to alter the mindset of humankind, and with that alteration brews unforeseen consequences. I had watched loved ones go from imprisonment to death and everything in between, and the only culprit that lingered in the shadows was alcohol.

This may cause me to lose a great level of support from some of my readers, but with my son entering his teenage years, every word has its value. If there is one set of words I can provide that will set his path straight, it is that alcohol is indeed a depressant, not the answer, and that a sober life is the greatest gift that anyone can give themselves. The choice is out there, we as individuals just need the wisdom and strength to make it. Even if our lives are midway through and our choices have put us in some dire situations, this does not mean in any way, shape or form that we can not change our ways. We all have the golden opportunity to be the people that we were born to be and there is no reason why we should stray from that.

I have clogged my system day in and day out since I was thirteen and I now recognize all of the errors that I have brought upon myself. The road ahead of me is riddled with trials and temptations, but with a new meaning in my life known squarely as Jesus Christ, I that know my sins will be forgiven because I have re-established my faith. Although God's forgiveness is one divine act that I could never expect from those whom I have burned, I just pray that time will turn their hearts the same way that it has turned mine. This novel is proof that the unachievable is achievable. I have finally started and finished something that took forty years of loss, pain, deception, lies, vices and humility to see through. A lot of hardships occurred in my life, but I stuck true to my intentions and seamlessly laced them all together into a work of art that I can be proud of.

As my story unraveled, I called notice towards many of the individuals who have made an impact on my life, but seldom did I mention anything about my thoughts and love for my son, Daniel. The haunting reality of my failures to Daniel is without a doubt the single greatest regret in my life. He was an inspiration for love to me and that alone should have been more than enough of a reason for me to change. Instead of striving to not let him down, I just buried his memory and what he had meant to me. I can not even imagine the magnitude of pain and confusion that I created for Daniel as he grew into a young man. The sentiment that I write now can never fix the wrong that I did to him, not even three lifetimes worth could fix that. He gave me more than enough opportunities to straighten my course and all that I did was let him down. All that his beautiful eyes ever witnessed was a stranger resembling his father and his selfish ways.

All that I could ask myself after this was how does an individual ever learn to forgive themselves after such a disgusting sin as mental and physical abandonment of one's own son or daughter? Well there is no solid answer, especially in my case when it is both. The only solution that I have learned that has any optimistic aura is to live the rest of my days trying relentlessly to fix those things which can never be undone. In all reality, Texas is only ten minutes away and very little is keeping me from making that much needed trip. I just want to see Daniel and be in his presence one more time. I want to be there to speak to him and share with him all of the words which are too extensive and personal to be compacted into these pages. All that I know is that my beautiful son Daniel deserves to be introduced to the father that he was always meant to have known.

So to all of those oblivious, ethnocentric fools out there, who are leaving their children behind, take an immediate stop to turn around and embrace the love that is so desperately out there to be given. Give them an opportunity for every minute of every day to be shared as a quality family and take advantage of each of these moments as though they were your last because otherwise, you are left with a world full of emptiness. This emptiness can always be refilled, as long as you give all of your family an unconditional love. All of life's awards should be present within itself.

Sobriety is the greatest tool that any of us can ever acquire. A sober, clear-headed mind allows us to step back from our everyday selves and see life for the bigger picture that it is. Form there, you can be more open-minded about the culmination of events that brought you to where you are today. As I wrote down these very thoughts, I was drawn to the words "shame and sadness from the class clown". All of my younger years, while sitting in the classroom, I sought for instant gratification instead of pursuing an education which could have ensured a lifetime of gratification. I then contemplated the educational goals that I have set out for myself and I am ashamed at how easily I cast aside such a beautiful gift as an education. An exercised mind is a powerful asset in each of our lives.

I was raised by a beautiful set of parents who only wanted my creative genius to flourish, but instead I used it for the means of self-glorification. As a rebellious youth, I surrounded myself with loving individuals who I could twist and manipulate to serve my own guilty pleasures. My children gave me every opportunity possible to love them and I only viewed them more like a burden and less like living blessings. I lost every woman in my life that took a chance and walked down the plank that was my love. Too many hearts were broken and the only factor that was amidst them all was the presence of alcohol. Twenty-five years of alcohol and all that I could credit to my ways was Lana alone in the world, my brother alone in prison and my parents alone at home still loving their long-lost son. With a lighter in hand, I burned every single bridge that I ever built and now no architect in the world could reconstruct them. Faith is my only option, faith that someday the good will that I express on these pages will somehow be absorbed and passed on to those that need it the most. I have laid my sins out for all to read and my repentance is all that I can hold dear.

So to every thirteen year old out there about to take his or her first drink, I beg of you to stop and reconsider your actions. Are you truly ready to accept the guilt and consequences associated with some legal poison? Is the gateway to the Pandora's Box of substances ready to be opened and if so, are you prepared for the pain that it entails? Save yourself from the temporary relief and prepare for the path of sobriety and enlightenment. I am not saying that everybody who drinks will suffer, but if you do, then do allocate it as an option. Ultimately, no good has ever come out of an empty bottle, just a false sense of security and a lot of pain to those you love. All of us have only been given one life to live and if we do not make it count towards something great, then it has not been lived to the fullest.

Everyone's life has a meaning, a Heaven and a Hell...This is just a piece of how I found meaning in my own life, not everything but more than nothing...An entire life created from a single vision.

AFTER WORD:
EYES OF THE CONFESSOR

As I read through what I have written over the past two years, what really grabbed my attention the most was how many times that I attempted to restart my life and failed. Then, a spark in my thoughts allowed me to realize that since this novel has been completed, my life has actually made a remarkable turn for the better. I have finally taken the initiative to prevent myself from making a mockery out of my life and hurting everyone around me. There have still been some harsh times in my world, but I have found the strength to tackle them with a sober mindset.

My son has shown me the way back to a loving home and my daughter has shown me the errors of my past. For their dedication and love, I am forever grateful.

I am still amazed that what started as a simple idea has grown into a cleansing of my soul and a reinvention of its purpose on this Earth. I think about all of the beautiful people in this world who are suffering this very minute from the effects of alcohol and drugs and anticipate how this novel can provide them with a meaningful influence. I pray that my ludicrous existence can actually motivate an individual to stop what they are doing and think that maybe, just maybe, the time for change is not too late.

I think of the young man who helped me complete this

tangible dream and the wonderful gift that he gave me through his relentless sacrifice. I can never thank you enough Michael for your unfailing desire to see this journey all of the way through.

My thoughts then turn to Lana and her immaculate recovery, allowing her to once again be a steadfast spirit of inspiration.

I think of my mentor, an irreplaceable man who taught me the very basic steps of being a better father and a better man. Thank you Stan, you have positively changed my life in countless ways.

My mind travels to the cell that occupies my brother and I pray that he does not lose his faith or hope in a life outside of those walls. Not a day passes that I neglect to envision him walking away from those steel doors, once and for all. This is one vision that I can always see so vividly.

I wonder how many parents will have to say goodbye to their children by either burial or incarceration and the loss that their hearts will have to suffer through. I believe that the children of this era are far more superior in intelligence than when I was a teenager and I wonder why they are still dying at such an increased rate. Why are they striking out so fast? The blind truth to this reality frightens me beyond belief.

Recognizing and accepting my failures as a father to all four of my children has allowed me to soften up my attitude and let the beauty of love and respect flow through me. This simple yet effective mentality has given me the chance to see the positive influence that I can provide as their father. Although I still spend much of my time thinking about them and being haunted by my past, at least by letting that negativity go, I can make my actions speak louder than my words.

If change is an action that you are truly ready for, then humbly reach out to the people who have your best interest in mind and let them know that you are receptive to their help.

I stand firm at this moment and tell every reader out there that a life without change is a terrible choice. There have been some interesting times in my life that have revolved around alcohol and drugs, but ultimately all that they ever really did was steered me directly into the path of an eternal addiction. This addiction only resulted in a lifetime of pain for both me and those whom I came into contact with.

The time for redemption is now and be confident in knowing that the sober life on the other side of the fence truly is better. I have made that leap into the green pastures of sobriety and I can honestly say that I have yet to look back. Through my clean and clear mind, I have demonstrated the humility needed to seek the forgiveness from those whom I have burned so greatly. Forgiveness is a wonderful blessing that warms the hearts of everyone involved. Both love and forgiveness are free, so spare no time in expressing them to everyone you encounter, friend or foe.

So with these final words, I bid all of my readers a pleasant goodbye. I thank each and every one of you for taking the time to take a walk in my footsteps, and I pray with all of my heart that my losses can be your guiding lessons.

ACKNOWLEDGMENTS:
MY ETERNAL LOVE FOR YOU

Heather, Joseph, Cheyenne, Juliano, Brandon, and Amanda – Thank you! Gerard and Michelle – For a life given, Shannah – For everything, Robert C. – My only brother, my sister Vicki, my pride, Yanira, Marissa, Teresa – For your strength, Auntie Bernadette, Ray, Bobby, Debi, Clark Moss, Gina, Madeline, Bernadette, Jeff and Sara Miller, Carmen, Debbie, Bobby Jr., Joey, Tony, September, Nigel, Mario, Violet, Toni, Francis, Katlyn, Nick, Vinnie, Rachael, Celeste, Kerrin, Ashley, Alex, Jayden, Missy, Caden, Rich Thomson – For never giving up on me, Kyle Jr., Natasha, Kayla, Emma and Liberty, Uncle Charlie, Kim Knox, Jacob, Sean – For the laughter, Bryn, Jaime, Junior, Danny, Angel, Trent, David, Stan – My mentor, Mr. Wells, Brittney, Joby, Derek, Taylor, Teresa Hampton, Lee Hoyes, Kyle Leake, Bathsheba, David Cassandra, Daniella Cassandra, Jerry Gooch, Bob Jones, Lady Di, Jaime McFarlane, Annie, Summer, Christian, Ian, Paxton, Tony Ciaflone, Eileen, Lisa, Jennifer Green, Lady Eddie, David and Michele Hallum, Yasmin, Sheli, Donna, Jeanette, Donnie, George, Sal, Tony Polselli, Danny Toledo, Ari, Shawnee, Jason, Cindy, Mike Kinney, Tim, Dan, Wes, Nancy Baldwin, Greg Rios, Tony Escuna, Korn Beef, Johnny Reed, Amy Reed, Matt C., Eddie Ridgeway, Cindy and Jessica G., Nicki,

Erica, Kathy, Bob H., my grandparents Nick, Don, Klara, Vera, Anne Marie, Larry Waggoner, Bobbi Murphy, Kurt and Bethene, Picasso, Ron Smith, Mike Rice, Colleen, Michael, Steven, Catherine, Janet and Larry, Bethany, Zac, Nick, Taryn, Chloe, Toby, Adam Brent, Anthony Burke, Clint Smith, Chipper, Steve Hieber, Meka, Stasha, Rose, Angela, Vanessa, Roman Kreminski, Melissa, Sandra, Eddie Moe, James and Loree, Allison, Lisa, Tina, Tony, Frank, Doreen, Dominic, Ian, Cody, Damian, Tracy, Ray Sidney, Elvis – My black Lab, Rosie, Jessica, Tisha, Jennifer, Mike, Scooter, Linda, Kaz, Teddy, Larry Torres, all of my teachers and the New York Yankees.

Amy, Crawford, Mike L., Les, Joe, Roberta, Frankie, Tony, Martin, Heidi, Joseph Murphy, Tug, Phyllis, Dave S., Karen, Bob Sr., Joe, Uncle Mikah, Little Ray, Leondro II, Uncle Ted – May you rest in peace always. To my sweet Lord - Thank you for never abandoning me!

CPSIA information can be obtained at www.ICGtesting.com
Printed in the USA
BVOW070938180712

295527BV00001B/230/P